Niernsee and Neilson, Architects of Baltimore

Niernsee and Neilson,

TWO CAREERS

RANDOLPH W. CHALFANT AND
CHARLES BELFOURE

INTRODUCTION BY MICHAEL J. LEWIS

Architects of Baltimore

ON THE EDGE OF THE FUTURE

Baltimore Architecture Foundation

BALTIMORE, MARYLAND

Chicago's Graham Foundation for Advanced Studies in the Fine Arts, the Baltimore and Ohio Railroad Museum, and Willard Hackerman, Baltimore, Maryland provided major funding for the publication of this book.

Baltimore Architecture Foundation
1016 Morton Street
Baltimore, MD 21201

Designed by Julie Burris

Frontispiece: John R. Niernsee (*left*) and J. Crawford Neilson, ca. 1873. *Baltimore chapter, American Institute of Architects*

Library of Congress Cataloging-in-Publication Data

Chalfant, Randolph W., 1919–2004
  Niernsee and Neilson, architects of Baltimore : two careers on the edge of the future / Randolph W. Chalfant and Charles Belfoure.
      p. cm.
    Includes bibliographical references and index.
    ISBN 0-9729743-1-8 (alk. paper)
    1. Niernsee and Neilson (Firm) 2. Niernsee, John Rudolph, 1814–1885. 3. Neilson, James Crawford, 1816–1900 4. Architecture—Maryland—Baltimore—19th century.
  I. Belfoure, Charles, 1954–II. Title.

NA737.N454C53 2006
720.92'2—dc22

                                        2006042712

Contents

Color plates follow page 78

Preface

Randolph W. Chalfant's interest in the firm of Niernsee & Neilson began in 1978, when he wrote an article on Calvert Station for the *Maryland Historical Magazine*. In doing the research, he came upon the diary of John Rudolph Niernsee and a biographical sketch of James Crawford Neilson, the architects of the building. This began a strong affinity for these two men that lasted over twenty-five years. Chalfant discovered the important role that Niernsee and Neilson had played in establishing the architectural profession in Baltimore, and he wanted to tell their fascinating story.

The history of Niernsee & Neilson is not just a description of Calvert Station and all the rest of their many splendid works. More importantly, it is about the creation of an architectural firm. This book illustrates the role of talent, hard work, and especially pure good fortune in achieving success in a profession that was basically in its infancy in the first half of the nineteenth century. It explains how the firm grew from a one-man operation into an architectural juggernaut that seemed to capture every important commission in Baltimore with almost unbelievable ease.

In a 2004 documentary film about Louis Kahn, the world-famous architect makes a comment about the important role that accidents play in our lives, about how much our lives are dictated by circumstance. This wise observation is the cornerstone of the story of Niernsee & Neilson. The history of the firm begins with an incredible stroke of luck—a job on the Baltimore & Ohio Railroad. At the time, John Niernsee thought it was just a last-minute, life-saving job offer for an unemployed engineer. But the

offer had a more fortuitous aspect to it. By pure chance, it came from Benjamin H. Latrobe Jr., an especially talented and influential man who would recognize Niernsee's ability and set him on a wonderful path of architectural success. Architecture is a business as well as an art, and an architect needs clients to sustain his practice and to create. The role of architectural patronage—how having the right first client can lead to a plethora of choice commissions from the city's wealthiest men—is a key part of the Niernsee & Neilson story.

Finding the right partner in life and business can also be a matter of luck. This job offer allowed Niernsee to meet J. Crawford Neilson, another engineer working for the B&O, on a tour of the line; the two took an immediate liking to each other. When it came time to choose a partner to help manage his burgeoning practice, Niernsee knew the right man for the job.

But the story also shows how success can be short lived and how professional decisions, which seem correct at the moment, can cast a shadow over careers and personal lives for decades to come. For John Niernsee, the chance to design the South Carolina State House in 1856 was the commission of a lifetime. He did not hesitate to dissolve his partnership and go south—long-distance architectural practices barely existed then—to devote his full attention to such an important project. In doing so, he gave up a successful practice and authorship of a very important building. But the Civil War brought the project to a halt and ravaged the South for years afterward, making continuation of the construction of his beloved building impossible. His commitment to finishing the State

House would have dire consequences for his and Neilson's architectural careers.

Architects in the 1850s in Baltimore and the United States were almost nonentities. Builders controlled both the design and construction even of public buildings. Very, very slowly, architects began to gain more influence in the building process. In Baltimore, it was the firm of Niernsee & Neilson that wrested control of the design and of building construction from the builders and established in the public's mind the idea that a professional, called the architect, designed the building and supervised its construction for the client. As much as architectural quality, they brought professionalism to Baltimore architecture. This legacy is probably the most important part of this story.

In a time when architectural schools did not exist and apprenticeship was the foundation of architectural training, Niernsee & Neilson trained scores of architects and imparted their sense of professionalism and their aesthetic and technical skills to those men, who in turn passed these on to other generations.

Chalfant knew that Niernsee & Neilson were quite skilled as designers, but he would never claim they were the most original or greatest designers in their time. He had a special admiration, however, for John Niernsee as an innovative engineer. Both Chalfant and Niernsee had an engineer's training and shared a keen structural intuition and a love of structural engineering. Whether it was a truss supporting a roof over a church nave or one in a great train shed, they appreciated finding the most elegant way to hold something up.

Chalfant felt another professional kinship with Niernsee: both men had been military engineers, with Chalfant serving in the U.S. Army Corps of Engineers in World War II and the Korean War, an experience that gave him a practical insight into the architectural profession. And, like Niernsee, Chalfant had to learn a second language to practice his profession when he was stationed in Germany.

His interest and admiration for Niernsee and Neilson were so deep that Chalfant took the greatest delight in the smallest detail the partners executed—a bolection molding on a door at Clifton or a Japanese-inspired piece of woodworking at Crimea.

In each city in America, there is probably a pioneering architectural firm that set the standard for professionalism and design for generations to come. In Baltimore, it was Niernsee & Neilson. And Randolph W. Chalfant believed that one could appreciate the architectural history of Baltimore even more by knowing their story.

James D. Dilts was the man responsible for bringing this rather complicated project to fruition. When debilitating illness overcame Randolph W. Chalfant while he was trying to write this work, the Baltimore Architecture Foundation made a wise choice in choosing Jim to take the helm of the project. He asked me whether I'd be willing to help, and I agreed.

It wasn't easy for Jim (or Ranny) to bring on another author, but with a great sense of diplomacy and a lot of good humor, he managed to pull it off. His experience as a writer and his editorial guidance proved very valuable. After Ranny's death, Jim encouraged me to go ahead and tell a story and make it interesting. Incorporating the insights Ranny had gathered over the last twenty-five years, I hope I've done that.

I'd like to thank Jim for his guidance and especially his patience with me. Walter Schamu was the one who recommended me to Jim, and I thank him very much for this opportunity. James T. Wollon Jr. was a great help, and so was Mary Ellen Hayward, who graciously reviewed my work. The efforts of Kevin A. Wiseniewski, who transcribed Ranny's audiotapes and did additional research, and Rosalind Shipley early on, are also deeply appreciated, and Barbara Lamb's editorial skills greatly improved my writing. Dee Dee Thompson, imaging services, the Maryland Historical Society, and Jeff Korman, of the Maryland Room, Enoch Pratt Free Library, were instrumental in providing photographs. The board of the Baltimore Architecture Foundation deserves much thanks, including executive director Adam Blumenthal. I am grateful to Jay and Fred Chalfant for their help in seeing Ranny's book come to light.

And finally, a special note of thanks goes out to John M. Bryan, whose very interesting and well-researched book *Creating the South Carolina State House* proved to be an extremely valuable resource when it came to writing about John R. Niernsee's ill-fated commission.

Charles Belfoure
Westminster, Maryland

Introduction

MICHAEL J. LEWIS

The world of architecture is in constant flux, but not all change is revolutionary change; much is merely the random oscillation of fashion, as each successive generation of architects strains to differentiate itself from its predecessors. Architecture may change and change again with no deeper meaning than a restless pursuit of novelty, like that which causes hemlines to rise and fall and fads in color to come and go. But sometimes genuine revolutionary change does occur, particularly when new ideas, new materials, and new money converge at a single point. Such a convergence occurred in Chicago during the 1880s, leading to the creation of the modern steel-frame skyscraper. This is quite properly regarded as one of the central events of American architecture, but who knows the parallel revolution that occurred in Baltimore half a century earlier?

With the Baltimore and Ohio Railroad, which began construction in 1828, Baltimore created the first rail link to the nation's interior. The railroad began operation two years later and gradually extended its reach to Harper's Ferry, West Virginia (1837), Cumberland, Maryland (1842), and Wheeling, West Virginia (1853). Now the wealth of the continent—which previously could only flow downstream along the Mississippi River or over the Erie Canal to New York—could speed overland to the port of Baltimore. Over the next two decades, Baltimore's population doubled, making it the second-largest city in the United States. To the architect, this meant opportunity of the most promising sort, particularly the lavish patronage offered by the railroads and their directors. Here was new money, in abundance, and here too was the challenge of finding forms appropriate to the new materials and building types associated with the railroad. How these forces converged on an obscure Vienna-born and Prague-educated architect, John Rudolph Niernsee (1814–1885), is the subject of this fascinating and poignant book.

Niernsee belongs to the first generation of architects to come of age in the Victorian era. He was born within a few years of such luminaries as A. J. Downing (1815), Samuel Sloan (1815), and James Renwick (1818), and like them, he entered a world in which the authority of classicism had collapsed and Victorian eclecticism was beginning. Yet while the others are widely known, Niernsee has remained obscure, despite such works as Baltimore's Calvert Station, the mighty Johns Hopkins Hospital, and the South Carolina State Capitol. Even to specialists he remains unstudied—and unpronounceable. This historical neglect is understandable: as a German-speaking immigrant, he already stood outside the mainstream of American culture, an isolation he compounded by fighting for the Confederacy during the Civil War. But it is only this accident of history and geography that makes Niernsee look like a minor provincial figure; he was, in fact, one of the great cosmopolitan figures in American architecture who opened it up to foreign influence.

Niernsee was apprenticed to the Prague architect Josef Andreas Kranner (1801–71), a pioneer of the Gothic Revival best known for his role in restoring and completing the Prague cathedral. Kranner was a proficient builder and stonemason, whose neo-Gothic work was always distinguished by a strongly structural

FIG. I.1. Green
Mount Cemetery
Chapel, Baltimore.
Susan McElhinney

INTRODUCTION

sense, mentally conceived in terms of the properties of masonry construction. Niernsee seems
to have kept an eye on the work of his mentor,
even after his emigration to the United States.
His 1857 Green Mount Cemetery Chapel (fig.

I.1, plate 11) was evidently inspired by Kranner's
Franz I monument in Prague, built from 1844
to 1850 on the banks on the Moldau (fig. I.2).
Each is a lofty stone spire, rising from a polygonal substructure to dissolve into a lacy play of

finials, based on the robust German Gothic of the thirteenth century.

But Niernsee's education was academic as well as practical. He trained at the Prague Polytechnic, where the language of higher education, as throughout the Austro-Hungarian Empire, was German. Prague was the first of the great German polytechnical schools, opening in 1806 and soon followed by others in Vienna, Karlsruhe, Hanover, and elsewhere. Education in these schools was a methodical and scientific affair, aimed at correcting the technical backwardness of the German-speaking states made apparent by the Industrial Revolution. Even architecture was taught as a rational discipline, and not as a primarily aesthetic affair, as at the Ecole des Beaux Arts in Paris. The student architect would progress through a sequential curriculum of mathematics and descriptive geometry, to construction and mechanics, and finally to architectural composition. He would become familiar with the historical styles of the past, learning them not as eternal verities, but rather as decorous coverings for a building that derived its form from technical and economic considerations. (And throughout his life, Niernsee meticulously tabulated his buildings according to their cost per cubic foot.)

Such a conception of architectural form, elastic and free of all servility to the authority of the past, was particularly suited to the design of the railroad station, that radical new building type, and it is only natural that Niernsee would soon provide the most progressive railroad architecture, both formally and technically, in the United States. Yet his path was not easy. After his 1836 emigration came several hardscrabble years as an itinerant surveyor and draftsman, at the end of which he was briefly suicidal. Not until 1839 did he come to the attention of Benjamin H. Latrobe Jr., the son of the celebrated architect and himself an engineer for the B&O Railroad. Latrobe was uniquely qualified to appreciate Niernsee, for his own family was of German descent and spoke fluent German, and his father was likewise an architect-engineer who struggled for professional recognition. Perhaps this accounts for his unusual solicitousness for Niernsee's pride, when he carefully warned him that his new job would not permit him to exercise his powers of design.

Nonetheless, Niernsee quickly proved himself a designer of imagination and boldness. His engine house in Frederick, Maryland (fig. 2),

FIG. I.2. Franz I monument, Prague. Dominika Marciniak

and freight warehouse in Washington, D.C., used a new system of prefabricated iron and zinc trussed roofs that were cheap and durable and could be sped by rail to the building site to be quickly bolted together. Both structures were sufficiently innovative to be published in 1842 in the *Allgemeine Bauzeitung*, the prestigious Vienna-based journal of architecture and engineering. Niernsee, perhaps frustrated by his lack of recognition in the United States, made certain that he was noticed in Europe.

And so he seems to have been, for shortly after the article appeared, the architect Leopold Eidlitz immigrated to New York. Born in Prague and trained in Vienna (the reverse of

Niernsee's trajectory), Eidlitz was a Jew, and he would have recognized that there was far more scope for professional advancement for a polytechnically trained architect in the United States than in the forbidding bureaucracy of the Austro-Hungarian Empire.[1] At any rate, Niernsee and Eidlitz opened the floodgates. During the next decade, German architects and engineers began to pour into the United States, a trickle that became a flood after the European revolutions of 1848. They settled in New York (Alexander Saeltzer, Friedrich A. Petersen, and Karl Gildemeister), Philadelphia (Gustav Runge and Edward Collins), Washington, D.C. (Adolph Cluss and Paul Schulze), Pittsburgh (Charles Barthberger), and Austin (Christoph Conrad Stremme)—to name only some of the most prominent.[2] During the 1850s, these German architects and the ideas they carried with them represented the most vital new impulse in American architecture.

Niernsee may have helped initiate this great architectural migration, but his own emergence as an architect came slowly and grudgingly; he had been in the United States for a decade before he finished his first architectural commission in 1846, a house on Mount Vernon Place for Latrobe, that prescient patron. By 1848 Niernsee was taking in enough work to form a partnership with his fellow B&O draftsman James Crawford Neilson. But clearly Niernsee was the principal designer, and he quickly found his personal voice. His first Italianate houses were rather conventional—efficiently planned and solidly built platitudes—but he soon discovered a gift for forceful composition. He learned to compose in terms of separate volumes, enjoying the play of bold blocky masses and crisp geometry. His 1851 B&O Railroad Depot at Washington, D.C. (fig. 60), his 1855 Central Presbyterian Church (plate 4 and fig. 44), and Clifton (1852) (fig. 25), his elegant villa for Johns Hopkins, all show the same bold cubic form offset by a taut campanile at the corner. In each Niernsee frankly showed the separateness of parts rather than working to draw them together into a graceful unity, an essentially neoclassical taste that must have been cultivated in Prague.

This bold blockiness is amply illustrated by Calvert Station (1850) (fig. 55), the Baltimore and Susquehanna Railroad terminal that is the only great station of pre–Civil War America to have been designed by an expert in railroad construction. At this time, railroad architecture was still in its infancy. The first generation of railroad architects played with the theme of the monumental entrance: Greek porticos (as at London's Euston Station) or Roman gates (as at Hamburg's Berliner Bahnhof). Neither would have been acceptable for a station in antebellum Baltimore.

Indeed, there was no clear and obvious model in antiquity for railroad stations, but Niernsee's education had inculcated in him no great reverence for the authority of the past. During his impressionable years in Prague, the most revolutionary doctrine was the idea that architectural style should not be based on historical precedent but on the objective properties of a building's materials and structural system.

This idea was first articulated by Heinrich Hübsch, the director of the Karlsruhe Polytechnical School, in his manifesto of 1828, *In Welchem Style Sollen Wir Bauen?* (In What Style Should We Build?). Weary of the debates about the proper form and use of the classical orders, Hübsch challenged the architect to concentrate on the "strictly objective skeleton" of its construction structure; ornament—which had previously been the focus of architectural education—was instead to be left to the "imagination of the individual artists." Rather than a recreation of a "historical and conventional style," he longed for an architectural style that would be appreciated in its directness and clarity by the layman—"without prior instruction in archaeology."[3] This style was to be based not on conventional historical form but upon rational masonry construction, arranged according to a vaulted arcuated system. The basic construction unit would be the round arch, and the style itself would have the objective designation "round-arched style"—*Rundbogenstil*, in German. Such a doctrine was ideally suited to the pragmatic curriculum of the polytechnical school, and the Rundbogenstil became a kind of universal, all-purpose architectural language during Niernsee's years of study.

In America, the style flourished for reasons of fashion rather than theory. After the long interlude of the Greek Revival, its forms seemed fresh and stylish, and in short order its academic German origins were forgotten (as was its name: Niernsee described the style of Calvert Station as Italian). The first great railroad station in the Rundbogenstil was Thomas Tefft's Union Depot in Providence, Rhode Island (1849).

Calvert Station, begun a year earlier, was a more radical building, purging itself of all historical nostalgia. If Tefft's station suggested the façade of a Romanesque cathedral, Niersee's offered an abstract essay in geometric composition: a compact cube was shouldered between two lofty towers, showing that characteristic tendency of the style to accentuate the periphery of a design (a distinctly anti-classical gesture). Here Calvert Station suggested a new kind of architectural monumentality, one that derived its formal power from the muscular array of its volumes rather than through sentimental allusions to the forms of the past. The Rundbogenstil now became the preferred style for train stations, and Niernsee's example was followed by Otto Matz's Illinois Central Depot in Chicago (1856), and Collins & Autenrieth's Union Station in Pittsburgh (1861).[4] Other railroads likewise hired polytechnically trained Germans to direct their architectural and engineering offices, as the Reading Railroad did when it hired Wilhelm Lorenz, Niernsee's Hanover-educated counterpart.[5]

It would have been satisfying to learn that Niernsee, whose career was made by the B&O, should have given the railroad its principal station, a building that would have been the fitting centerpiece of Niernsee's career. Yet his 1853 project for the B&O's Camden Station commission ended unhappily. This would have been a mighty and sprawling block that suggested the concentrated industrial power of its three barrel-vaulted trainsheds to the rear (fig. 62). But here Niernsee's impatience got the best of him. After three years of waiting for his plans to be approved, in May 1856 he impetuously left for Columbia, South Carolina, in order to design and build the South Carolina State House. Immediately the railroad entrusted the building of Niernsee's station to Joseph F. Kemp, a draftsman-architect of diligence rather than brilliance. Kemp executed Niernsee's design in a pared-down version, making a rather drab and utilitarian performance out of what would surely have been a masterpiece of the Rundbogenstil. The building is still impressive, but Niernsee must have grieved.

Niernsee had no better luck with the South Carolina State House. A conventional and rather old-fashioned Palladian scheme was already determined before Niernsee took over the project, and he set about updating it, adding a richly sculpted tower behind the central pediment (Fig. 79). This, alas, was never built. Niernsee

struggled to build the State House throughout the war, even as he served the Confederate Army as a military engineer. In the final days of the war, he helped fortify Columbia against William Tecumseh Sherman's army, leading his team of craftsmen to form a battlefield unit. When the city fell, his office was burned, destroying his drawings, private papers, and collection of architectural books. A chastened Niernsee returned to Baltimore to pick up the pieces of his practice and resume his partnership with Neilson.

Niernsee's work was now distinctly dated, and he found himself losing the most fashionable commissions to upcoming Victorian architects, such as Edmund G. Lind and the firm Dixon and Carson. Two of his competitors even came from his own office: Bruce Price and E. Francis Baldwin, the latter now the favorite architect of the B&O.[6] Niernsee adapted as best he could, and the stylistic flexibility of his polytechnical education stood him in good stead. His 1872 Young Men's Christian Association Building shows his facility with the Venice-tinged High Victorian Gothic of the 1870s (fig. 97). Yet this was a style that younger architects like Baldwin and Price handled with far more conviction and ease, and while Niernsee was still valued for his technical acumen, his grasp of style was beginning to seem rather musty.

This is the sad fate of his design for the Johns Hopkins Hospital, in consultation with Dr. John Shaw Billings (1838–1913). Billings was a physician of extraordinary imagination, whose achievements range from the development of the pavilion-plan hospital to the use of punch cards to process aggregate information—that forerunner of the computer. Together Niernsee and Billings toiled on the plans from 1874 to 1876, producing the country's most sophisticated hospital design, with independent heating and ventilation for each of the detached pavilions in order to prevent the spread of contagious diseases by air (figs. 104, 105). Yet for all its functional brilliance, the elevations (if Niernsee produced them at all) must have struck the hospital's trustees as rather dowdy; in any case, in 1877 the execution of Niernsee's buildings was turned over to Cabot & Chandler, an elegant firm of Boston architects whose specialty was a stately Queen Anne. As with Camden Station, once Niernsee's schematic design had been finalized, its execution could be assigned to others.

For this, perhaps, Niernsee had only his own method to blame. By beginning with the determinants of plan, construction, and cost, from which the façade emerged as a kind of byproduct, he did not impart the exaggerated sense of individuality that the overheated Victorian visual world demanded. A certain schematic quality clung to his work, which suited it for utilitarian needs but not for the peculiar specificity of expression required for more important buildings. Precisely because his buildings were so rational and judicious and because they solved their technical problems so effortlessly, they were seldom memorable—and certainly not in the way that makes for architectural celebrity. This surely contributes to Niernsee's undeserved obscurity.

In the end, Niernsee's achievement was to open American architecture to the lessons of the practice and theory of modern German architecture. Because of its early leadership in railroad development, Baltimore was the first city to assimilate these new lessons, although the Civil War would soon relegate the city to a secondary role. But for this fleeting moment around 1848, when wealth, technology, and a progressive new architectural doctrine aligned, Baltimore was at the epicenter of American architecture, and Niernsee was its principal figure.

Why does a biographer write a book, if not because of some personal sympathy with his subject? I believe this book would never have come into being were it not for Randolph W. Chalfant's conspicuous personal identification with John Rudolph Niernsee.

Chalfant—whose friends knew him as Ranny —could not have helped but notice that his own education at the Carnegie Institute of Technology in Pittsburgh followed a curriculum much like Niernsee's polytechnical program in Prague. Like his subject, Chalfant shifted between architecture and building and was pulled from architecture to war. He served in India during the Second World War and in Germany during the Korean War. During his second stint he learned his superb German, which permitted him to read Niernsee's diaries, the impetus for this book. All these coincidences and parallels form the book's invisible scaffolding and give it its underlying sense of being a pleasant obligation.

I met Ranny Chalfant in person just once, in 1983, when he and his wife kindly put me up for the night while I was researching my master's thesis on Bruce Price. An impoverished graduate student, thankful for any gift of lodging and research assistance, I was welcomed as if I was an old friend. There was no fuss or formality; we were both comrades in the same cause, and that was that. More than twenty years later, I am grateful to be able to repay that debt. Could it be that Niernsee, working in a different age and under very different pressures, was as kindly as his jovial and open-handed biographer?

Chronology

1814 John Rudolph Niernsee is born in Vienna.

1816 James Crawford Neilson is born in Baltimore.

1821–32 Neilson and his family reside in England and Brussels.

1832–36 Niernsee studies engineering at the University of Prague.

1833–34 Neilson returns to Baltimore and attends St. Mary's College.

1835 Neilson works for Benjamin H. Latrobe Jr. surveying for the Baltimore and Port Deposit Railroad.

1836 Niernsee emigrates to the United States.

1836–39 Niernsee conducts railroad surveys and works as an engineer on coastal fortifications for the U.S. government in the American South.

1837–42 Neilson works as an engineer for the Baltimore and Ohio Railroad engineering staff in Martinsburg, VA.

1839–45 Niernsee is hired as a draftsman by Latrobe for the Baltimore and Ohio Railroad engineering staff in Baltimore.

1839 Niernsee meets Neilson on a tour of the B&O Railroad line to Cumberland.

1840 Neilson marries Rosa Williams of Harford County, MD.

1841 Niernsee marries Emily Bradenbaugh of Baltimore.

1842–48 Neilson works for the U.S. Coastal Survey.

1846 Niernsee begins his architectural practice, designing two houses for Benjamin H. Latrobe Jr.

1848 Niernsee and Neilson form a partnership.

1853 Niernsee becomes a founding member of the American Institute of Architects.

1855 Niernsee consults on structural problems of the new South Carolina State House under construction and is appointed a consulting architect.

1856 Niernsee is appointed architect of the State House effective January 1 and dissolves partnership with Neilson. Niernsee permanently moves to Columbia, SC, in June.

1856–65 Neilson goes into sole architectural practice.

1856–64 Niernsee designs the new South Carolina State House and supervises its construction.

1864–65 Niernsee joins the Confederate Army as a military engineer and is ordered to conduct reconnaissances of western South Carolina and plan for the defense of Columbia.

1865–74 Niernsee returns to Baltimore and forms second partnership with Neilson.

1873 Niernsee is appointed U.S. representative to the Vienna International Exposition.

1874 Niernsee and Neilson dissolve partnership.

1874–85 Niernsee forms new practice with his son Frank as Niernsee & Son.

1874–1900 Neilson goes into sole practice.

1885 Niernsee returns to South Carolina to resume work on the State House but dies in June and is buried in Columbia.

1900 Neilson dies and is buried at Priestford in Harford County, MD.

Niernsee and Neilson, Architects of Baltimore

ONE

Coming to America and the B&O Years

The view was definitely worth the few cents admission and the 230-step climb. Standing at the top of the Washington Monument, John Rudolph Niernsee was enjoying the 360-degree vista of Baltimore. "From here, one has a wonderful view over the whole city with its wonderful buildings, the surroundings, and the Chesapeake Bay," he wrote in his diary for Saturday, August 31, 1839.[1]

The twenty-five-year-old engineer from Austria was in high spirits, and for good reason—the following Monday he would start his new job as a draftsman with the Baltimore & Ohio Railroad, a position that would last at least three years with the possibility of a raise. Only two months earlier, with no prospect of employment and in a fit of depression, he wrote that he had stopped thinking of the past and the future because he could not see anything but "thunderstorms on all sides" (end of June, 1839). As he looked out over the landscape from the observation deck of the great Doric column Robert Mills had designed in honor of George Washington, Niernsee was optimistic that his professional and personal life would finally have a sense of stability. His peripatetic existence as a surveyor in the South and the hand-to-mouth drafting jobs hopefully were over. With a steady job with good prospects, he could even consider getting married. The city that lay below him just could be the start of a new life.

Niernsee saw that there were no buildings for several blocks south of the monument. The city's development had halted more or less at the intersection of Mulberry and Cathedral Streets, where Benjamin Henry Latrobe's great cathedral stood. The reason for this pause was that the city waterworks had not yet created a system of reservoirs for domestic water supply or fire-fighting. Looking to the north, Niernsee saw a savanna of meadows and trees, almost totally empty of buildings. But Baltimore, which he described as "a handsomely located commercial city of 102,000 inhabitants on the Chesapeake Bay," was on the cusp of industrial and mercantile greatness.

Below Latrobe's cathedral was a port city that was being transformed by an American industrial revolution driven by steam, coal, and iron. The week of Niernsee's arrival saw clipper ships departing with goods bound for England and the West Indies, a great parade of two hundred horsemen to welcome Henry Clay, the famous senator and orator from Kentucky, and the circus at the Aetna Theatre, with the first giraffe ever seen in Baltimore. The city was gaining notoriety as a handsome place of great monuments. Frances Trollope, an acid-tongued Englishwoman visiting America, praised the city: "The noble column erected to the memory of Washington, and the Catholic Cathedral, with its beautiful dome, being built on a commanding eminence, are seen at a great distance."[2] Niernsee's new employer, the Baltimore & Ohio Railroad, was a key catalyst for Baltimore's new industrial strength. Its shops employed more than a thousand workers to build and equip the railroad's new line to Cumberland. Dozens of businesses fabricating locomotive and machine parts had sprung up throughout the city.

Young Niernsee could not have imagined what lay in store for him. If he had climbed to the top of the monument fifteen years later, he would have seen a much different city, its blocks packed with buildings and houses of all descriptions—the most prominent having been designed by him. The immigrant, who in 1839 was nearly penniless and desperately in need of steady employment, would become a partner in Baltimore's first truly professional and most successful pre–Civil War architectural firm, with James Crawford Neilson, another B&O engineer whom he would soon meet on the job. Their firm, Niernsee & Neilson, completely dominated the design of Baltimore architecture as well as completing many other commissions from Maryland and Virginia into the Carolinas and Georgia.

Architectural practice in America at this time was making its painstakingly slow evolution into a separate, full-fledged profession on a par with medicine, law, and engineering. During colonial times and at the founding of the republic, the professionally trained architect did not exist. The design of buildings was in the hands of either the gentleman-architect or the master builder. Members of the elite class, such as planters, attorneys, and merchants, designed residences and public buildings for their own pleasure, not to earn a living. Thomas Jefferson, Peter Harrison, and Dr. William Thornton were among the most prominent gentlemen-architects who achieved a reputation for their designs. And because new buildings were needed to establish settlements, carpenters were among the most highly valued colonists in seventeenth-century America. They designed the buildings as well as built them, and this began the tradition of the builder-designer in America.[3]

Beginning in the early 1800s, immigrant engineers and architects like Maximilian Godefroy and Benjamin Henry Latrobe first countered this tradition, and Niernsee, a formally trained engineer, would continue the transformation of architecture into a respected and valued profession. Niernsee & Neilson greatly advanced architectural practice in its formative years in Baltimore through dedication to excellence in design and engineering and above all, professionalism. The firm would make another long-lasting mark on Baltimore architecture by becoming the progenitor of generations of the city's future architectural talent. Several architects who apprenticed in their office would go on to design some of the city's finest buildings.

But on August 31, 1839, all John Niernsee really cared about was his new job. He climbed down the Washington Monument and signed his name in the visitor's book, then went back to his room in a boardinghouse on Liberty Street. That night, he made a pen and ink sketch of the monument and the "prettily decorated" fence that enclosed it (fig. 1). As he made his entry in his diary, he may have felt that his perseverance had finally paid off. In the past three years, there had been times when he was about to give up his quest for success in America. "As a disconsolate wanderer, I must fight my way through the thorny paths of this world, without a home and without a guiding star … I don't know what a vicious fate has ordained for me," he wrote in November 1838 upon the news of his father's death, probably the lowest point of his American sojourn. Despite his loneliness and uncertainty about the future, he was determined to go on. His journey to Baltimore had been long and circuitous.

John Rudolph Niernsee was born in Vienna on April 29, 1814, and little is known of his early education, family background, or social status. His father, Johann, was a minor official in the city and his mother, Barbara, whose family name is unknown, is reported to have been from Trieste. The second of four children, he had an older brother and a younger brother and sister. When it was time to continue his formal education, Niernsee did not attend the Polytechnic in Vienna, but rather enrolled in the Polytechnic in Prague, the oldest such institute in the German-speaking world.

The Prague Polytechnic was founded in 1803 by the Austrian empire's most important astronomer, physicist, and most practical applicator of science, Franz Joseph von Gerstner, who was known as "the great achiever." The school had already matriculated over seven thousand pupils by the time Niernsee graduated. It was totally different from a classical university, which was oriented to teaching young men to become churchmen. Classical universities were an outgrowth of the Christian Church; polytechnics came into being as a result of the French Revolution and the Age of Reason, which considered the natural and practical sciences to be of primary importance. Therefore, the Prague Polytechnic taught such subjects as engineering and surveying, mathematics, and political science.

Railroad engineering was an especially prized discipline to study. Austria was a land-locked country, connected to the sea only by conquests of principalities in northern Italy, including Venice. The prime aim of the new monarchy was to reliably connect the nation with the Mediterranean Sea. Austria was therefore extremely interested in the extension of railroads across mountains, especially in overcoming the Alps that lay between Vienna and Trieste. Delegations including von Gerstner and his son were, in fact, sent from Austria from 1838 to 1840 to study railroads in America, in particular the Baltimore & Ohio Railroad, and how it was conquering the steep grades between Baltimore and Cumberland.

Graduates from the school were expected to provide the talent to build railroads and solve the other considerable internal problems of the Austro-Hungarian empire, not to travel to the United States as Niernsee did. He may have emigrated to leave Austria's tightly structured class society, realizing he could never break through this strict societal barrier. At the time, preferences for positions in the government and the bureaucracy were given to people with the proper social breeding and family connections rather than to persons of self-achievement. A detailed search of the *Almanac de Gotha*, the Bible of social status in Europe, found that Niernsee had no claim to nobility or membership in the upper classes.

In addition to his studies at the Polytechnic, Niernsee also held an apprenticeship, either while in school or just after graduation, to a celebrated Prague stonemason named Joseph Andreas Kranner. The education Niernsee received from Kranner would greatly contribute to his sense of the Gothic style and its masonry construction techniques, a knowledge that would prove valuable in his architectural career. Kranner, the third-generation owner of a stoneworks in Prague, had studied landscape painting in Italy and done an extensive apprenticeship on his own account in the French cathedrals before returning to Prague. He returned to his hometown to take up residence and actively began reconstructing elements of Prague's own architecture, including work on the city's cathedral, St. Vitas, and other Gothic Revival structures.

It is quite likely that Niernsee sat in on lectures at the university given by the famous son of von Gerstner, who made himself an expert and author on railroad transportation and may have given Niernsee the idea that money and experience were to be gained by immigrating to the United States.[4] After completion of the apprenticeship with Kranner, Niernsee returned to Vienna, where he requested a portion of his inheritance from his family. With the money

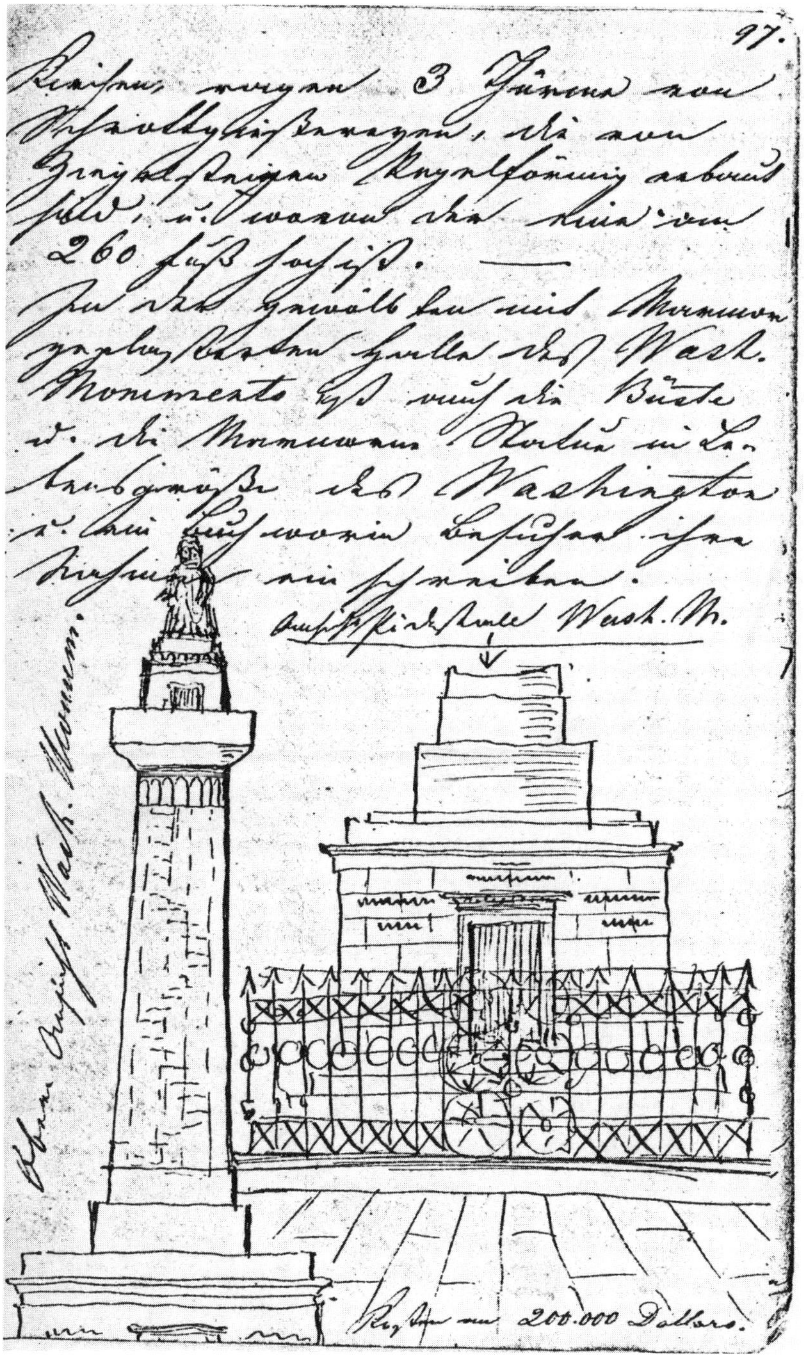

FIG. 1. Washington Monument, Baltimore. Diary of John R. Niernsee, 1839. Maryland Historical Society, Baltimore, Maryland

given to him by his father, Niernsee, along with two friends, was on his way to America. He was twenty-two years old when he and Alphonse de Pammstein, a distant cousin from Niernsee's mother's side, and Angelo Zyre, a classmate from Prague, first set out from Prague to Hamburg. It took them sixty-two days in 1836 to sail from Hamburg, probably to New York. Niernsee would not return to his native country until 1873, when he was nominated by President Ulysses S. Grant as his personal delegate to the International Exposition of 1873 in Vienna.

After barnstorming up and down the American eastern seaboard looking for work, the trio all found temporary government jobs in a program building coastal forts for the defense of the nation in response to the Napoleonic Wars and the British assault on Washington, D.C., in 1814. Niernsee would travel back and forth through the southeastern United States from South Carolina to Alabama at least three times between 1836 and 1839. He recorded the mileage of his travels in the back of the final volume of his diary. The diary begins in mid-1838, when Niernsee is completing some survey work and making field notes for the future construction of the Alabama-Georgia-Florida Railroad Company. Niernsee traveled from Montgomery, Alabama, to Pensacola, Florida, and back in late 1838, a four-hundred-mile trek on horseback through the wilderness. Unfortunately, the railroad soon filed for bankruptcy because of the effects of the Panic of 1837, but Niernsee was paid to continue his survey work.

Niernsee's complete diary, which spans the years 1838 to 1841, documents his hand-to-mouth existence. Most importantly, it records his keen and often eloquent descriptions of life in the American South, which did not always make for pleasant working conditions. As a European, unused to high heat and humidity, he often complained that "the heat begins to be severe and almost unendurable for us Europeans. The thermometer reads 100 degrees here in New Orleans and even farther north it is that hot."[5] His time in Alabama was especially miserable: "There was no one in camp who did not want to get out of the region of the Pigion River and the wilderness after this half year of torture" (May 6, 1838). He was also unaccustomed to snakes: "We killed many of them from two to five feet long and of the thickness of a man's arm" (May 5).

Despite the harshness of the southern climate, Niernsee had great admiration for the scenic beauty of the country and enjoyed visiting cities like New Orleans, "a confluence of almost all nations." He was fascinated by many Americans' habit of whittling, and he especially enjoyed chatting up young Southern belles and observing the curious habits of Creoles. "He drinks, eats, runs, works and sits in the sun as much and as long as he desires without paying any attention to the climate. He is always well unless he takes too much to the bottle," wrote Niernsee of the Creoles, admiring their "cold-blooded indifference" (July 1, 1838) to the harsh Louisiana climate.

The young engineer did not have to live out in the wild all the time. In cities like Pensacola, he stayed in a hotel or rented a room in a fine house for thirty dollars a month including meals. His journey through the South was more than mere employment for Niernsee; it was an education that enabled him to visit all manner of industry, study the architecture of the New World, and also read and draw. Except at the time of his father's death, he was never homesick for Austria; rather, he unequivocally believed that America offered him the greatest opportunity for success.[6]

Because the country's declining economic conditions in the late 1830s made the future of his surveying work in the South quite uncertain, Niernsee had a plan in case this work dried up. He would try his hand as an architect in New Orleans or in the northern states. His decision to do this seemed to stem from his criticism of the military architecture he encountered in the South. In Pensacola, a new military hospital prompted him to comment that "the architectural taste of the buildings is as bad as it can be only in the case of American military engineers who at the same time like to be architects" (Oct. 8, 1838). Niernsee bemoaned the lack of design skills in the engineering profession (a charge architects make to the present day) and was eager to get an opportunity to display his own architectural skills:

Thus here too, in this country, many thousands of dollars are spent without creating something really beautiful in the way of architecture. This is because of the same reason as in Austria; namely that one leaves the drafts (designs) and executions of them to the government engineer because one believes that a lieutenant or a major of a regiment of engineers must have—without fail—the best taste in architecture and all other talents. I believe, without flattering myself, that I would have been able to produce more useful and cheaper buildings for the fifth part of the money and salary which these engineers got during the many years of construction. They would also have been able to claim the appearance of a tasteful style in the art of architecture. (Oct. 18, 1838)

Formal engineering education in America was dominated in the beginning of the nineteenth century by one institution—the U.S. Military Academy at West Point, New York.

The U.S. Army Corps of Engineers, like the academy, was founded in 1802, and both were the country's training grounds for its engineers, especially in constructing coastal fortifications and defenses. The military engineers were also responsible for public works in peacetime.[7] Before gaining fame as a Civil War general, Robert E. Lee was a highly regarded engineer. At West Point, architectural training was only a sidelight to engineering studies, unlike the curriculums in European polytechnics, which gave more weight to design. Niernsee's education had given him a far broader training when it came to architecture, and in addition, the European cities where the schools were located had rich architectural heritages themselves. Niernsee's European design sophistication was a continuation of the superior education that the first immigrant architects like Benjamin Henry Latrobe and Maximilian Godefroy brought to America in the early 1800s. Compared to most of his American counterparts, Niernsee was exceptionally well educated. His obituary in *American Architect and Building News* in 1885 pointed out that it was rare to find an engineer with such formal training in the United States in the 1830s and 1840s. But it would be another eight years before Niernsee would be able to demonstrate his skill as an architect.

After an unsuccessful month-long search for employment in New Orleans at the beginning of 1839, Niernsee decided that he had exhausted his southern opportunities for work and bought passage aboard a riverboat traveling up the Mississippi and Ohio Rivers. From Wheeling, Virginia (now West Virginia), an important port on the Ohio, he took a stagecoach to Frederick, Maryland, then finally arrived at Philadelphia in March. To his great disappointment, there was no work to be had: "The place of which I expected so much, I found all my expectations and ideas to be in vain." With his last four dollars, he made his way to New York but, despite going from office to office, could not find any work. To complicate matters, he had fallen in love, but with no money or employment prospects, marriage was out of the question. "I am about to starve. I am thinking of powder and lead, " he wailed into his diary.

Almost two months later, Niernsee got a temporary drafting job in Washington for the U.S Army Corps of Engineers. He sent out dozens of employment queries in search of a permanent position. In August, with work about

to run out, his luck finally changed. He received a letter from Benjamin H. Latrobe Jr., a field engineer for the B&O railroad who was looking for a draftsman. With a promise of at least three years work and an eventual pay raise from three to five dollars a day, Niernsee quickly accepted the position.[8]

Niernsee was fortunate to find any engineering work at all. The Panic of 1837 had spawned a depression that lingered on into 1839. "Credit in this country does not seem to have recovered. People who have extra money don't seem to care to invest it in railroads, buildings, or canals," he complained when he got to Philadelphia.[9] But the young engineer's path luckily crossed with one of the country's greatest engineering efforts—the building of the Baltimore & Ohio Railroad. The railroad, despite the economic conditions and rudimentary state of railroad technology, was determined to build its line from Baltimore to Wheeling.

The success of New York State's Erie Canal in 1825 had made canals the preferred commercial pathways in the United States, and railroad investment was considered a great financial risk. On July 4, 1828, the same day that the B&O began work, the Chesapeake & Ohio Canal started construction on its water route along the Potomac River to the Ohio River. Nevertheless, the B&O's board of directors risked their financial fortunes on the railroad. At the time, it seemed a ludicrous choice. The only real rail technology used at the time in America was short haul railroads that carried stone and coal, and steam locomotives were laughably primitive. Since no one had actually built a rail line, railroad engineering literally was invented each day. Niernsee and his fellow B&O engineers would create the core of the profession for future generations of railroad men. Latrobe's offer of employment would change his life forever. This one incredible stroke of good luck would not just provide Niernsee with a job, but set him on the path to his future success as an architect.

He also had the great good fortune to work under an exceptional man. In his letter to Niernsee, Latrobe explained the duties of an office draftsman—basically, drawing plans and sections and making copies of plans (there was no blueprinting). There was a caveat, however; the position "would not permit you to exercise to much extent at least your powers of design or bringing actual contact with works in course of construction."[10] This may have irked Niernsee, but it was a promising job, and he knew it was a start with eventual possibilities for designing, especially the depots and other ancillary structures the railroad would need.

Latrobe was a son of Benjamin Henry Latrobe, who is considered the father of the American architectural profession and was the architect of the Baltimore cathedral and the old House and Senate chambers in the U.S. Capitol, among other early American architectural masterworks. Latrobe, who inherited his talent from his brilliant father, initially trained to be a lawyer at Georgetown College and St. Mary's College in Baltimore. Discovering that he was more interested in surveying and engineering than law, he secured a position with the B&O in 1830 through his brother John H. B. Latrobe, the company's attorney, who had studied engineering at West Point (the brothers had made opposite career choices—"a swap between us,"[11] John later explained). Latrobe, along with his brother, would spend most of his professional life with the B&O, his main achievement being the construction of the line from Harpers Ferry to Wheeling. In building this line, he became America's pioneer railroad engineer. On August 31, 1839, before his visit to the Washington Monument, Niernsee had walked out to the Thomas Viaduct, which carried the railroad over the Patapsco River. The 704-foot-long arched structure, which Niernsee described as a "pretty bridge made of granite," was designed by Latrobe, who had never designed a bridge or taken an engineering course. The $200,000 bridge was America's largest in 1835 and the first to be constructed on a curving alignment. But most importantly for Niernsee, Latrobe was a man who recognized talent, and he would prove to be the most important influence in the young man's career.[12]

Niernsee made a home for himself in Baltimore and with the B&O, and he quickly proved himself to be highly qualified as a draftsman, a surveyor, an engineer, and an estimator. Nor was he confined to the office as Latrobe's letter had predicted. By December 1839, he had gained the confidence of the B&O's chief engineer, Jonathan Knight, who invited him to tour the rail line to Cumberland, which he described in great detail in his diary. Niernsee traveled the eighty-two miles from Baltimore to Harpers Ferry on a locomotive at a speed of twelve to eighteen miles an hour. His account details the hardships of early railroad construction; steep grades made travel difficult, and mountains had to be tunneled through with black powder at a cost of millions of dollars. He understood the great impact the railroads would have on the nation, observing that the B&O would connect the east with the southern and western states. "From Wheeling one can go by boat to New Orleans, a distance of over 3,000 miles which can be covered in 5 or 6 days including even two nights of rest."[13]

The inspection tour was valuable because it gave Niernsee his first overview of the entire route, but more significantly, on it he met the man who would play the most important role in his professional life—his future partner, James Crawford Neilson, the B&O's resident engineer stationed at Martinsburg, Virginia (now West Virginia). Their friendship began with a pleasant evening at an inn on the night of December 5, 1839, "talking to the pretty daughters of the innkeeper" (Dec. 5, 1839).

Niernsee was so busy with his railroad work that he stopped his diary entries for almost two years, from December 1839 to October 1841. When he took up his pen again, his diary was of a more personal nature. He wrote of his lodgings, the boardinghouse of a Mrs. Bradenbough, which was located on Fayette Street. The Bradenboughs were ordinary Baltimore folk of German descent, but Mrs. Bradenbough was descended from Peter Dennis, a French planter from Santo Domingo, who had been driven out, like most Frenchmen, by the black slave revolt of 1801, which led to the formation of Haiti. Mrs. Bradenbough had a daughter named Emily, with whom Niernsee was very much enchanted. She was bright and interesting and lively, and he volunteered to send her to the female academy in Emmitsburg for her education. Judging from his earlier diary entries, Niernsee was always falling in love, but he never considered proposing because of his dire financial straits. But marriage was an important goal in life for the young Austrian, almost as important as professional success.

When Emily returned to Baltimore in 1842, Niernsee married the fifteen-year-old.[14] He romantically documented their courtship in his diary, though several of these pages were sentimentally torn out by his wife. His social life in Baltimore was also made more pleasurable because more than 20,000 German immigrants arrived in the city during the 1830s, making up one fifth of Baltimore's population. His years traveling in the South had given Niernsee the opportunity to perfect his English, unlike the 5,000 Baltimore Germans who could not speak English. In the same year he arrived in Baltimore, a proposal before the city council unsuccessfully attempted to have all laws and legal documents printed in German. More Germans were to come; from 1840 to 1860, most of the 170,000 immigrants who arrived were from German-speaking countries. Throughout his life, Niernsee would remain well connected to the city's German community.[15] Niernsee's life, both professionally and personally, now seemed set. But he still did not know what good fortune lay ahead for both him and the B&O engineer from Martinsburg.

Although James Crawford Neilson was born in Baltimore in 1816, his early life and education, in part, mirrored his future partner's foreign upbringing. After his birth, he was immediately taken to England, where his mother and father moved to various places in the western part of the country in Devonshire, chiefly settling in Exeter and in Dullish, a seaside town on the Cornish coast. Neilson was baptized in Exeter along with his sisters at the Church of St. Mary's Steps, which still stands. Neilson's father was in poor health and when he died, Mrs. Neilson, who was by birth a Dutch citizen and of Belgian origin (the Kingdom of Holland then included Belgium), left with the children for Brussels to live with her sister and brother-in-law, a retired English Army officer named von Barley.

Neilson was schooled and tutored until the age of sixteen in Belgium. He must have been fluent in French, as one could not live in a city like Brussels without at least a moderate knowledge of either the Flemish or the French language. When a revolution broke out in 1836, Mrs. Neilson sent her two oldest children back to Baltimore. James was enrolled at St. Mary's College, the alma mater of Benjamin H. Latrobe Jr., apparently to study engineering, including mathematics and surveying, the specialties of the school at the time. When Neilson had completed his courses at St. Mary's, he was hired by Latrobe as an apprentice-surveyor assisting him in the surveys of the Baltimore and Port Deposit Railroad. Latrobe saw the young man's ability, and when Latrobe began the surveys for the extension of the B&O from Point of Rocks to Cumberland, Neilson was promoted to field engineer, and he completed the surveys from

which the railroad was built. Latrobe very soon called him into service for the surveys of the proposed line to Pittsburgh.[16]

Meanwhile, Neilson's future partner dove into his new B&O job with great enthusiasm. After Niernsee arrived for work on Monday, September 2, 1839, he quickly settled into the office's routine. "I spent the months of September, October, and November rather undisturbed ... I went to the office regularly, where I drew plans and maps to the best of my ability and where I performed the duties of an office engineer," he recorded in his diary in December 1839. Soon after he began work and probably to his great pleasure, there came an opportunity to design two buildings for the Frederick and Washington branches of the railroad. In the early years of railroad development, there was little need for passenger stations. Passengers at the B&O's first depot at Ellicotts' Mills, thirteen miles west of Baltimore, waited for trains at the adjacent Patapsco Hotel. But freight houses and buildings for equipment storage were essential. Niernsee soon developed a special design expertise for these utilitarian structures; most significantly, they were of iron rather than timber.

Prior to the mid-1840s, few American buildings used iron except for fasteners or columns. The use of iron then greatly increased when it was applied to bridges, storefronts, and lighthouses. The years 1850–51 were a watershed for ironwork in America. Iron became the standard material for railroad bridges and for lighthouses built by the U.S. Army Corps of Engineers. The federal government specified that all its new buildings have iron internal frames. Niernsee would be technologically ahead of his time in the use of this new material in America, because Europeans, especially the French and the British, had been using iron technology for at least fifty years.[17]

Although his early railroad buildings are no longer extant, Niernsee wrote a detailed description of their construction in the summer of 1842 for publication in the *Allgemeine Bauzeitung*, a Viennese engineering magazine. The article, which describes the structures in the ponderous, learned style of that period, is accompanied by a single plate, which details the structural frames for the two buildings (fig. 2).

The first of the two was a small engine house in Frederick, Maryland, which was only about thirty feet wide. The early locomotives for the

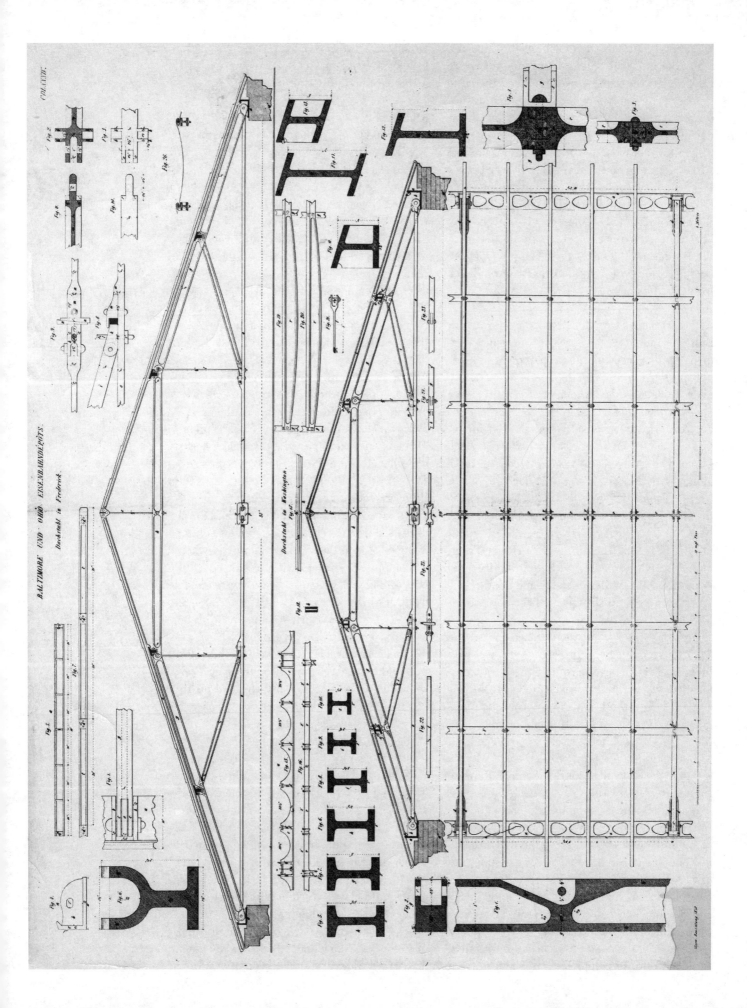

BALTIMORE UND OHIO EISENBAHNDEPÔTS.

Durchschnitt in Frederick.

Durchschnitt in Washington.

B&O were the so-called Grasshoppers, whose operating machinery was exposed, so they needed to be stored in an engine house. It was the design of the roof and especially its cast-iron and wrought-iron construction that shows that Niernsee's innate structural intuition. The roof trusses were totally constructed of iron, a sophisticated combination of wrought iron tie bars and cast-iron castings for web and chord members. Using wrought-iron pins, the structure could move freely as the temperature changed. A turnbuckle on the bottom chord and other fasteners could be tightened to make all the components work together as one strong structural unit. Totally different from English types of roof structures, they were quite similar to many European trusses of the time and were, in fact, somewhat unstable, depending solely upon bending at a critical point for the development of the full stability of the truss. Niernsee knew that railroad buildings had to be easy and inexpensive to construct. The ingenious quality of these trusses was that they were designed simply to be hoisted in place and connected with roof purlins, then covered with zinc sheets to make a complete roof. The zinc roofing had flanges on the outer end. These fit into grooves in the top chord of the truss, treated as a small U-shaped gutter, which was covered by a supplementary piece of zinc to hold the sheet in place.[18]

The other building was much more ambitious, a 350-foot-long freight warehouse in Washington, D.C. This building was on a curving section of the B&O line, which originally ran to a depot on what is presently Constitution Avenue. Designed with a track running through it and a platform alongside for the handling of freight, the freight house was fitted with doors at each end to prevent theft.

The trusses for both buildings are nearly identical in design; those for the Washington building had cast-iron I-beam members for the top chord and struts. But because the building was built on a curve, it could not be roofed in a similar fashion as the Frederick structure; preformed zinc sheets would have had to be made in two sizes and would have involved considerable waste of material. The roofing was made of thick slate slabs, which were laid on purlins spanning the trusses. The joint at this point of support was decked by metal covers. Niernsee carefully explains to the readers why he chose the roof pitches for both buildings that he did. Because he felt that a steep North European

roof slope for a building whose walls were only nineteen feet high would be ungainly, he chose instead a low-slope pediment, which he adopted on the assumption that snow accumulations in Washington and Frederick were not that severe. In an age in which structural testing was practically nonexistent, Niernsee actually performed a load test on the I-beams at three times the design load.[19] This building and its roof existed until the early 1930s, when it was cleared away for the completion of the Federal Triangle and the plaza of Union Station.

The article closes with an extensive analysis of the weights of the members of the roofs and their costs. Niernsee also explains the economy and speed obtained by doing such work in the railroad's own shops and transporting it to the site in the field for erection. Ironically, Niernsee's skill in designing these two structures was recognized in Europe, but in America, where engineering publications were almost nonexistent, his work went unnoticed. Niernsee may not have been the first to incorporate an iron roof into a design, but it is certain that these were the first thoroughly documented iron roofed buildings built in the United States. His engineering reputation has suffered, since few knew of his contribution to the introduction of structural iron into American building practice. In addition to the descriptions of the buildings, he included a summary of the rest of his B&O work, listing a number of buildings on the drawing board, such as two 150-foot-diameter prefabricated round-houses to be built at Harpers Ferry and at Cumberland.

The engineering process that went into the design of the buildings was atypical for the time. Niernsee, a formally trained engineer with a background in mathematics and structural design, teamed with James Murray, the foundry chief at the B&O Railroad's Mount Clare shops, a mechanic whose structural sense was entirely empirical. It was rare for a man of Niernsee's training to be designing railroad structures. Most structural design in this period was handled entirely by builders with no formal engineering training and whose knowledge of materials prior to about 1850 was largely confined to wood and stone.

Mathematically based engineering science in America was in its infancy. There were still very few formally trained engineers, especially structural engineers, even from West Point or new engineering colleges like Rensselaer Polytechnic

FIG. 2. *(opposite)*
B&O Railroad Engine
House, Frederick,
MD. From *Allgemeine
Bauzeitung*, 1842.
Smithsonian Institution, National Museum
of American History

9

Institute, which granted its first engineering degree in 1835. Even by 1870, formal education was a rarity; of the approximately four thousand engineers working in America, only seventy-five had an engineering degree. There were no independent engineering firms in America during Niernsee's years with the B&O. The railroads and canals employed engineers, and the men who designed the B&O bridges, like Latrobe and most famously, Wendel Bollman, were self-taught. In the absence of mathematically based engineering, early iron structures were overbuilt.

In contrast, Niernsee had sufficient knowledge of mathematics and structural analysis to do an accurate calculation of the stresses. He could design an economical yet structurally safe truss. Niernsee's article demonstrates his sophisticated knowledge of the actions of trusses, their lateral and longitudinal compressive forces, the transfer of loads, and the problems of wall settlement at the truss-bearing points. Murray provided practical advice on the fabrication and the assembly of the components. Niernsee gave Murray credit in his article, and both jointly held the patent on the design. It is clear that all of these parts of the roof trusses could be cast and assembled in the Mount Clare works, put on a freight car, transported to the destination, and easily erected. There is no other record of any prefabricated building of the period of this magnitude which was transported by rail to the site of construction.[20]

Niernsee would design more B&O buildings: a roundhouse at Martinsburg, another engine house that was re-erected in Martinsburg, and freight houses and roundhouses at both Cumberland and Martinsburg in 1858 when he was in private practice. He contributed one more article to the *Allgemeine Bauzeitung* in the summer of 1842, on B&O construction methods—the building of the right-of-way of the railroad and the details of experiments in cross ties and the support of iron rails, most of which were abandoned later in favor of the ubiquitous wooden cross ties set in rock ballast.

Both Niernsee and Neilson were kept quite busy as the B&O drove west toward Cumberland. By 1842, the promise of a two-dollar raise seemed just that. B&O records list Niernsee as an office draftsman in the engineering department still earning three dollars per day. His future partner also made three dollars per day as a resident engineer.[21] Aside from the buildings described in his article, no records of Niernsee's

other design work for the B&O exist; some of the company's records from that period were destroyed in the Baltimore Fire of 1904, when the railroad's headquarters burned down. When the railroad was actually completed to Cumberland in 1842, there came a hiatus in construction in which time was sought to seek additional funds and to reap the income from the railroad's new expansion to the rich coalmines of the Georges Creek region west of Cumberland.

Neilson's job at Martinsburg came to an end after the completion of the road to Cumberland. In those days, railroad engineers were immediately laid off once their services were no longer required. Niernsee was luckier; his employment with Latrobe lasted until 1845, probably because of his design talent.

Neilson applied to the U.S. Army Corps of Engineer's Coastal Survey, which had employed Niernsee in the late 1830s. His first project for the survey was charting the Chesapeake Bay; Neilson's name appears on each of these charts, along with the rest of the staff who prepared them. Neilson went out on the survey schooners, and nearly lost his life one afternoon near Sandy Point, Anne Arundel County, Maryland, when a squall capsized the vessel. Neilson was occupied in the winter drawing the charts. At the same time, he also stayed at his new wife's family home called Priestford, in Deer Creek in Harford County, Maryland. He had married well, in June of 1840; Rosa Williams was the daughter of James W. Williams, a congressman from Maryland.

The B&O Railroad transformed Baltimore into an economic power. The construction and equipping of the railroad not only created jobs and new businesses for the city but also attracted a unique array of engineering talent to build the line and design the rolling stock and the scores of bridges it needed. Young engineers like Niernsee and Neilson had the great fortune to be part of this pioneering effort of American engineering. They learned a great deal from their B&O work, which laid the foundation for their future success. When Niernsee's B&O tenure was finally up in 1845, he was back looking for a job as he had been six years earlier. He wrote to Colonel Joseph Totten of the U.S. Army Corps of Engineers in Washington about employment, but there were no positions available. The prospects for work now seemed dim, but once again, Benjamin H. Latrobe Jr. came to his aid. He had plans of his own for the young engineer.

TWO

The First Partnership and Town Houses in Mount Vernon

By the mid 1840s, the land around the Washington Monument was being transformed into Baltimore's most prestigious residential district, Mount Vernon Place. The new neighborhood would be built on land at the south end of Belvidere, the estate of the Revolutionary War hero John Eager Howard, who in 1815 had donated a small parcel for the erection of the monument. After his death in 1827, his heirs laid out the land around the monument into building lots facing four parks surrounding the monument.

Baltimore's housing patterns, which dated from its founding in 1729, were slowly changing. Men of wealth no longer wanted to live cheek by jowl with the working classes near the harbor. They now desired to live away from the city's commercial center in more spacious quarters befitting their status. The nature of the business class was undergoing a change as well. Instead of traditional merchants actively involved in the day-to-day running of shipping concerns and small businesses in the city, "men of capital," who made their money from investments came to dominate Baltimore's business community, becoming the city's wealthiest citizens. These were the men who came to live in Mount Vernon.

The streets defining Mount Vernon had been laid out when John Niernsee visited the monument in 1839, but the blocks were mostly vacant. The lots would soon be filled with grand town houses, designed in the latest architectural fashion—the Greek Revival. And Benjamin H. Latrobe Jr. desired to live in such a house in Mount Vernon. Latrobe had prospered with the B&O, becoming the chief engineer in 1842. He had risen in Baltimore society by proving

to the wealthy directors of the B&O what an exceptionally talented man he was. The driving force behind the construction of the line to Cumberland and to Wheeling, Latrobe kept a firm hand on all aspects of the project, including construction, surveying, cost estimates and economic forecasts, which convinced stockholders that all this work would prove profitable. Many men, as well as the City of Baltimore and the State of Maryland, had invested heavily in the B&O. They realized that Latrobe was the one indispensable man who could bring the great enterprise to completion and thus financial success. The entire cost of the expansion to Wheeling would be $22 million, only 6 percent over Latrobe's original estimate—an extraordinary feat given that he was building a railroad for the first time and over mountainous terrain.[1]

Latrobe would build two houses, at 606 and 608 South Washington Place, one for himself and the other to sell. The architectural profession was slowly gaining a foothold in Baltimore, and there were a few men who had made the transition from carpenter-builder or gentleman-architect to true practitioner of architecture. Latrobe could have chosen a local architect like Robert Cary Long Jr. to design his houses, but instead he gave the opportunity to his former B&O engineer. The choice was probably based in part on his admiration of Niernsee's ability and the lower fee the young architect probably charged to get his start in the profession. Niernsee had been waiting for this opportunity since his days surveying in the South. He could not have wished for a better first client to begin his career. To garner important commissions, an architect needs clients with connections and influence, and Latrobe, with his ties to the Baltimore business community and society gave Niernsee an excellent entry to this very privileged world. Niernsee's career would be a textbook case of how the right architectural patronage could pave the way for a very successful practice.

Latrobe's houses were prominent enough to be described in the *Baltimore Sun* in 1846. The *Sun*, which had begun regularly reporting on the building activities around Mount Vernon about this time, commented, "Taking it throughout, Baltimore can boast few finer buildings than this."[2] The buildings were quite large, with twenty-eight-foot fronts, three stories, and an attic; with back buildings, the total depth was ninety-seven feet. The interiors were trimmed in marble and heated by hot air furnaces. The façades of the houses, which were not identical, were done in the Greek Revival style; marble steps led to a columned Greek Doric portico beyond which lay the vestibule, opening to a double parlor and elegant staircase. There were two large bedrooms in the second story and three in the third. The attic story held servant's quarters and storage rooms. The fireplaces throughout the house were done in marble, and a boiler in the basement kitchen sent hot water to the "bath house" in the third story of the back building.[3]

Niernsee needed design guidance as to what was "au courant" and may have turned to builders' guides for inspiration (there were no architectural publications at this time). In 1840, one year after Niernsee had settled in Baltimore, John Hall, a builder-architect and furniture designer published *A Series of Select and Original Modern Designs for Dwelling Houses*, providing designs and floor plans for fashionable Greek Revival style houses. He also published a book detailing compatible interior decorating schemes, including suitable furniture and the production of appropriate moldings. A third book was a guide for carpenters on developing elaborate curving staircases and their geometry.

Most row housing in the city was "designed" by carpenter-builders, who depended heavily on such guides. Niernsee likely took his design cues from earlier high-style Greek Revival houses in the neighborhood. John Eager Howard's sons, William and Charles, had erected Greek Revival row houses in the early 1830s, which set the architectural standard for much of the future residential development. Both boasted Ionic porticos

with low-pitched roofs and attic windows. The Morton House at 107 West Monument Street was another important Greek Revival composition of the late 1830s—five bays wide with an attic story and a free-standing portico and tiny attic windows. In 1842, William Tiffany commissioned an unknown architect to design a five-bay-wide house at 8 West Mount Vernon Place that had a tall English basement and a bold four-columned Doric entrance portico.[4]

The influence of these buildings is apparent in Niernsee's early residential designs and would set a precedent for his design approach for the rest of his career. Niernsee was never to be a highly innovative architect, but one who was very adept at manipulating current and past styles into dynamic compositions. One of Latrobe's houses eventually became an annex to the original Walters Art Gallery, and both were later torn down to provide the site for the present 1909 museum building at the northwest corner of Charles and Centre Streets. Aside from the description of the Latrobe House, the *Sun* article contained two very important sentences— "This splendid mansion has been erected for B. H. Latrobe, Esq. It was constructed under the superintendence of Mr. John R. Niernsee, architect."[5] It was the very first mention of Niernsee's work in the press. Many more complimentary articles would appear in Baltimore newspapers over Niernsee's career, making his talent and ability known to the public and playing a major role in garnering him new commissions.

With the Latrobe House, Niernsee established a precedent that architects follow to this day—he supervised the actual construction of the project to make sure his design was executed properly. Latrobe paid him $1,800 for the supervision alone. In that era, there were usually no general contractors who handled entire projects; instead, Niernsee would hire the subcontractors and act as superintendent, a practice that no architect would follow today.

Without Latrobe's commission, Niernsee probably would have left Baltimore in search of an engineer's position after he was let go by the B&O. Instead, with this first job from an influential member of Baltimore society, he was able to put up his shingle and advertise that he would do architectural and engineering work (including steam engineering, a discipline that was never taken up).

Other than Latrobe's houses, there is no record of work done by Niernsee on his own

THE FIRST
PARTNERSHIP AND
TOWN HOUSES IN
MOUNT VERNON

account between 1846 and 1848. His work for Latrobe began to pay dividends in 1848, however, when he garnered three important residential commissions in Mount Vernon. Again the *Sun* took note of the new work and in November 1849 commented on "the splendid places of residence recently erected thereon, which, for general beauty of exterior, elegant workmanship, and convenience of interior arrangements would lose nothing in comparison with any similar edifices in the Union."[6] All three followed the Greek Revival model; the Edmund Didier House at 16 West Mount Vernon Place had a "chaste Greek front and portico of classic taste and beauty." The house was drastically altered in 1888 and 1896 to reflect the current Romanesque revival style. The George Tiffany House at 12 West Mount Vernon Place was also a Greek Revival composition with a lavish interior; the floors were done in marble with the main stair lit by a dome of stained glass (fig. 3). The façade was ornamented by an elaborate balcony of cast iron, a material that was beginning to come into use by the end of the 1840s.

The John H. Duvall House, across the street at 5 West Mount Vernon Place, had a similar Greek Revival exterior (fig. 4). It is one of the very few buildings for which Niernsee's original drawings still exist. Found in the posses-

sion of the Historical Society of Pennsylvania, the drawings, which were submitted with an application for insurance to the Franklin Fire Insurance Company of Philadelphia in 1848, show the original design including a cross section through the depth of the house (fig. 5).

The design was standard for a high-style row house of the period with a spacious stair hall, a double parlor, forty-six feet in length, and a large dining room in the back building from which a rear stair led to the kitchen and scullery in the basement. Bedrooms and a study were located in the second and third stories. The servant's room at the rear of the third story of the back building was connected to the rest of the levels with a stair, and behind the main stair was another servant's stair to the basement. At the rear of the main block, a balcony on the first and second stories overlooked the garden. The house was well proportioned with a three-bay-wide, thirty-foot frontage and fifteen- and fourteen-foot ceilings on the first and second levels, respectively. Instead of being a cramped space, the basement, housing the kitchen, had a twelve-foot ceiling and its own outside entry located where the back building joined the main block. All of Niernsee's Mount Vernon houses had indoor bathrooms, a luxury only the wealthy could afford at the time. The bathroom would not

FIG. 5. John R.
Niernsee, Duvall
House, Baltimore,
plans. Historical
Society of Pennsyl-
vania

NIERNSEE
AND NEILSON

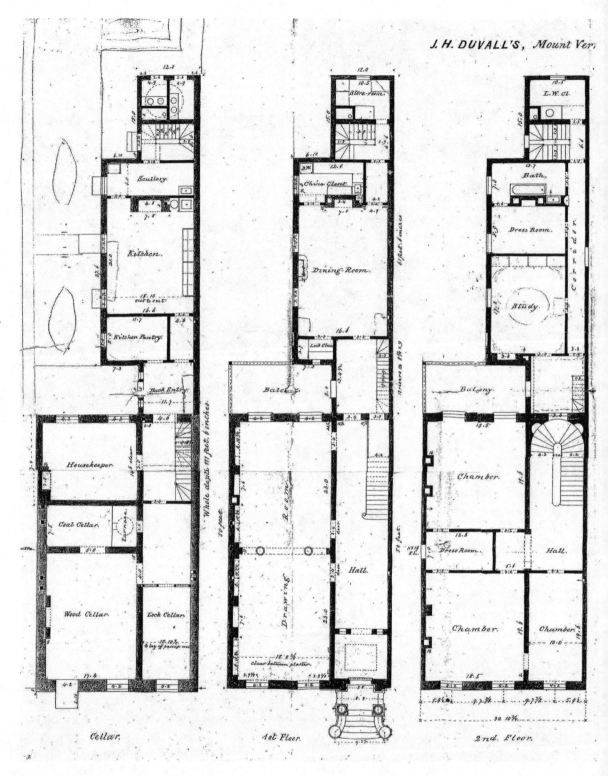

J.H. DUVALL'S, Mount Ver

Cellar. *1st Floor.* *2nd. Floor.*

become a middle-class convenience until after the Civil War.[7]

Assuming that Niernsee did the drawings himself (he signed them), they clearly show his fine drafting ability. Many architectural drawings of this period were just crude pencil sketches by carpenters. Any detailing was drawn in chalk at full scale on a floor or wall at the building site. It is readily apparent from Niernsee's drawings that he had been trained in drafts-

manship at the Polytechnic in Prague. Done in ink on linen, as was the practice of the time, the line work is crisp, accurate, and professional. Instead of single lines to delineate the walls, he gave them properly scaled thicknesses as well as "pocheing" them, or coloring the walls with ink. All dimensions are indicated, including those for the doors, windows, and stairs, with the lettering done in an European-influenced cursive manner. The section indicates the design

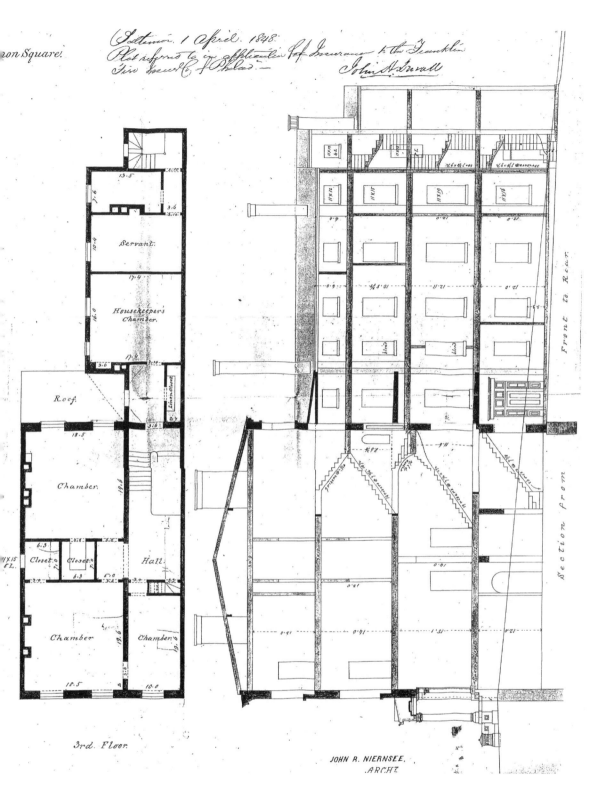

of the entry portico and calls out the three-inch by twelve-inch wood floor joists. Compared to today's construction documents, which spell out the tiniest detail in order to avoid liability problems, nineteenth-century drawings give the bare minimum of information, leaving the construction methods and interior and exterior detailing to the craftsmen.

Architects in this era spent much more time at the building site than architects do today,

answering questions and sketching out details on the spot. The *Sun* routinely listed the subcontractors on every job, and it is clear that Niernsee liked to use particular craftsmen again and again, like John E. Davis, a carpenter, Dieter Barger, a bricklayer, and Bell & Packie, marble cutters, probably because he knew they were trustworthy and did high-quality work. The Duvall, Didier, and Tiffany Houses were very expensive for the time—a total cost of

FIG. 6. Thomas House, Baltimore, ca. 1860. Maryland Historical Society, Baltimore, Maryland

$60,000 ($1.4 million in 2004). The newspaper praised all three houses, but most importantly, it acknowledged the designer, "they were designed and superintended in all their details by John R. Niernsee, Esq. Architect." Positive publicity of this kind gave momentum to Niernsee's practice and very soon his plate was full of commissions—all from affluent influential Baltimoreans, which in turn would lead to even more commissions.

But it would be his next house that would secure his reputation. The Thomas House, later known as the Jencks House and now called the Hackerman House, at 1 West Mount Vernon Place, is considered Niernsee's masterpiece (fig. 6). The house, built for the wealthy physician and banker Dr. John Hansen Thomas, was noteworthy from the beginning for its size and its expense. The building, the *Sun* reported when construction began, "has already attracted considerable attention from both artisans and property holders" (Dec. 14, 1848). The building was, at the time of its construction, extremely

sumptuous in its decoration and fittings, and a landmark of domestic architecture in Baltimore.

The house also marked an important stylistic transition in Baltimore. Instead of strictly adhering to the Greek Revival models of previous years, Niernsee cautiously introduced Italianate features to residential design in the Thomas House. The Italianate had been used in commercial buildings and townhouses in New York since the mid 1840s and by the 1850s supplanted the Greek Revival across the country. The house continued the basic proportions and elements of the old style; five bays wide with attic windows, measuring fifty-nine feet across and sixty-three feet deep with a raised entrance portico of four Corinthian columns, "of the purist white Italian marble," reported the *Sun*. But it was the embellishment of the north and east façades that was novel in its use of a new architectural material. The tall windows are topped with Italianate-style cast-iron architraves molded in a Greek Revival motif.

16

The most arresting new feature, however, is the deep overhanging Italianate cornice, supported by scroll brackets. In a nod to the old style, the top edge of the cornice is decorated with Greek acanthus leaf ornaments. The original stucco exterior, painted a classical dove gray, was later removed.[8]

The interior, as well, broke away from the Greek Revival and the mold set by John Hall. The focus inside the house is on a magnificent, semicircular oak staircase, which rises out of a large stair hall decorated in the Corinthian style. "Above the staircase," reported the *Sun*, "rises a superb oval dome, supported from the second floor by Corinthian columns of the same style as those below" (Jan. 24, 1851). The public rooms on the main floor are lit by French windows, glazed doors that extend from floor to ceiling and can be opened to allow full ventilation to the room. Each window opens onto a shallow cast-iron balcony, which gives a sense of privacy from the sidewalk only a few feet below. The second floor windows on the north and east façades also have similar cast-iron balconies. The floor plan revolves around the central staircase (fig. 7).

To the right of the stair hall is the usual double parlor, brilliantly decorated in stucco with its sixty-foot length broken up by two pairs of marbleized Corinthian columns. On the left, at the center of the house, was once a breakfast or morning room leading to the library in the front of the house, which was originally decorated in the Gothic Revival manner, with elaborately carved mahogany bookcases and trim, including carved wooden heads of famous authors such as Robert Burns and William Shakespeare, attached to the tops of the pilasters. Insets over the bookcases and doors were painted in trompe l'oeil fashion. The other door from the morning room led to the dining room at the rear, which was also designed in the Gothic Revival style, with plaster walls and ceiling painted in imitation of wood.

It was the insertion of these airy, central rooms, which focused on drawing room requirements, that was such a departure from the Greek Revival interiors published by John Hall. Entertaining in this period had a strict code of behavior, with women retiring to drawing rooms leaving the men in the dining room with port and cigars. The arrival of guests in the great hall created a sense of drama all its own with the monumental curving stair acting almost as a stage piece where the hostess stood to welcome her guests.

The house, completed in 1851, was remodeled in 1892 by Charles Platt, the architect and brother-in-law of Francis Jencks, the new owner of the house. The east façade was modified by the addition of a bay window to the dining room, as well as several other small changes to the exterior. An open rear porch with cast-iron railings was converted into a conservatory. The interior was changed to the extent that Platt seriously diminished the amount of decoration that was originally part of the architects' plan of 1848. This building has been renovated, including restoring its original color scheme, for use by the Walters Art Gallery, whose Asian art collection it now houses.

Niernsee's inclusion of fashionable Italianate elements in the Thomas House of 1848 shows that he was well up to date on current architectural trends sweeping the nation. Influenced by

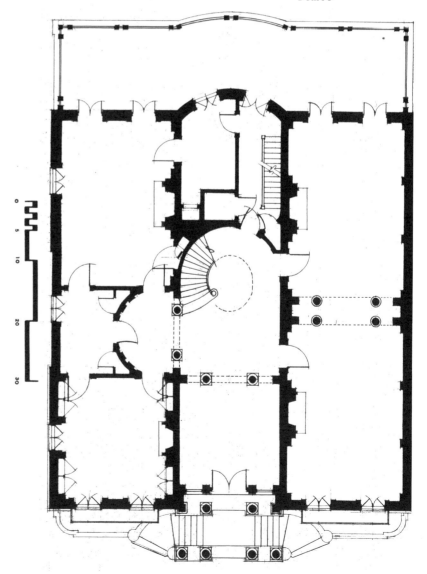

FIG. 7. Thomas House, Baltimore, first-floor plans. Peter Pearre

the Renaissance palazzo designs of the English architect Charles Barry, the Scottish born architect John Notman introduced the Italianate style to America as early as 1837 with the Bishop Doane House in Burlington, New Jersey, and the Philadelphia Atheneum of 1845. It is doubtful that Niernsee ever saw these buildings; instead, he relied on architectural books. In an age before architectural periodicals, architects and builders relied on books that illustrated the new styles. One early English work available in Baltimore in 1836 was *Encyclopedia of Cottage Farm and Villa Architecture*, by J. C. Loudon. American architect Alexander Jackson Davis published his designs in *Rural Architecture* in 1837. But the most influential architectural books of the period were Andrew Jackson Downing's *A Treatise on the Theory and Practice of Landscape Gardening*, published in 1841, and *Cottage Residences*, published in 1842, which introduced romantic styles, including the Italianate, to America. All these books were available to Niernsee, which undoubtedly helped him master the details of the new style, as evidenced by his handling of the Thomas House. At this time, Robert Cary Long Jr. designed an Athenaeum for Baltimore—the first building to bring the palazzo style to the city. Standing at the northwest corner of St. Paul and Saratoga Streets, the gleaming white marble building could not but have influenced Niernsee in his experiments with Italianate design.[9]

As the Thomas House was going up, Niernsee was working on a substantial dwelling for another important Baltimore businessman and banker, John S. Gittings, at the northeast corner of St. Paul and Monument Streets. Three stories in height and trimmed in marble, the forty-nine-foot-wide house had thirty rooms and cost $23,000. Gittings was so pleased with the results he took the hundred or so men involved in the construction out for a night on the town at John Himesley's Public House, where "everything that the epicurean palate of man could desire was provided in abundance, and the character of the feast was highly creditable to all concerned."[10]

Gittings, like Latrobe, also saw profit in building speculatively in Mount Vernon. He had already built rows of working-class houses in Fells Point and Federal Hill and now eyed a wealthier clientele. In 1851, he commissioned Niernsee to design six row houses for him at 104–112 East Madison Street, spacious three-story, three-bay-wide buildings with Italianate cornices (fig. 8). Originally stuccoed brown and scored in imitation of brownstone, the row still survives with the stucco removed from the brick façades. Though it was a speculative venture, the houses were not inexpensive—$100,000 in total cost. Beginning in the late 1840s, both the carpenter-builder who built for the working classes and the professional architect, like Niernsee, who designed for the wealthy, now bought a great many prefabricated architectural items, such as Gittings' wood cornices and arched entry surrounds, from established millwork dealers who mass produced their products with steam-powered machinery rather than by hand.[11]

The *Sun* article of December 14, 1848, credited both the Thomas and Gittings houses to the firm of Niernsee & Neilson. This was the first mention of the partnership in the press. Niernsee's good fortune in securing commissions meant he had more work than he could handle by himself and needed help, a reliable right-hand man. He knew Neilson's ability from their railroad days together. Neilson had come into Niernsee's office to assist him as early as April 1848 and certainly proved to be an able lieutenant, supervising the work and taking care of the office correspondence. The firm of Niernsee & Neilson legally began when partnership documents were signed in July 1848, and business started up at 16 East Fayette Street.

A successful partnership in any business comes about when each partner has a definite talent that the other does not. Their respective strengths must complement each other. In an architectural firm, these talents usually divide into design, business procurement, and construction administration. The melding of these separate abilities creates an effective working relationship, and this is exactly what happened with Niernsee & Neilson. It is clear that Niernsee presided over all of the design work of the firm until its dissolution in 1855. Neilson had no formal training in architecture, but being of a quick mind and an analytical nature, he may have contributed to the critiques of the works in progress but more likely served as construction supervisor. Meticulous and detail oriented, he was well suited to this role. The engineering experience he gained from the B&O Railroad gave Neilson a complete understanding of the building process. But at the same time, Neilson was actually serving an architectural

FIG. 8. Row Houses, Madison Street, Baltimore. Charles Belfoure

apprenticeship and learning the design side of the profession, something that would be quite beneficial to him in the future.

As opposed to being a firm run by a sole practitioner with very little drafting help, as was the norm for early architectural firms in America, Niernsee & Neilson became Baltimore's first full-service firm, with a drafting staff and a business structure that could handle the volume of work that poured in from 1848 to 1855. Processing the enormous amounts of paperwork for the accounting, contracting, and inspecting that all these projects generated could not have been accomplished without the able assistance of a staff. Part of the firm's success was the thoroughness with which it supervised the various contracts for its clients. Though no accounting or project records of the firm remain, there is evidence in the form of records from clients' daybooks that both partners were scrupulous in their control of the work of various contractors. The work was inspected, approved, and the owner billed only when satisfactory completion was achieved. Bills from the alteration of the Thomas Swann House, for example, show where the architects wrote "correct" and signed their name below the bottom line figure of an invoice authorizing payment (fig. 9).[12]

Architectural partnerships were rare in pre–Civil War America. The most prominent one

was that of Ithiel Town and Alexander Jackson Davis, which began in 1829. Town secured business and Davis remained in New York City to design, manage the office, and teach students. The partnership, which briefly had branch offices in Washington and Baltimore between 1832 and 1833, ended in 1835, when Town decided to concentrate on bridge engineering. Niernsee & Neilson were among the very few architectural partnerships in this period to survive and become successful. The practice was run as a business instead of an artistic cottage industry.

Baltimore's rapid industrial growth meant it needed to house the workers and immigrants who came to the city to work. Housing construction rose to a peak of about two thousand new houses a year in 1848, then leveled off to about eighteen hundred units built annually until 1851.[13] Except for the six houses for Gittings, Niernsee & Neilson would design none of this speculative housing.

The design of such houses had traditionally been the province of the building mechanics, the nineteenth-century term for builder—either masons who built houses and incorporated the work of carpenters or carpenters who employed masons and other tradesmen to do the work. The buildings were designed from sets of instructions for building a particular kind of house, exactly what John Hall and other pattern book

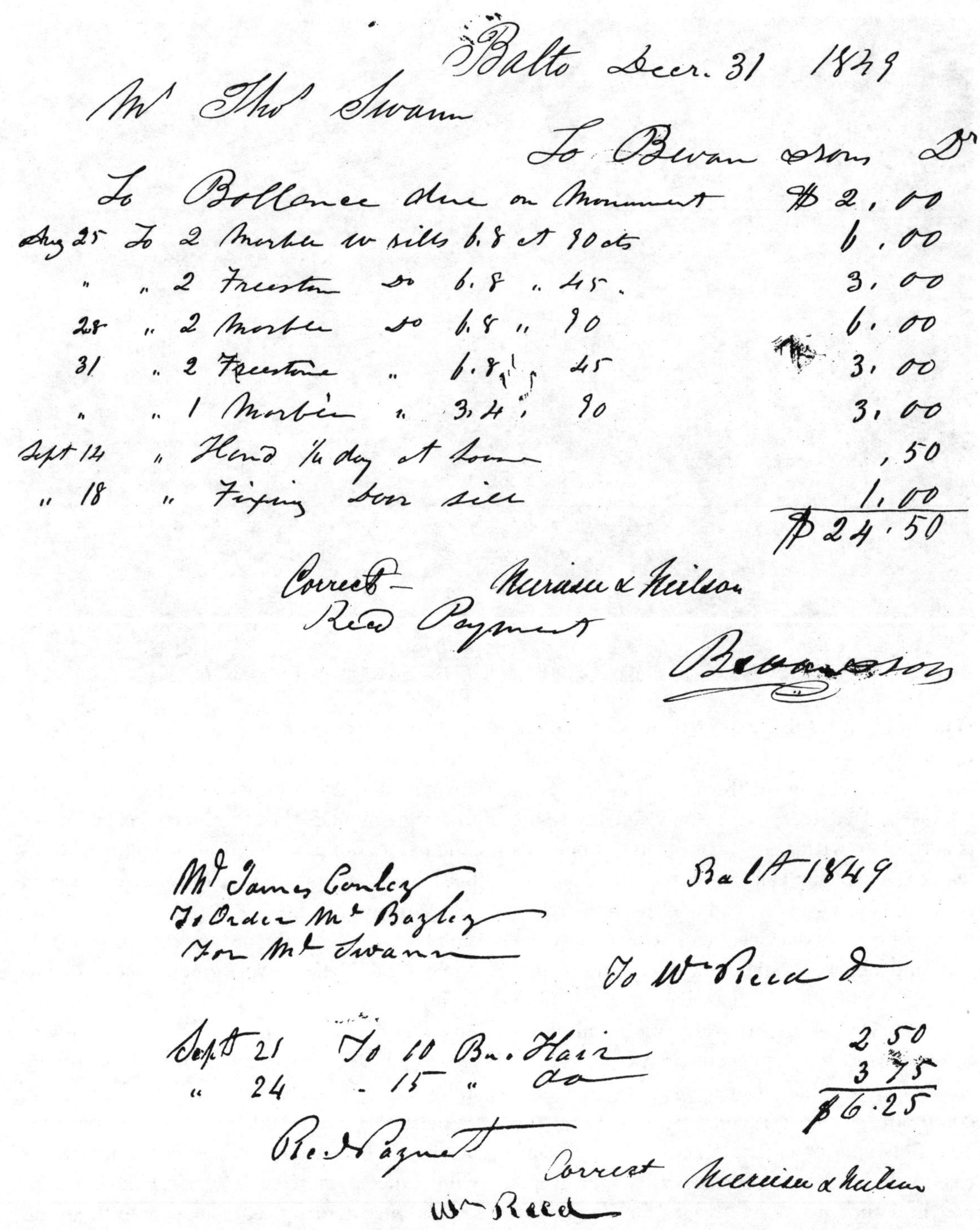

FIG. 9. Swann House, Baltimore, invoice, 1849. Maryland Historical Society, Baltimore, Maryland

NIERNSEE AND NEILSON

Balto Decr. 31 1849

Mr Thos Swann

To Bevan & sons Dr

To Ballance due on Monument $ 2,00
Aug 25 To 2 Marble w sills 6.8 at 90cts 6.00
" " 2 Freestone do 6.8 " 45 . 3,00
28 " 2 Marble do 6.8 " 90 6.00
31 " 2 Freestone " 6.8 " 45 3,00
" " 1 Marble " 3.4 " 90 3,00
Sept 14 " Hand ½ day at home ,50
" 18 " Fixing door sill 1,00
$ 24.50

Correct — Niernsee & Neilson
Recd Payment

Bevan & sons

Mr James Conley
To Order Mr Bazley
For Mr Swann

Balt 1849

To Wm Reed Dr

Sept 21 To 10 Bu. Hair 2 50
" 24 — 15 " do 3 75
$6.25

Recd Payment
Wm Reed

Correct Niernsee & Neilson

authors provided in their ready-made plans. The size of the framing and the thickness of walls were empirical in nature, passed down from one mechanic to another over generations.

As buildings became more complex, especially nonresidential building types, the public slowly turned to the very few professional architects in America like Niernsee, a person who not only possessed artistic talent but also had a scientific knowledge of the strength and qualities of various materials and a well-rounded knowledge of construction. Niernsee & Neilson would establish a truly professional level of architectural services, quite different from that of a draftsman working for a builder. They would act as the client's agent, insuring that the building was constructed as designed with a high level of craftsmanship. The firm would guard against shoddy building practices and overcharging by the contractor or subcontractors. The services they offered were contrary to the norm in Baltimore, where architects had had very little influence. Builders possessed all the power over design and construction super-

vision, sometimes hiring architects to do the most minimal of drafting for their projects. This led to an almost universal lack of appreciation of the value of an architect's services and skills. Niernsee & Neilson was the first firm to counter this trend.

On his next major commission, Niernsee would completely abandon the Greek Revival style and produce a fully developed Italianate design. In 1851, the Decatur Miller House, which still stands at 700 Cathedral Street at the northwest corner of Monument and Cathe-

FIG. 12. Miller House, Baltimore (interior, second-floor front)

front allowed the visitor to enter a foyer and then a hall, from which an attractive elliptical stairway rose in a gentle looping fashion in a counter-clockwise direction to the second story, then to the third. A stylish skylight of stained glass made by H. T. Gernhardt of Baltimore lights the stair. The principal room of the ground floor was the office/library/den of the owner Decatur Miller, a well-known merchant and shipper. This room was done in what was referred to then as the Elizabethan manner, with a deeply coffered ceiling, involving not only rectangular but diagonal patterns. A small room to the west still contains the original safe.

Some of the rooms were altered in the process of conversion, making it difficult to fully appreciate the grand parade of rooms on the *piano nobile* that originally existed in 1853. Behind these rooms, there was a small conservatory overlooking the alley behind the lot. The saloon ceiling, which is still extant, is very handsomely laid out in molded panels decorated with paintings and is an excellent example of the sumptuous decoration of this mid-century house (fig. 12).

There was very little description of this house in the local press, but the Decatur Miller House is unusual in that a ledger listing the building firms and costs still survives. The brownstone work cost $3,792, with the lumber and carpentry amounting to $10,770. The local firm of Hayward, Bartlett & Company fabricated the iron veranda for $385. The architects' 5 percent fee on an estimated cost of $26,314 amounted to $1,315. The final construction cost was $32,000.[15] Architects in pre–Civil War America thought 5 percent was a fair fee. Benjamin Henry Latrobe and later Richard Upjohn first promoted the idea of a percentage fee tied to building costs as opposed to the lump sum payment the subcontractors received. The American Institute of Architects finally adopted the 5 percent fee in 1866.

The firm's next commission continued the valuable B&O connection that began with Benjamin H. Latrobe Jr. The 1850 $3,300 addition and alteration to a house originally designed by Robert Cary Long Jr. for Thomas Swann in the 200 block of West Franklin Street, gave Niernsee another opportunity to design a two-story cast-iron veranda (fig. 13). It cost $517 and faced the garden.

Swann, a lawyer who became the B&O's president in 1848, played an important role in securing financing for the line's expansion from Cumberland to Wheeling. His success would

dral Streets, would also provide him his first opportunity to use real brownstone instead of brown painted stucco (figs. 10, 11). Once again, Niernsee was aware of the latest architectural fashion. Brownstone, a member of the sandstone family, became a popular building veneer in the 1840s. There were four main quarries on the eastern seaboard from which to buy the material: Portland, Connecticut; Hummelstown, Pennsylvania; East Meadow, Massachusetts; and the largest in New Jersey, a thirty-two-mile belt along the Delaware River above Trenton from the Palisades on the Hudson River to Suffern, New York. The last provided the stone for Richard Upjohn's Trinity Church on Wall Street, built in 1846. The mania for the material would last until about 1900. It was easily cut to a four-inch thickness and applied as a veneer to a brick back-up wall.

Niernsee gave the Miller House an English basement and a brownstone entrance façade with a rusticated basement, molded window surrounds, and a handsome bracketed cornice. The brownstone was not continued around the Monument Street façade; here the brick was painted in imitation of brownstone. The windows on Monument Street are protected from the sun by an elaborate series of cast-iron balconies, a style that tends to be associated with New Orleans, but was at the time of its construction just as original to Baltimore.[14]

The interior of the Miller House was quite elaborate, and it is fortunate that very little of the original decoration has been altered, including the ceiling and wall decorations of the *piano nobile* in the second story. The three-bay-wide open up the world of politics to him; he became mayor of Baltimore in 1854. The Prince of Wales, the future King Edward VII, sat on Niernsee's balcony during a celebration in his honor when he came to Baltimore in 1860. The list of final costs for the house, which late in the century housed the Maryland Academy of Sciences, show that again, the firm received a healthy 5 percent fee of $165. As mentioned earlier, the Swann job is notable for the extensive itemized bills now in the Maryland Historical Society, which show the firm's approval process for paying contractors.[16]

The Albert H. Schumacher House, at 10 East Mount Vernon Place, now known as Asbury House, is another Italianate design in brownstone, "a grand and costly" residence of the "Roman style," noted the *Sun*.[17] Schumacher, one of the city's first successful German businessmen, was the managing director of the North German Lloyd Line, the main steamship company that brought immigrants to Baltimore. Built in 1855, the three-bay-wide house has a rusticated English basement containing an arched doorway and two arched windows (fig. 14). Its *piano nobile* is treated in an entirely original manner, a very large bay window with a deep brownstone balcony stretches across the entire façade, providing the only fenestration. The bay contains tall narrow arched windows framed by decorative niches. Two-story pilasters run up to the underside of a dramatic overhanging Italianate cornice.

The interior is a repetition of the sumptuousness of the Thomas and Miller Houses. Instead of opening onto a very narrow stair hall, the ground floor entrance vestibule leads to a beautiful semicircular stair hall, which runs the full width of the house, the stairs rising clockwise to the *piano nobile* (fig. 15). In the vestibule, there is a very exuberant yellow-orange marble dado framed in wood. The marble was probably supplied by Niernsee's lifelong friend Hugh Sisson, the stone dealer, who dealt in exotic marble and stones and contributed greatly to the decorative effect of many of Niernsee's buildings. The ground story office, with its decorative Elizabethan ceiling of geometric moldings and its comfortable Victorian fireplace, is where Schumacher conducted much of his business. The staircase leads to the principal room of the *piano nobile*, an octagonal saloon boasting four niches, filled with built-in furniture and a fireplace. The dining room and a bedroom or sunroom are also done in an octagon shape. The

curved stair continues to the third story, where it is lit by a magnificent and spacious glazed dome supported by Corinthian columns.

The firm's William Mayhew House, located next door at 12 East Mount Vernon Place and built the same year, was also designed in "the Roman style" but without the dramatic bay window. Looking similar to a speculative Manhattan brownstone, the house has plain window trim but an ornate arched entry with double doors set beneath an arched transom. The cornice was removed to install windows in the fourth story. Both houses had four-story back buildings, where the bathrooms, kitchen, and servants' quarters were located.[18] Other brownstones were built in Mount Vernon around the same time. On the same block as the Schumacher and Mayhew houses, Louis Long designed six speculative Italianate brownstone houses for Richard E. France, who sold all of them before they were finished.[19]

FIG. 13. Swann House, Baltimore, balcony. Maryland Historical Society, Baltimore, Maryland

demolished in 1914. At the time of their construction Niernsee was living in his own house (not of his own design) at 922 St. Paul Street.

Niernsee and Neilson's Mount Vernon residences became the cornerstone of their practice, establishing their reputation for quality and dependability with Baltimore's elite. The publicity they garnered for these houses solidified their reputation as the architectural firm of choice for the wealthy. An architect could not have dreamed of a more successful start to a new practice. Instead of struggling, as most new architects did (and still do), to get even the most mundane of commissions to launch their careers, Niernsee's first projects were of the highest quality one could have. Beginning with Benjamin H. Latrobe Jr.'s pair of houses, the firm produced one handsome design after another, making a smooth transition from the Greek Revival to the Italianate style. Niernsee's elegant palazzo for Albert Schumacher, in particular, showed what sophisticated design skills he possessed. In addition, the firm did much in this period to further the separation of the professional architect from the builder, particularly with regard to the design and construction administration of a project. In the public's mind, the architectural firm of Niernsee & Neilson, not the carpenters or masons, created the design of the houses. Their practice was set to explode with work.

FIG. 14. *(above)* Schumacher House, Baltimore. Charles Belfoure

FIG. 15. *(right)* Schumacher House, Baltimore. James D. Dilts

The Latrobe family continued to use Niernsee for their own residences. The firm designed a house in 1851 for John H. B. Latrobe at 901 North Charles Street; it was demolished before World War I and replaced by a tall apartment house named after Latrobe.[20] A pair of three-story houses that had imitation brownstone façades was built for James Carroll at the southwest corner of Howard and Monument Streets in 1852. The buildings that now stand at this location, however, bear no resemblance to the early newspaper descriptions.[21] After 1852–53, commissions for city houses slowed down.

Niernsee, who had mainly lived in boarding houses, now had the financial means and the time to build his own speculative houses. In 1853, he built three houses at 404–408 Courtland Street, and he lived at 406 from 1866 to 1870. All were

THREE

Country Houses and Estates

The class of men for whom Niernsee designed luxurious town houses preferred to summer in the country, away from the heat and humidity of Baltimore. Because of his success in Mount Vernon, these wealthy clients naturally turned to Niernsee to design their country residences. But the very first known country house Niernsee designed was not outside Baltimore but in Virginia. He designed Elmington, a large plantation house on the York River north of Gloucester Point, in 1847 (fig. 16).[1] The house was built for Dr. John Prosser Tabb as a wedding gift to his bride. Though the Italianate and other romantic styles popularized by Downing in the 1840s slowly found favor in America, Greek Revival structures still remained popular in the South. It is difficult to discern Niernsee's original design because Elmington was remodeled in the late nineteenth century by Thomas Dixon, the author of *Birth of a Nation*, into an almost stereotypical Southern plantation house, with a Palladian-inspired projecting two-story portico supported by four Corinthian columns. A pedimented entry framed by sidelights and pilasters is probably part of Niernsee's original design. It leads into a grand hall, where rises a beautiful curving stairway, similar to the one in the Thomas House. The interior spaces seem to have been unaltered; the first floor rooms are well proportioned, with tall ceilings, grand fireplaces, and French windows—a common amenity in large southern mansions to allow natural airflow. Elmington features what would become a favorite Niernsee design element for a country house, a roof top gazebo large enough to host a small party in the summertime, to sit and enjoy the river view.

FIG. 16. Elmington, Virginia. From Robert A. Lancaster Jr., *Historic Virginia Homes*, 1915

The most impressive country house designed by Niernsee & Neilson was Alexandroffsky, built for Thomas de Kay Winans, near the B&O Railroad's Mount Clare shops in west Baltimore. The client was the son of Ross Winans, who provided the B&O and other railroads in America with locomotives and rolling stock in the 1830s and 1840s. The elder Winans was asked by the Russian government to plan work on a new railway from St. Petersburg to Moscow, but he declined and suggested that his sons take his place. So Thomas de Kay Winans and his brother, William, went to Russia in 1842 with two Philadelphia engineers to supply the rolling stock for the railroad, which was laid out by Colonel George Washington Whistler. Whistler, an engineer with much experience planning railroads in Baltimore and Massachusetts, was the father of the artist James McNeill Whistler. Winans formed a consortium to

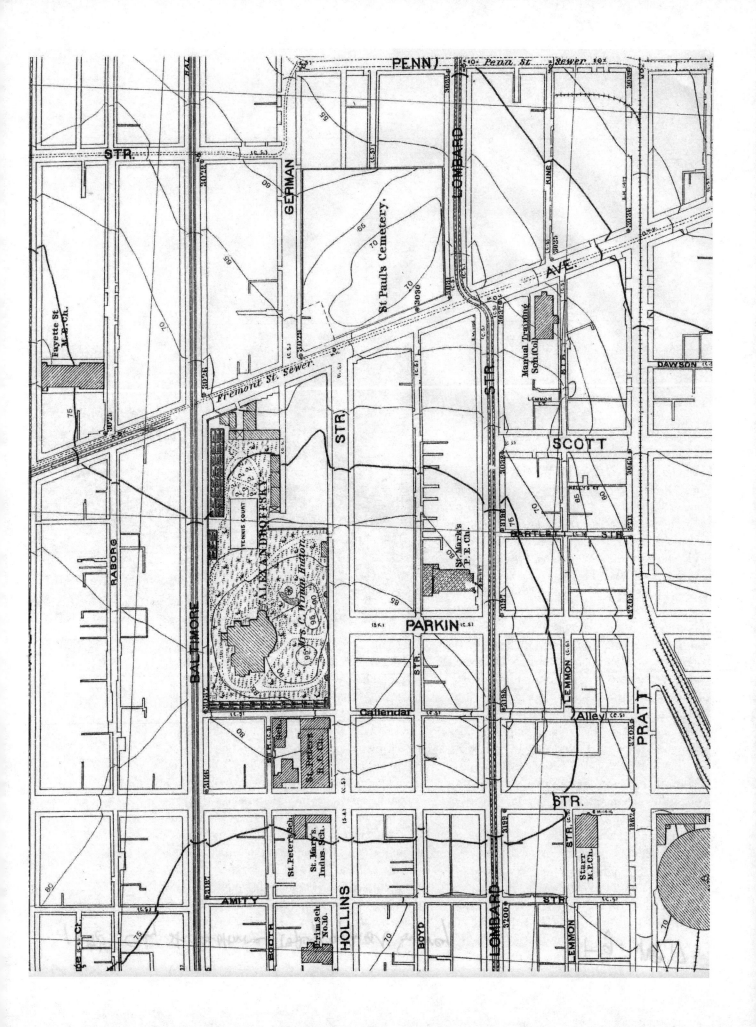

turn a former fabric factory at Alexandroffsky in Russia into a locomotive works. The enterprise was a great success and as a consequence, the partners made a huge fortune, enhanced by a contract they received to operate the railroad for the following ten years. Thomas Winans' house, named after the Russian locomotive works, was built from this cash flow.[2]

The four-story house that Niernsee designed for Winans was actually an addition to a Federal style villa called Fayetteville, built about 1803, which Winans had bought from the McHenry family in 1850. James McHenry, a surgeon during the Revolutionary War and Secretary of War from 1796 to 1800, named the estate in honor of the Marquis de Lafayette, a wartime compatriot. The building, a hip-roofed house with projecting semioctagonal entrance bay, had been used as a boarding school.[3] By the time Winans purchased it, the estate was a curious anomaly, a house with a cruciform footprint on a large tract of land within the city's grid of blocks, which was being surrounded by working-class row houses built for B&O employees who worked at the nearby shops at Mount Clare. For privacy, a twelve-foot-high brick wall was constructed around the entire property. Winans' wife, the former Celeste Revillon, a lady in waiting to the Tsarina of Russia, was unwilling to indulge the American public in its habit of entering into and using large, private grounds as public parks for recreation and leisure. People in this period were not inhibited about walking onto the grounds of estates to picnic or sightsee, as there were no public parks in Baltimore until Druid Hill Park was created in 1860.[4]

The new building was an extremely robust Italianate composition featuring a tall hip-roofed tower and semicircular bays. The front entrance faced Baltimore Street to the north and was accessed by a very long serpentine driveway, which began at the intersection of Parkin and Hollins streets and completely circled the house, returning to another gate further east on Hollins Street (fig. 17). Visitors entered the mansion under a semicircular porch based on Niernsee's favorite arcade, one that fronted Brunelleschi's Foundling Hospital in Florence, built circa 1419 (fig. 18).

The new plan of Alexandroffsky completely obscured the Fayetteville villa. The entrance hall was flanked by separate-sex reception rooms that led into what was the original house, which

Niernsee divided into the "Green Parlor" and Winans' office. A great saloon, the main entertainment space, opened off the west side of the parlor; to its south, the Marble Hall housed the grand staircase. The Marble Hall led to the formal dining room with its circular apse at the southern end, which in turn opened into a magnificent sixty-two-foot diameter semicircular iron and glass winter garden, very early for such construction in the United States, especially considering that this room was built in the summer of 1851, at the same time as the Crystal Palace in London. The conservatory was fitted with sliding glass windows, but its other features are unknown. The south façade presented a striking symmetrical elevation showing how Niernsee knit the entire building together with semicircular projections and towers (fig. 19). Each gabled end of the main house boasted a hip-roofed tower similar to the one at Elmington. Gaining access from the grand stair, the Winans family could climb to the top of the towers and take in the view from all directions through arched windows, which could be opened to catch the breezes in summer. Above the conservatory, a semicircular balcony opened from the circular apse located at the end of the ballroom set directly above the dining room. The exterior of the apse matched the front porch. The ballroom was flanked by another dining area and a library that had a circular boudoir attached to the east elevation (fig. 20).

The house was unique not only for its size but also for its amenities, especially its central-heating system, an exhaust draft design built by Hayward, Bartlett & Company. Fresh air was drawn over heating coils placed between the floors and then rose into the rooms above. It took eight hundred pounds of coal per day to operate.[5]

The influence of Downing's work is apparent in Alexandroffsky in both its Italianate massing and its detailing. The major design element was the tower, with its bracketed hip roof and arched windows, a familiar Northern Italian feature illustrated in Downing's publications. The cornices of the main block were also heavily bracketed; small balconies appeared in the gable ends, with small square windows in the third story. The exterior finish echoed Italian building techniques: brick stuccoed and painted gray to resemble stone. Niernsee's design was an early example of the Italian villa style architec-

FIG. 17. *(opposite)* Alexandroffsky, Baltimore, 1896. *City of Baltimore Topographical Survey*

27

FIG. 20. *(top)*
Alexandroffsky,
Baltimore, east
elevation. Maryland
Historical Society,
Baltimore, Maryland

FIG. 21. *(bottom)*
Alexandroffsky,
Baltimore, garden.
Maryland Historical
Society, Baltimore,
Maryland

COUNTRY HOUSES
AND ESTATES

ture in the region. The form became very popular by the mid–1850s, with great houses such as Wilton, El Monte, and Chatham, designed by Norris G. Starkweather for the Dorsey family, and the greatest of all Italianate mansions of the period, Guilford, designed by Lind & Murdoch for William McDonald and later owned by A. S. Abell, owner of the *Baltimore Sun*.

The extensive gardens of Alexandroffsky also followed Downing's landscaping philosophy (fig. 21). The gardens and lawns flowed around the house, providing a parklike setting, recreating a romantic image of nature—picturesque and wild. Interspersed within the grounds were gazebos, statuary, greenhouses, and a stream with bridges. The entire landscaping design successfully cloistered the estate from the busy city that had grown around it, allowing the Winans to live in their own separate world. The estate fascinated the public. A contemporary guidebook noted that "spacious grounds surrounding it are tastefully laid out and adorned in a style that would do credit to the home of a European prince."[6]

The grounds of Alexandroffsky played a small role in the history of American art. James McNeill Whistler, a friend of the family who had been dismissed from West Point because of his poor academic record, visited the Winans' new home in July of 1854. He spent time sketching the classical statues in the gardens and also the Mount Clare shops. In November, he secured a job with the Drawing Division of the U.S. Coast Survey Office, which he held until February of 1855, when he returned to Alexandroffsky. With Thomas Winans' encouragement and financial help, Whistler left for Paris to study art. Winans would buy some of his friend's early paintings, including one entitled *Wapping*, which hung in the house until its demolition.[7]

What little information exists concerning the new house is contained in the private journal of Thomas de Kay Winans, who recorded the construction stages, such as setting the first-floor joists and building the garden wall. He also noted the three payments to Niernsee & Neilson totaling $2,200 for the project ($52,000 in 2004). Construction of such of a large house was surprisingly quick; it began on March 23, 1851, and Winans first slept in his new home on February 24, 1852.[8]

The final piece of work completed by Niernsee & Neilson for Winans at Alexandroffsky

FIG. 22. Crimea, Baltimore. Maryland Historical Society, Baltimore, Maryland

would come in 1871, when they designed a vast concert room thirty feet by sixty feet, which contained a pipe organ and musicians' gallery. At that particular time, Winans was an enthusiastic musician who played the organ himself and experimented with the construction and design of organs. Part of the design for this music room was an eighty-foot-tall square chimney. It provided thermospheric air pressure, which may have been used to assist the organ supply but was probably used to draw off the gas fumes from the many gas chandeliers that lit this large festival room. The chimney became a landmark in the neighborhood.

The public (by invitation only) finally got its chance to look inside the great house and walk the grounds in 1923, when Winans' daughter, Celeste Hutton, held a benefit for the South Baltimore General Hospital. Two years later, Mrs. Hutton died and her two daughters decided to sell the estate and auction off its contents. Alexandroffsky was thrown open to the public, and Baltimoreans by the hundreds entered a mysterious world they had only glimpsed over a twelve-foot brick wall. The *Sun* reported that "Alexandroffsky had no secrets today," and noted the visitors' reactions to the world of the rich: "Surely this couldn't have been a bathroom. It is as big as our whole house."[9] The neighborhood eventually became a Lithuanian enclave, and in 1925, the house was torn down.

Alexandroffsky having turned out to be too close to the rapidly growing west side of Baltimore to remain comfortable for summer living, Winans bought a nine-hundred-acre property much further west, now known as Leakin Park. There he built a true summerhouse, which was to be named Orianda, after the Tsarina's summer home in Yalta on the Black Sea, though the estate itself was known as Crimea. Sited on a hillside overlooking the Franklin Town Road (now obscured by vegetation), the house was designed by Niernsee and construction began in June of 1856. The architect simplified the Italianate style and designed a simple cube, three stories high, with a hipped roof and a large gazebo at its apex, flanked by four chimney stacks (fig. 22). The house, built of unadorned native fieldstone, has an idiosyncratic style, somewhat resembling an Asian pagoda, with its wide eaves and simple plan. On the ground floor, directly opposite the entrance, a large parlor runs across the entire south face, its French windows opening onto the verandas that encircle this end of the house. There are twin staircases, one for the servants and one for the owners and their guests. The dining room and study are located on either side of the entryway.

Crimea has handsome verandas on three sides of the first story, and a second-story veranda on the south side. All are very simply detailed in a mock Asian style, achieved by extraordinarily

simple means with machine-made pieces of wood (fig. 23). The balustrades for the porches are solid wood, perforated with a decorative cutout. The brackets supporting the roof overhangs are modeled on those of Asian temples. The roof eaves extend well beyond the walls of the house and in each corner, a large carved wood pendant hangs down in the form of a traditional Japanese temple lantern (fig. 24). The house stands on a slope, so its basement story, which houses the kitchen, is fully visible on the south side, at the rear of the house.

Niernsee's favorite roof top gazebo is accessed by a handsome oak stairway. He designed it not only to be a cool place to sit but to also to act as a thermo-siphon to ventilate the whole house. Crimea was surrounded by other buildings, including a farmhouse, stables, and a charming chapel in a Gothic board-and-batten style (which Neilson designed). The house was completed about 1857 at a cost of $9,170, but Mrs. Winans died in 1861. Out of choice, Winans remained a widower for the rest of his life. His daughter Celeste became his hostess and companion and did not marry until after her father's death in 1878, at which time she

married an Irish-born American diplomat to the court of Czar Alexander. Crimea is now used as the headquarters for Outward Bound in Baltimore.

The design of the house was completed before Niernsee left for South Carolina in 1856 (see Chapter 7), and the work was probably superintended by Neilson, who represented the firm in Baltimore after Niernsee's departure. There could be another Niernsee design for the Winans family; a simple, stark, large timber house built at Newport, Rhode Island, shortly after the Civil War by Thomas Winans. There is no documentation that Niernsee provided this design, but it has a kind of directness and simplicity that suggests that it could have been done by Niernsee & Neilson. It was called Bleak House, after Charles Dickens' novel, this somber title due to Winans' widowhood.

As a result of its work for the city's wealthy, Niernsee and Neilson's practice picked up more and more momentum, and quickly gained new clients. In 1852, they garnered a commission from one of the city's richest and most important merchants, Johns Hopkins. A B&O Railroad director, Hopkins had purchased a 166-

acre property in 1841 on Harford Road, then outside the city limits, for a country residence. The land came with a circa 1800 two-story brick farmhouse, which Hopkins wanted renovated. This house was remodeled by Niernsee into an imposing Italianate villa by adding a third story, an arcaded veranda all around, and mostly notably, a tower (fig. 25). "The exterior of the villa is rough casted to imitate free stone work and develops the graceful proportions of the 'Italian Villa' style of architecture with massive arcades, projecting cornices and brackets, depending for its effect on the varied masses and outlines of the whole rather than on the minuteness of its details," wrote the *Sun* in 1852.[10] The interior was handled with great subtlety and skill. Clifton is very idiosyncratic in its arrangement and at the same time very comfortable and even grand in many of its features. As with Alexandroffsky, Niernsee did a remarkable job of incorporating the original house into a dynamic composition. In both cas-

es, he probably would have preferred to knock the old buildings down and start with a clean slate. It is a measure of an architect's skill as to how well he can work with the existing buildings his clients insist upon keeping.

From the porte cochere at the west end of the house, through a pair of heavily molded doors having square panels with hollow corners and heavy bolection moldings, one enters the base of the great tower, where the main stair, with a balustrade in black walnut, is located (fig. 26). At the lobby level of the first story, there is a mural depicting the Bay of Naples, now covered by many layers of paint. Climbing a short flight of stairs brings the visitor to the main corridor, to the south (right) of which is the main parlor and breakfast room of the original house. To the north (left) is the dining room, with its semioctagonal end, and the salon, with a library attached. The dining room, located in an early addition to the original house, has a plaster ceiling of unique quality

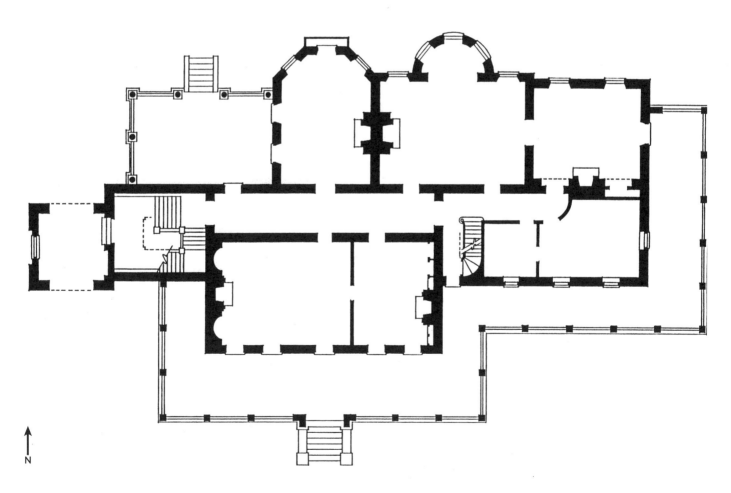

FIRST FLOOR PLAN - 1852

0   5   10   15   20

FIG. 26. Clifton, Baltimore, first-floor plan. Peter Pearre

Stonleigh
The Residence of R. P. Brown Esq.

FIG. 27. (above) Stoneleigh, Baltimore, vignette. From Robert Taylor, *Map of the City and County of Baltimore, Maryland*, 1857.

FIG. 28. (opposite, top) "Plain Timber Cottage Villa." From A. J. Downing, *The Architecture of Country Houses*, 1850

FIG. 29. (opposite, bottom) Fairy Knowe, Elkridge, Maryland. Maryland Historical Society, Baltimore, Maryland

frescoed in the manner of an Italian terrace, as might have existed in Amalfi or Sorrento. The roof beams are arrayed in lush vegetation. The decoration was most likely done by Ernst Dreyer, who did a great deal of decorative fresco work for Niernsee & Neilson in many of their houses. In the northwest corner of the house, off the main corridor beside the dining room, is a large open porch, where meals were taken during the summertime.[11]

In the second story, the room above the dining room, also with a semioctagonal north end, became Hopkins' bedroom and dressing room; guestrooms occupied the other side of the corridor. Hopkins, being a bachelor, had a rather large retinue of extended family as guests and nearly permanent residents. Over the salon and library was another open porch. In later years, this porch was enclosed with glass and transformed into a study library. The windows of the second story were fitted with painted or stained-glass panels. The third story, as in most villa designs, housed the servants, with a back stair connecting downstairs. The narrow, steep stair to the gazebo platform ascends from a room on the second-floor landing. Clifton's tower is taller and far more dramatic than Alexandroffsky's.

Niernsee skillfully pulled the entire composition together with another Italianate villa design element, the arcaded veranda. It wraps around the building on the east, south and west façades, once again inspired by Brunelleschi's Foundling Hospital porch in Florence. All the chimneys at Clifton are grouped together and have prominent flaring tops and chimney pots. The large Italianate palazzo takes charge of its site with great authority. The mansion stands atop a gentle rise. The land falls away from the house then slopes up to Harford Road, where an arched gateway made a formal entry onto the grounds (since demolished) (plate 12). The house was one of the most memorable Italianate country estates in America in the 1850s. The 1852 *Sun* article about Clifton attested to the fame the firm had garnered over the previous four years: "The entire improvements reflect credit upon the well known architects, Messrs. Niernsee & Neilson" (Feb. 5, 1852). Over the next twenty years, Hopkins would become Baltimore's most important benefactor. The fact that the firm did work for such an influential man would not be lost on the rest of the city's wealthy citizens. Owned by the City of Baltimore, Clifton is now the headquarters of Civic Works, a youth program.

Another country house designed around 1852 was Stoneleigh, which was built for Robert P. Brown, a wealthy importer (fig. 27). The house of stuccoed brick survived until the mid 1950s when it was demolished for a residential development of the same name. It was probably another one of Niernsee's transformations of an existing country house. The photographs of the twenty-seven-room mansion indicate that the northern half was an existing country farmhouse. A lower annex with some public rooms was added at the south end, and an L-shaped stair and the familiar Niernsee device of a rooftop gazebo at the east end. A veranda tied all the elements together. The house, at a cost of about $16,000, was a subdued Italianate design with the usual bracketing and hip-roofed gazebo. It did not achieve the kind of monumentality that Clifton, Alexandroffsky, and Crimea did, but it must have been a very comfortable country retreat suited to the times. Photographs taken by the newspaper show that the original interior decoration was virtually intact in 1952, when the last member of the Brown family died.[12]

Niernsee & Neilson did work for the Latrobe brothers outside the city as well. Fairy Knowe, a rambling half Gothic and half Greek country house, was designed by Robert Cary Long Jr. in 1843 for John H. B. Latrobe on Lawyers' Hill near Elkridge, Maryland. This house was completely destroyed in a fire in 1851 and was reconstructed on the original's foundations by Niernsee & Neilson. The design, although it is attributed to Long, was actually derived from a watercolor, made by John H. B. Latrobe himself. Latrobe was one of the most experienced watercolorists of his time, as befits the son of a great architect, even though he was an attorney by practice. Shortly after the fire, Latrobe "sent to town for an architect and he came … Sunday." Together, he and Niernsee chose an image from A. J. Downing's 1850 *The Architecture of Country Houses,* as the model for the new house (fig. 28). Niernsee added a tower to the board-and-batten design with its two front-facing gables. The next day construction began and Fairy Knowe

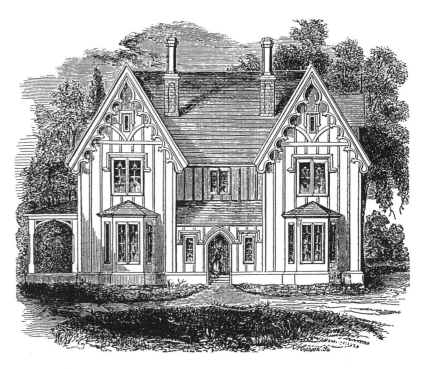

was completed in fifty-four working days (fig. 29).[13] The house has been demolished.

Downing's new book was immensely successful across America, far more than his earlier works. Americans of modest means wishing to build a new house could simply choose a design as Latrobe did and tell the carpenter to follow the model with some modifications. *Country Houses* was the progenitor of the house-plan magazines found today at supermarket checkouts and bookstores, in which the architect is completely bypassed in favor of a building contractor or, as in Niernsee's case, is asked by the client to revise the design. Beginning in 1850, the architect became less involved in speculative residential design in America, and more a luxury associated with the wealthy and the upper middle class.

Niernsee may have done several more country houses before he left the firm in 1856, including additions and alterations in 1853 to Dumbarton, a mansion in what is now the Rodgers Forge section of Baltimore County, and to Anneslie, another country house near Towson. Niernsee may also have been the architect of one of the city's best-known country houses, the Wyman Villa, which was demolished in 1955 by the Johns Hopkins University.

In 1851, William Wyman, the son of a rich draper in Baltimore, approached Richard Upjohn to design a house for him. He admired Upjohn's 1845 Italianate villa for Edward King in Newport, Rhode Island (fig. 30). This had been published as design 28 in Downing's *Architecture of Country Houses* in 1850 (fig. 31). The house was also reproduced in wood and masonry and with varying degrees of refinement and success in several places in the Carolinas and Virginia. When Herman Aldrich, Wyman's brother-in-law, heard that Wyman was planning to build a house, Aldrich met Upjohn and also visited houses that Upjohn had designed. The architect quoted a price of $20,000 to build the house; Aldrich knew that his brother-in-law would not spend a penny more than $10,000.

Although Wyman began construction in the fall of 1851 using a local builder who tried to copy the house from Downing's book, he ran into difficulties. Wyman then did an underhanded thing—he plagiarized Upjohn's drawings. Because Upjohn always took his drawings back when his houses were completed so that people could not copy his designs, Wyman asked his cousin, George H. Cary of Boston, to get Francis Wilbar, the carpenter on the Edward King house, to go around the actual house and take some measurements. But that did not make matters any easier. In a letter to his brother-in-law, Herman Aldrich added a tart reminder that time was wasting and that Wyman had better

find a local architect to draw up the plans in the winter so that when the spring season came, he could start construction.[14]

Although the major elements have been transposed, there is no question that the Wyman Villa is based on Upjohn's Edward King house; the massing and certain details, such as the second-story tower balcony, are exactly the same. The local architect Wyman most likely hired was Niernsee. The porches at the Wyman Villa are exact copies of the design at Clifton. There are definite improvements over Upjohn's design in its proportion and detailing, such as the height of the towers and the addition of a bay window (fig. 32). No documentation has been found to prove that Niernsee's office did this building, but there was only one architect working at this time who could have brought such skill to another man's design. The firm may not have claimed authorship because of professional ethics. Upjohn was an architect of national reputation, and it would seem extremely unprofessional for Niernsee, an architect of great promise, to admit to blatantly copying his design. This was quite different from helping John H. B. Latrobe adapt a vernacular house from a builder's guide.

Niernsee & Neilson's country houses for such powerful men as Winans and Hopkins led to more and more work, including the most prestigious building type of all in this era—the church. All men of wealth in Baltimore had strong connections to their church. It was as important to them as their families and their businesses and investments. The elite that lived in luxurious residences in wealthy neighborhoods fully expected their churches to be of the same or of even higher architectural quality. Almost all denominations in Baltimore would build as extravagantly as their purses allowed. Niernsee & Neilson would be called upon by society's most powerful religious denomination, the Protestant Episcopal Church, as well as almost every other religious group in the city to design houses of worship.

FOUR

Churches

Baltimore had become a major American city by 1850, and its public buildings now reflected this rising growth and status. Churches were an especially important barometer of a city's architectural sophistication. Construction of new religious buildings was a sure sign the city was expanding. "No city in the Union has evidenced more improvement in the department of church architecture than Baltimore," the *Baltimore Sun* reported in an article in 1854.[1]

Until the early 1850s, the city's most prestigious churches were located within half a mile of the center of town. But the churches began to parallel the movement of housing away from downtown. The center city was becoming completely commercialized, driving out those who had the financial means to live elsewhere. For some downtown churches this meant a full exodus of parishioners who now found their old church inconvenient to get to. Each congregation had to fend for itself financially, mainly through the sale or rental of pews. (Today's practice of pledged donations was not followed then.) Only a small percentage of pews was set aside as free, since this was the major source of income for the church. When the parishioners left, income dwindled, so most congregations willingly sold their buildings, which had become valuable city real estate, and moved.

Often, the new churches preceded much of the new housing in outlying neighborhoods; large elaborate structures would be surrounded by vacant lots until real estate development caught up. There was a demand for new churches in the Mount Vernon area and in east and west Baltimore. This was met by a number of architects, with Niernsee & Neilson designing many of these structures. With their connections to the city's wealthy, the firm was well placed to secure the most prestigious church commissions.[2]

The idea that architecture could influence the spiritual tone of people had a history dating back to the ziggurats in Mesopotamia and the great cathedral age of northern Europe. The power of such things had great currency in an age when religion was an inextricable part of Americans' lives. The southern colonies—Virginia, Maryland, North Carolina, and South Carolina—were primarily affiliated with the Church of England, or what was then called the Protestant Episcopal Church. The founding of the Maryland colony, based on a doctrine of religious freedom in 1634 by the Roman Catholic Calvert family, laid the foundation for a strong Roman Catholic Church, especially in Baltimore. For all denominations, the aesthetics of the place of worship were extremely important.

Baltimore churches of the eighteenth and early nineteenth centuries, though, were usually just one-room buildings with no architectural embellishment and, in some cases, not even a steeple or tower. As the need for space for Sunday school, missionary society meetings, and prayer groups arose, new churches incorporated rooms in basements and ground stories or in auxiliary buildings (often called chapels) adjacent to the main church. After about 1840, Protestant churches slowly made the transition to more architecturally distinctive buildings, mostly of the Greek Revival style. Sometimes this trend was challenged from within a particular denomination. A few religious leaders felt the pretentiousness and high cost of the new churches were in conflict with the virtue of piety and diverted money from evangelism. The *Baltimore Baptist* weekly newspaper warned that the extravagance of churches was "squandering the Lord's money on useless ornaments and costly appendages." One particular style, the Gothic Revival, was singled out for its lavishness. Nevertheless, it would become the most popular style for churches in America in the late 1840s and 1850s.[3]

In the 1830s, the English universities of Cambridge and Oxford spawned a Neo-Gothic revival. The young intelligentsia in the English universities believed that the Gothic period represented a purity and spiritual unity that appeared to be missing in the contemporary atmosphere of churches and religions. But most importantly, the church should be restored to its original Gothic form, a hall or nave for the congregation and a chancel for the clergy. Ecclesiology, as the early Gothic Revival movement came to be known, favored not only the return of the liturgical architectural form but also the use of the Middle English period of Gothic architecture. This style was devoid of the rich excesses of tracery and detailing associated with the perpendicular English Gothic style.[4]

The Episcopal bishop of Maryland, William R. Whittingham, urged his parishes in Maryland to emulate this Gothic style. The bishop, who led the Episcopal Church in Maryland from 1840 to 1879, was a founding member of the New York Ecclesiological Society (1848). It advocated a simple, asymmetrical form of the Gothic and even had a list of approved church architects whom it felt properly executed the style. Whittingham was a friend of America's greatest practitioner of the Gothic, Richard Upjohn, whose masterpiece was New York's Trinity Church (1839–46). He had first visited Upjohn's office in New York in 1843 to obtain designs for churches. Upjohn made the Ecclesiological Society's list in 1852.

The Gothic had been used in Baltimore since the early 1800s. Latrobe presented a Gothic design for the Roman Catholic cathedral, which was rejected in favor of a classical scheme. Maximilian Godefroy's Gothic design for St. Mary's Chapel was built in 1806. The style had even been used on residential projects such as Alexander Jackson Davis's house for Robert Gilmor, called Glen Ellen, in 1832. By the 1840s, Robert Cary Long Jr., who had become the city's preeminent church architect, used the Gothic vocabulary for St. Alphonsus Roman Catholic Church of 1842, the Franklin Street Presbyterian Church of 1844–48, and Mount Calvary Episcopal Church in 1844. In the mid 1840s, Long also designed at least five small parish churches for the Episcopal Church that followed the picturesque aesthetic of Church of England country parishes. This theory of religious architecture was imposed by those churchmen in power in Baltimore at the beginning of the late 1840s and early 1850s. Niernsee & Neilson immediately adopted the style, designing exemplary churches for all denominations.[5]

Though the Protestant Episcopal Church was the religion of the power fraternity in Baltimore, Niernsee's first church commission was Saint Charles Borromeo in Pikesville in 1848 (fig. 33). This was a church built to house a Roman Catholic parish that had no church of its own but used a private chapel on the estate of a well to do Catholic Baltimore County farmer. He had received permission from the archdiocese to employ a priest at his own chapel, but the congregation grew too large, so a two-acre site was acquired on what is now called Church Lane, off Reisterstown Road in Pikesville.

The Church of St. Charles Borromeo was a very simple church, fifty-five feet long and thirty feet wide, with a covered porch in place at its entrance. "It is built of brick, in the Gothic style, according to a plan furnished by Mr. Niernsee, of Baltimore, who is well known for his taste and skill in the profession of architecture," reported

FIG. 33. St. Charles Borromeo Roman Catholic Church, Pikesville, Maryland. James T. Wollon Jr. Collection

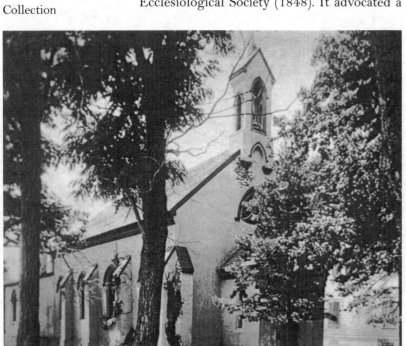

U.S. Catholic Magazine in 1849.⁶ Its Gothic vaulted nave ceiling had ribs that sprang from ornamental brackets on the walls—all covered with plaster. The chancel had a triple-arched Gothic tracery window, fitted with stained glass. The nave windows were also fitted with wooden Gothic tracery and painted glass. The church exterior was unadorned stuccoed brick, with a steep gabled roof and a Gothic window in the gable above the porch. The buttresses had stone caps. There was a small vestry on one side of the church, and there may have been a similar extension on the other side. The church was demolished in 1895 and replaced by the present one, designed by Thomas C. Kennedy, of Baltimore.

Baltimore had a substantial and growing Jewish population in the eastern part of the city next to the Jones' Falls, known as Old Town, which now wanted more formal places of worship instead of using converted buildings. The next religious structure designed by Niernsee was the Har Sinai Verein Synagogue, on High Street (fig. 34). Described as being in "the Norman style" by the *Sun* in an article on the temple's dedication in 1849, the simple gable-roofed synagogue could seat 350 and also had a schoolroom in the ground story.⁷ Niernsee must have made the decision that the Gothic style was not historically correct for Judaism and chose an earlier medieval form influenced by the Lombardic Romanesque, with a front gable outlined in raked corbeling. The front façade had another Lombardic feature, a large center arch over the entry that contained a "wheel" window of stained glass flanked by smaller arched windows. Buttresses stood between the arches.

One impressive feature of the temple was the elaborate ark, which held the Torah. The drapery in front of the ark was a scarlet silk velvet curtain embroidered in gold. Har Sinai was the first reformed temple built in the city and in the *Sun* article, the rabbi, Morris Brown, made the distinction between his ritual and methods used by other movements to promote understanding. A striking pipe organ was also installed in the temple, as there was a good deal of choral singing in a reformed congregation. There was no separation of the sexes, and therefore no need for balconies for women. Har Sinai found this temple too small for its needs and ordered an addition to be built six years later. Soon this, too, proved to be inadequate for the growing population of worshipers, who

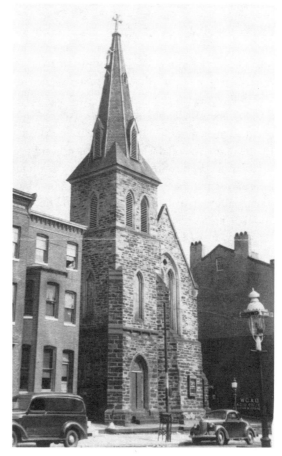

FIG. 34. (*top*) Har Sinai Verein Synagogue, Baltimore. Jewish Museum of Maryland, Har Sinai Collection

FIG. 35. (*bottom*) St. Mark's Episcopal Church, Baltimore. Randolph W. Chalfant Collection

FIG. 36. Grace and St. Peter's Episcopal Church, Baltimore, ca. 1910. Grace and St. Peter's Church

moved uptown and sold the temple to another Jewish congregation. The building was eventually demolished.

The next church would be Niernsee & Neilson's earliest pure Gothic church, St. Mark's Protestant Episcopal Church on West Lombard Street near Parkin Street (fig. 35). It was on an interior lot, purchased by the Rev. Malcolm MacFarlane for a mission church, which he was sponsoring at his own expense. According to his diary in the Diocesan archives, MacFarlane went to New York to consult with Richard Upjohn on the design of this church, but returned to Baltimore without hiring him. When the church was about to be built in 1850, it was announced that Niernsee would be the architect. MacFarlane bargained with Niernsee to design a small church that would not exceed $10,000. St. Mark's had a very elegant façade, with the gable end facing Lombard Street and a powerful short stone tower capped by a broach spire. The church had aisles, but no clerestory; the aisles simply had a shallower roof pitch than

that of the nave. Six triangular dormers in the steeper roof provided light to the nave. At the consecration, Bishop Whittingham called the design "solid, spacious, lofty and seemly in all its parts."[8] The church, which was used to broadcast services on the radio in the 1930s, was demolished in the 1950s.

Well-to-do Protestants and Catholics alike appreciated the Gothic Revival and chose the fashionable style for their new churches, hoping to attract new members. The most important surviving church in Baltimore built in the midst of the Gothic Revival vogue and designed in 1850 by Niernsee & Neilson is Grace Church, now, after a merger, Grace and St. Peter's Episcopal Church, at the northeast corner of West Monument Street and Park Avenue (fig. 36). It was the first church in the city to be faced with brownstone, like the Decatur Miller House one block east.

The design is a bold three-dimensional expression of the picturesque country parish church style of England, with a dramatic steep roof, buttresses, and a projecting vestibule. The front pointed-arched window set above the gabled entrance porch gives the church a powerful simplicity, and the tall buttresses that frame the façade reinforce its sense of strength. The first story of a side tower on Park Avenue, its intended spire never built, serves as another entrance porch.

It has a distinguished floor plan—a seven-bay basilican nave with a semioctagonal chancel. Arches in the English Perpendicular style define the nave and aisles and support the clerestory. A passage connected the chancel with the sacristy (then called a vestry), a twenty-four-foot diameter semidetached polygonal building on Park Avenue (later demolished for a rectangular replacement designed by Henry M. Congdon, of New York). This polygonal structure may have been a reference to the polygonal chapter houses of many English Gothic cathedrals.

The most dramatic interior feature is the fine hammer-beam ceiling, which rests on beautifully carved brackets flanking the elegant clerestory windows (fig. 37). Historically, such decorative trusses were used not only for churches but

also for market halls, barns, and great rooms in palaces. The dark stained wood of the trusses provides a dramatic contrast with the plastered walls. On either side of the chancel are beautifully crafted wrought-iron gates. Neilson's pew remains in the church (plate 2).

In the 1850s, churches like Grace Church were installing such modern conveniences as hot-air heating and gas lighting. Niernsee placed the furnace in the basement and incorporated flues in the exterior walls to bring the heat and outside air to the main story. A limited amount of space was "a difficulty common to churches in this city," reported the *Baltimore American*.[9] But Grace Church, which originally cost $52,000, works quite well on its small lot. Many of the same subcontractors who worked on the firm's Mount Vernon residences were used for the church. Unfortunately, Niernsee's tower was never completed. The design was severely criticized by the purists of the Ecclesiological Movement as being less than desirable.

Some architectural historians are of the opinion that Niernsee & Neilson made a breach of architectural proprietary by plagiarizing the plans of St. Mark's Church in Philadelphia, designed by John Notman. Although there are superficial resemblances between that church and Grace Church, it cannot be said to be a copy of St. Mark's. Many details from both churches, such as the tracery of the clerestory windows, are copied from the same model, plates in A. W. N. Pugin's *Examples of Gothic Architecture*, the most popular reference for Gothic detail of the time. Grace Church is partially a paraphrase of St. Mark's, but a better effort, especially the hammer-beam trusses of the nave. If the tower had been completed, the design would have stood on its own without any comparisons to Notman's work.[10]

The exterior of the church has not weathered well. Because brownstone was a new material, Niernsee (and many other architects) did not understand the importance of proper bedding orientation of the stone. Brownstone is a sedimentary stone that formed over the centuries in layers, so it is of the utmost importance to orient the layers, or bedding planes, perpendicular to the wall of the structure instead of parallel, which allows moisture to infiltrate and cause delamination—as happened to Grace Church and countless other brownstone buildings.[11]

In 1852, the Second Presbyterian Church at the southwest corner of Baltimore and Lloyd Streets found that its 1803 hall church was becoming too small and so it was decided to build a new one (fig. 38). Niernsee's design was in a very simplified Neo-Gothic style carried out in stuccoed brick with brownstone trim. The *Sun* quoted the firm as describing the church "in the style of the buildings constructed during the transition from the Norman to the Romanesque to the pure Gothic—a style that admits the general use of the pointed arch, in connection with some of the most agreeable features of the Romanesque."[12] It was a simple gabled building with triple windows facing Baltimore Street set between two 142-foot towers and spires and a narthex porch; the 76-foot-wide front had three entrances. The broaches were gabled above the four corners of the towers. The interior, with seating for one thousand, featured large arcades on both sides of the nave which supported the roof. There was also a small niche chancel set into the Sunday school building at the rear of the church. The church, which cost $25,000 to build, lasted until 1926, when the congregation moved to a new church in Guilford, and the old building was sold and ultimately torn down.

There is very little description of the appearance of St. Michael's, a Roman Catholic Church, built on the site of a former cemetery, on the northeast corner of Pratt and Regester Streets. The only newspaper account of the new church appears briefly in a *Sun* article in January 12, 1852, describing it as being built in brick having a 76-foot frontage on Regester Street with steeples at each corner and running back 100 feet on Pratt Street. The new church was necessary because St. Michael's German immigrant parish needed more space. The arrival of immigrants from Germany and Ireland was the main reason for the Catholic Church's rapid expansion in Baltimore from 1839 to 1860, when it built eleven churches along with schools, convents, and orphanages. The Church proclaimed the rise of Catholicism by building architecturally distinctive parish churches in the newly developing neighborhoods, such as St. Michael's in east Baltimore. Robert Cary Long Jr.'s St. Alphonsus Church at Saratoga Street and Park Avenue was the grandest of all new Catholic churches with its High Gothic style and richly detailed interior. The new churches provided a sense of stability and permanence in a time when anti-Catholic and anti-immigrant hostility ran high, especially in the 1850s.[13]

FIG. 38. Second
Presbyterian Church,
Baltimore, ca. 1890.
Second Presbyterian
Church

CHURCHES

When the Episcopal congregation of Mount Calvary Church discovered that their church, designed by Robert Cary Long, Jr. in 1844, was already too small they employed Niernsee to expand the structure's northern face in 1852. (Long had died of cholera in 1849.) The church was originally designed in a simplified Gothic style on a triangular lot between Madison Avenue and Eutaw Street. It consisted of a nave measuring about sixty-feet long with a tower

FIG. 39. St. Luke's Church, Baltimore, ca. 1914. William Hollifield Collection

centered on the long south side of the nave and a small chancel projecting from the long north side. This form fit the triangular site admirably but must have presented some difficulties in creating a direction for ritual. Niernsee's design transformed the church into a "pure hall," square in plan. This was accomplished by removing the north bearing sidewall of the church opposite the tower and supplanting it with a bridge truss of considerable ingenuity. The new addition was then built to the north with a shallow projecting chancel. In order to make the addition work, another system of two trusses intersected the truss supporting the roof at the original wall line, almost suggesting a modern space frame.

This roof remains in place, although in recent years anxiety over this innovative roof-framing plan called for investigation by modern engineers, who were completely baffled by the design. They dictated that columns be placed under each of the panel points of the truss, so the church now has a series of extremely slender columns extending from the floor up to the truss, which, though they do not obstruct the congregation's view, are a distraction. Niernsee's chancel was enlarged in the 1880s by T. Buckler Ghequier, an architect trained by Neilson, who designed it in a muscular English Gothic style.

The vestry of St. Luke's Church commissioned Niernsee & Neilson in 1851 to design St. Luke's Church on Carey Street near Lexington Street and Franklin Square, in west Baltimore, to serve Episcopal communicants working at the B&O shops at Mount Clare, only a few blocks away (fig. 39). The quest for this commission was a strange and circuitous journey of misunderstanding between architect and client.

The vestry of St. Luke's had begun as early as 1848 to inquire if Robert Cary Long Jr. would provide a design in the Gothic Revival manner. Long refused their terms, and the day following his meeting with the vestry, Niernsee & Neilson presented two designs for the prospective St. Luke's Church. It is unknown whether these designs were drawn specifically for St. Luke's or were drawings of previous churches they had executed, such as St. Charles Borromeo or St. Mark's.

After the presentation was made, the vestry declined their services because a senior warden was eager to have the Philadelphia architect John Notman design the church. Notman asked for the standard 5 percent fee, which included construction supervision. Instead of producing drawings specifically for St. Luke's, he presented designs for a church that he had been commissioned to do in Savannah, Georgia.

A bitter debate then arose with the vestry over whether Notman should act as contractor, but being totally unfamiliar with the Baltimore labor market and prices, he declined to do so. In a spirit of compromise, he offered the drawings for $225 on a $15,000 estimate. A price of $150 was agreed upon, but on condition that Notman supply the specifications, which he refused to do. In addition, the vestry demanded that the design of the furniture be included in the price.

Notman threw up his hands and walked away, asking that his drawings be returned. The vestry felt it had not been treated "with proper frankness and ingenuousness" and threatened to file a lawsuit. Eventually, St. Luke's did comply with the request and returned the drawings for the church. Unfortunately, by that time Notman had lost his Savannah project.[14]

The church then approached New York architect Frank Wills who was on the Ecclesiological Society list, but they could not agree on a price. When it was announced that Niernsee & Neilson would do the final work, it was with the understanding that the church would be built to the barest minimum. The firm agreed to a 2.5 percent fee with provision in the contract raising it to 5 percent "if the architects gave a contribution of money or materials equivalent to additional rate." Niernsee & Neilson provided the design for a complete church, costing about $15,000, but only $11,000 was available. The reduced plan consisted simply of a nave and aisles, the base of a future tower, the chancel arch, and two transepts, which were to be used as temporary vestries.

Niernsee's design was executed in granite with a very high nave supported on octagonal granite columns. The clerestory is pierced with quatrefoil windows. The side aisles are lit by richly colored stained glass windows, which were designed by William Butterfield, the English architect of the most influential Gothic Revival church, All Saints', Margaret Street, in London in 1849. In a strange twist, the rector, the Rev. Asbury Baker, became a convert to the Roman Catholic Church, and in April 1853, he announced to the assembled congregation that he was stepping down and going to Rome, as it was referred to in those days. This caused considerable consternation, and work on the church was summarily stopped. Thus, the state of the church after this episode was that the chancel arch had been filled with a temporary wall, probably of wood, stucco, and plaster, with a temporary window leaving the church feeling cold and drafty.[15]

The architects were paid off and in 1857 the job was handed over to John W. Priest, another New York architect recommended by the New York Ecclesiological Society, who demanded a 5 percent fee, stating that this "was the rate for new buildings and old ones were harder to manage." He met with the vestry and proceeded to severely criticize Niernsee's design, declaring that it would have resulted in a church "abnormal in design and grotesque in execution" and that the nave was too high for its width. He also condemned the construction quality and materials of Niernsee's work.

Priest was one of the relatively few out-of-town architects to come to Baltimore to work in the pre–Civil War period. Most commissions were handled by local architects. If an outside architect was chosen, he was invariably from New York, the prevailing belief being that New York had higher aesthetic standards and more talented architects than a provincial place like Baltimore. This practice caused a resentment that lasts to this day. Usually a new architect is diplomatic when critiquing a predecessor's work, unless he was deceased. In Priest's case, he didn't seem to care at all what Niernsee

thought. In the end, St. Luke's was completed to Priest's design, but Niernsee had some consolation, since Priest died the following year, in 1858, and the work was turned over to his partner, Henry M. Congdon. Before his demise, Priest had added a chancel, one of good proportions.[16]

The mélange of Niernsee's and Priest's work, when completed, produced the largest Protestant Episcopal church in Baltimore (fig. 40). The change of architects was due to Rev. G. Edgerton, the new rector, who did not favor the completion of the design as prepared by Niernsee & Neilson. The design, in his estimation, did not adhere to the theories of the new Ecclesiological movement, which was then gathering force in the United States and which proposed the reinstallation of the correct Gothic of thirteenth century England as the ideal house of worship for the Protestant Episcopal Church. Despite all the problems securing the project and executing the scaled-back design, the *Sun* reported that Niernsee & Neilson "maintained their high reputation as architects."[17]

Another important Protestant Episcopal church commission came in 1853 with Emmanuel Church, to be built at the southeast corner of Read and Cathedral Streets near Mount Vernon Place (fig. 41). This congregation was typical

FIG. 40. St. Luke's Church, interior. James D. Dilts

of the migration pattern from downtown in the 1850s. Baltimore's second Protestant Episcopal Church, Christ Church, was located at Gay and Fayette Streets. By 1850, few of its parishioners still lived in the neighborhood. Many had moved uptown, with the wealthier members settling in Mount Vernon.

Until the introduction of horse cars in 1859, most people walked in Baltimore, and the trek back downtown to church was inconvenient. In 1851, the parish was granted a petition by the diocese to form a new church uptown, Emmanuel Episcopal Church, within walking distance of their residences. The new church was almost a mile from Christ Church. After Emmanuel opened, the rector, the entire vestry, and almost half the pew-holders left, and by 1868, Christ Church was almost bankrupt, with only 82 out of 198 pews rented.[18]

The exodus from other downtown Protestant churches increased; from 1858 to 1870, eleven moved out. Bishop Whittingham, an ardent supporter of church architecture, was disturbed by the migration, criticizing those who "forsake unfashionable neighborhoods and desecrate consecrated buildings by selling out GOD's property and go where thriving building speculations promise high pew-rent rolls or where the aggregation of genteel society has massed together pew-holders of sufficient pretensions to suit their taste."[19] Nevertheless, such demographic shifts meant new commissions to architects, and Emmanuel Church was a choice project for Niernsee & Neilson, which

FIG. 41. Emmanuel Church, Baltimore, ca. 1880s. Randolph W. Chalfant Collection

got the opportunity after Richard Upjohn declined the Rev. Henry Van Dyke Johns' request for a design. Upjohn refused to waste his time with congregations that had no money in hand to build. Instead, he published *Rural Architecture* in 1852 to give poor congregations designs for low-cost wood-framed churches.

Emmanuel Church, built of rough-faced granite with bluestone trim, was a very progressive design for its time. The vestry did not want to go into debt with the new building, and as a result,

the unadorned exterior was a simple and strong Gothic statement. Congregants entered at the bottom of its most impressive feature, Niernsee's unique soaring tower and belfry, which had very few window openings.

The large nave of Emmanuel Church, over sixty feet wide, had side galleries but no aisles (fig. 42). The architects roofed the building in the manner of St. Mark's with an expression of aisles under roofs of a lower pitch flanking the steeper nave roof. Later, dormers inserted at

FIG. 43. Emmanuel
Church. James D.
Dilts

The most striking feature of the nave was the roof support system: two extraordinary compound Howe trusses, spanning 100 feet, with vertical rods in tension between the bottom chord and the top chord, plus diagonal wrought-iron tension rods. The roof of Emmanuel was supported entirely on these two great timber and metal trusses. Each of the wooden beams of the steeper pitched nave bore on a panel point of the longitudinal truss. The purlins ran parallel to the trusses, and rafters over the aisles were also supported on the upper chord of the trusses. Below the trusses hung wooden tracery in the form of mock Gothic arches.

The church was an immediate success, with all its pews selling for a total of $34,000. Emmanuel Church was later completely altered by the work of two architects. The vestry in 1914 commissioned the noted ecclesiastical architect Ralph Adams Cram to design and execute a real Gothic stone arcade; the galleries and trusses were removed, totally obliterating Niernsee's original interior design. In 1919, Boston architect Woldemar H. Ritter was employed to reconstruct the tower and add flanking narthexes, decorating it in a confection of Flemish high Gothic with sculptural figures telling the Christmas story (fig. 43).

Not very much is known about First Constitutional Presbyterian Church on Greene and German (later Redwood) Streets, another commission Niernsee & Neilson received in 1854. A single three-story tower reminiscent of Reims Cathedral topped the portico gable. The church was later sold to the Beth Tfiloh congregation and became a synagogue before it was eventually torn down and replaced by a warehouse building.[21]

Niernsee executed a near duplicate of his 1852 Second Presbyterian Church design in 1854 in Frederick, Maryland, for the Evangelical Lutheran Church of Frederick (plate 3). Here the twin 150-foot octagonal towers with spires are somewhat more slender and more widely spaced across a 97-foot-wide façade, but the same technique was used to create the head gables of the corner broaches of the steeples. Centered between the towers is a similar gabled entry porch. The triple window arrangement of the front façade is also similar. The interior of the original church was slightly remodeled after Niernsee's initial design, with an enlarged chancel, and Ernst Dreyer's frescoes have been destroyed. The Union Army used the church as a

the change of pitch brought light into the nave. The interior of the church was that of a single preaching hall, which held 850 worshippers facing a large Gothic arch, opening into the chancel. The side galleries, which could seat 400, were suspended from the roof structure—an arrangement, the *Sun* noted in 1854, "to avoid the disagreeable interposition of pillars between the pastor and many of the congregation."[20] The plaster faces of the wall on either side of the chancel arch had frescoes by Ernst Dreyer showing a choir of angels. Above the chancel arch, a circular window housed a stained-glass image of an eternal flame. The projecting (or "recessed," to use the word of the day) chancel had a triple Gothic window in its east end facing Charles Street; it was flanked by sacristies. The church did spend lavishly on the interior furnishings, which were done entirely in black walnut.

CHURCHES

hospital during the Battle of Antietam in 1862. The church commission was a case of near replication by Niernsee, who often used similar forms for different projects, but rarely copied another building verbatim. Even if asked by clients to recycle previous designs, most architects rework them to stand on their own. Nevertheless, the church survives, and its towers have become a beloved landmark of Frederick's skyline.[22]

The firm continued to do important downtown Baltimore Presbyterian churches. Presbyterian congregations also favored elaborate church architecture, and in the Central Presbyterian Church, they got more than they had imagined. Located on the southwest corner of Liberty and Saratoga Streets, it opened in 1855 with thirteen hundred people attending the first service (plate 4). Two hundred and two pews arranged in eight rows brought in much income for the church. Costing $63,000 for the lot, building, and furnishings, the church, the most expensive in the city, was Italianate in design, constructed of stuccoed brick with brownstone trim. Its main feature, a 133-foot tower topped by a 75-foot-tall wooden spire at the northeast corner of the building, was quite controversial. Some Presbyterians called the tower "monstrous." Although the main tower, with its triple arched belfry, was huge, it was well proportioned, but the steeple seems almost an afterthought. It had the feel of a skyscraper next to the surrounding row houses. (A later

photograph of the church shows the tower without the spire; fig. 44) Italianate details, like elaborately molded hoods, appear on segmentally arched windows on the side façade. A gallery located in front of the organ loft was supported on brackets. Ernst Dreyer did the fresco work, and the floors of the chancel and aisles were covered in Brussels carpeting. A large chandelier was suspended from the 45-foot-high ceiling. The church had only been in existence for twenty-two years when it was destroyed by the Clay Street fire, in 1873.[23]

Niernsee & Neilson used the Italianate style again in 1855 for St. John the Evangelist, a Roman Catholic Church at Eager and Valley Streets in East Baltimore, a burgeoning immigrant parish (fig. 45). Like the Second Presbyterian Church, St. John's has twin towers, here capped by short concave pyramidal roofs that closely resemble those of Ludwigskirche of Munich, designed by Friedrich von Gartner. The church was built of brick covered with stucco. The sixty-five-foot-wide main façade is composed of a series of tall half-round arched openings and arched windows that carry around the clerestory and side aisles. The interior alludes to an early Christian basilica with its high-ceilinged nave with the clerestory arches supported on cast-iron columns. The finishes were described by the *Sun*: "The sidewalls and ceilings are painted in fresco colors and present a chaste and decorated appearance. The pews are

FIG. 45. St. John the Evangelist, Baltimore. Collections of the Associated Archives at St. Mary's Seminary and University

52

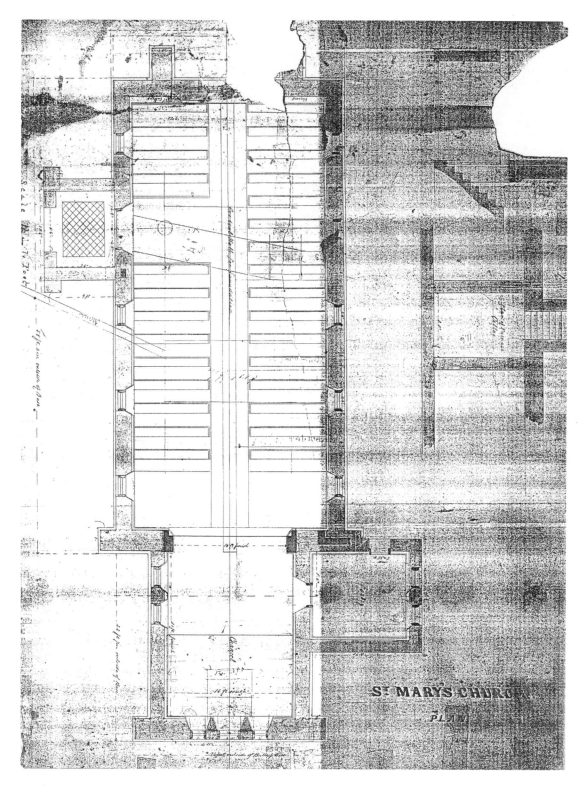

FIG. 46. St. Mary's Church, Emmorton, Harford County, Maryland, plan, J. Crawford Neilson. Historical Society of Harford County, Inc.

CHURCHES

painted and grained in oak and are convenient and very neat. The altar railing is of handsome walnut. The most striking feature to the visitor is the beautiful altar of colored marbles—the tabernacle of which is a rare piece of workmanship, both for the engraving as well as the head of the Saviour over the door, carved from one piece of marble and which for artistic skill is unsurpassed in its way."[24]

Construction went quickly for a building of this size; it took just over a year to build. Instead of a workforce of subcontractors, a general contractor, Samuel H. Adams, was hired. The church was lengthened in 1892 by E. Francis Baldwin, but the original design remained unchanged. The building, now owned by Baltimore City, is a food distribution center.[25]

FIG. 47. *(top)*
St. George's Parish Church, Spesutia, Perryman, Maryland. Kevin Wisniewski

FIG. 48. *(bottom)*
St. George's Parish Church, interior, 1931. James T. Wollon Jr. Collection

Niernsee & Neilson's work for the Protestant Episcopal Church was not confined to Baltimore. They designed two country churches of extraordinary character, both done in 1851 and located in Harford County. The first of these, St. Mary's Church at Emmorton (plate 5; fig. 46), is designed in the pure Gothic style after the manner of the Ecclesiological Society's model church, St. James the Less outside Philadelphia.

St. Mary's, built of very fine fieldstone, is beautifully detailed in all its parts and achieves a great dignity and character. It has a simple nave without aisles and with a well-defined chancel (plates 6 and 7). The church has been augmented over the years by stained-glass windows, which were contributed out of the private fund of the Rev. William Francis Brand, who had initially attempted to hire William Butterfield

for the project. Between 1851 and 1870, he did buy fifteen stained-glass windows designed by Butterfield, depicting the life of Christ. Brand had persuaded congregants to donate land and his wife's family to pay for the entire church. Phoebe Stanton, in *The Gothic Style and American Church Architecture*, called it the "finest rural church in the diocese of Maryland." An original watercolor rendering for this project at the Maryland Historical Society shows the church as it was intended to have been completed with a small obliquely positioned tabernacle spire containing the church bell at the peak of the west gable (plate 8).

Most parishes left designing to Niernsee, but Brand and Whittingham had a prototype in mind when they hired the firm—"The First Pointed Church," an image in the October 1849 issue of *New York Ecclesiologist*. Brand subsequently made some adjustments that actually improved the original design. Such illustrations were used to provide guidance to congregations on aesthetics. The roof beams at St. Mary's, for example, were left bare because the magazine said that exposed roof timbers, not plastered ceilings, expressed "truth and beauty." Architects in general hate to be told to copy a design, but in dealing with such a tandem of religious authority as Brand and Whittingham, Niernsee seems to have acquiesced.[26]

In 1851, Bishop Whittingham offered to raise funds for another Episcopal church, Spesutia,[27] to be built in Perryman, Harford County, Maryland, for St. George's parish (fig. 47). The new building was the fourth church of this seventeenth-century parish, one of the original thirty parishes in Maryland. Niernsee & Neilson's church is built of stuccoed brick and has tall narrow round-arched windows and a small south porch. Buttresses between the windows give the one-story building a feeling of solidity and strength. It has a single nave without aisles and a handsome, well-proportioned two-story tower, the upper belfry story being octagonal with louvered openings. The semioctagonal chancel is lit by three round-arched windows (fig. 48). St. George's Parish Church resonated in the architectural world as successfully as did Niernsee's Thomas House in the residential field. A number of copies or near copies exist.

The last three important Episcopal churches designed by Niernsee & Neilson are Martin's Brandon Church in Burrowsville, Virginia; Saint Paul's in Petersburg, Virginia; and Christ

Church in Elizabeth City, North Carolina. Nearly identical in design to St. George's, Martin's Brandon Church was a simple rural parish church composition of stuccoed brick with a tower adjoining the roof gable (fig. 49). Its round arched windows and side porch echo the ones on the Harford County church. The church, built in 1855, replaced an earlier building.[28]

St. Paul's Church of 1857 was completed by Neilson after his partner departed for South Carolina (plate 13). It is clear that Niernsee did contribute to its design, which was planned before the two separated. The church replaced Calvin Pollard's elegant Greek Revival church of 1838, which burned in 1854, on an exciting hilltop site, overlooking the valley below. The design has a classic central steeple set before a wide gabled nave. Inside, balconies supported on slender columns lead the eye to an open-beam truss roof. As originally built, it had a very small chancel, which was enlarged over the years. Although St. Paul's now faces a six-story telephone building of considerable proportions, it must originally have had a commanding effect on the city skyline. It is one of the most successful and yet simplest of Niernsee & Neilson's Neo-Gothic buildings. It has the simplicity of St. Mark's in Baltimore but is finished in stucco on brick rather than fieldstone. The spire is very well proportioned and its overall effect is one of enormous dignity and picturesque expression. The interior of the church is much less emphatic in its design, and its structure is more ethereal in detail than the strong elements of buttresses and wall panels of the exterior might suggest. Because Robert E. Lee worshipped there during the siege of Petersburg, the church has a special status and is very often referred to as the Lee Church.

Christ Church in Elizabeth City, North Carolina, built in 1857, is a handsome edifice of brick with stone trim of excellent detail and has a single, very well proportioned tower rising to the right of the gabled nave (fig. 50). Above the entry is a triple set of Gothic windows. Here the interior details are also more slender and ethereal than the battlemented brickwork outside would indicate. The nave has a hammer-beam truss ceiling similar to that of Grace Church in Baltimore.

While working later in South Carolina, Niernsee took on some side projects, which included two Roman Catholic churches. The first is St. Mary's Church, located in the town of Edgefield,

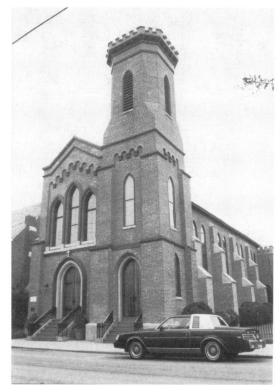

FIG. 49. *(top)* St. Martin's Brandon Church, Burrowsville, Virginia. Randolph W. Chalfant Collection

FIG. 50. *(bottom)* Christ Church, Elizabeth City, North Carolina. Frederic C. Chalfant

an important county town south of Columbia (fig. 51). The parishioners raised $3,000 for the site and construction costs. Built in 1857, St. Mary's is a simple stone church with a nave, a small chancel, and a gable-roofed tower centered on the front façade. Niernsee, most likely, had a stonemason working on his state capitol project cut the stone for the tower and its cross. The marble altars were imported from Italy. It took ten months to complete construction.[29]

The Church of the Most Holy Trinity, a Catholic church in Augusta, Georgia, was an 1863 work in which Niernsee provided a Roman-

NIERNSEE
AND NEILSON

buttresses. The church has a basilican plan with two aisles, a balcony and a spacious chancel lit by round-arched windows in its rear wall. The interior is quite elegant and awe inspiring; the transverse arches, which are covered in plaster, are supported by twelve cast-iron columns, painted in gilt and dark coral (plate 10). The marble altars were carved in Baltimore by John MacMurphy and had to be smuggled through the Union army blockade during the Civil War to be installed for the consecration in 1863. In 1886, the church stood firm without a crack during an earthquake.[30]

The number of churches Niernsee & Neilson designed from 1848 to 1856 is staggering, considering all the other commissions that came into the office. Their churches may be their most enduring legacy; the one building type that is still the most used and the best preserved. Congregations like those of Grace and St. Peter's in Baltimore, St. Paul's in Virginia, and the Church of the Most Holy Trinity in Georgia treasure their buildings and are proud to worship in such beautifully designed churches. Niernsee was not an innovative designer, but beginning with St. Charles Borromeo, he displayed a great skill in interpreting the Gothic Revival and Italianate ecclesiastical forms of the day. The churches are all well proportioned and handsomely detailed, often displaying an innovative structural system that in itself was quite beautiful.

But as impressive as Niernsee & Neilson's church architecture is, their very best ecclesiastical work of the period celebrated the ritual of death.

esque design at his own expense (plate 9). Built of brick finished in stucco, it has an asymmetrically placed tower with an octagonal belfry and spire. The round-arched window and door openings include a set of carved wood, double-entry doors. A central traceried stained-glass window over the entry lights the nave along with three small rose windows. The side facades have six stained-glass windows separated by

FIVE

Green Mount Cemetery Chapel

American attitudes toward death in the mid-nineteenth century were greatly influenced by Victorian England, where there was a deep preoccupation with the subject. Unlike today, the ritual of death was taken very seriously and with great ceremony. The shorter life expectancy, high infant and child mortality, and Christian beliefs all played a role in this thinking. Grief, mourning, and especially the rite of interment were considered quite important, and families went to great lengths to give the deceased a "proper" departure to the hereafter.

Age, gender, religion, and circumstance of the death determined how funerals were conducted. There were "good deaths," like dying of old age, and "bad deaths," like suicide or death from a disease like syphilis, which meant a quiet modest funeral. Class also played a key factor. The wealthier the family, the more elaborate the funeral, and the centerpiece of the burial ritual

FIG. 52. Green Mount Cemetery, Baltimore, 1936. Photograph by A. Aubrey Bodine, © Jennifer B. Bodine

in mid–nineteenth century cemeteries was the ornate Gothic mortuary chapel, which satisfied the Victorian fascination with death and the afterlife.[1]

In Baltimore, the well-to-do preferred interment in Green Mount Cemetery, established in 1839 on the former Robert Oliver estate outside the city limits. But by 1850, the cemetery needed a more elaborate and ceremonial setting for funeral services befitting the wealthy, and Niernsee & Neilson were called upon to design a mortuary chapel. Niernsee designed it in the manner of the southern German Gothic, a style he was well acquainted with from his apprenticeship with Kranner, the Gothic Revival stonemason (plate 11). Built from 1851 to 1857, a dramatic 102-foot spire of brownstone surrounded by freestanding pinnacles and flying buttresses rises above an octagonal chapel that is entered from a porte cochere (fig. 52). Niernsee took a spire from a cathedral and literally brought it down to earth. The chapel is actually a very small building, but it has a dynamic presence.[2]

In the center of the interior space, above where the coffin is placed for ceremonial interment, is a dome, flooding the chapel with natural light and enhancing the feeling of openness and lightness of the space. The plan of the chapel is very simple. An octagonal aisle defined by eight slender columns surrounds an octagonal sanctuary covered by a vault representing the heavens (fig. 53). The aisle is twelve feet wide and about twenty-four feet tall; the sanctuary is double that height. The eight columns support the tower above. The effect upon entering the space, which is completely ringed by solid walls pierced by a door or window on each facet of the octagon, is that of a shaded walk within an illuminated sanctuary. It is the quality of illumination in the sanctuary, which seems quite separate from the surrounding aisle, that gives the chapel its special dignity. The exterior walls and buttresses are decorated with conventional representations of aedicules; those on the lower buttresses are blind. With a stained-glass dome directly under the tower, the chapel, itself is one big aedicule.

The significance of the chapel's design relates directly to the final ceremony before burial, when the coffin containing the deceased is placed upon the bier in the center of the sanctuary and is lowered beneath the floor. The bereaved are comforted by the sense that the re-

cently departed are already in the shelter of God. It is this special quality that gives the chapel its particular poignancy.

Other mortuary chapels had been built in America. John Notman's 1837 chapel for Laurel Hill Cemetery, Philadelphia (demolished) and the 1843 Bigelow Chapel in Mount Auburn Cemetery in Cambridge, Massachusetts, were among the most notable examples of the period. But Niernsee's design, and its innovative iconography of interment at a parklike cemetery, remains the sole example of such planning for a mortuary chapel.

Green Mount Cemetery is an example of a metropolitan development of the early nineteenth century, when American cities were beginning to get too large to continue the traditional habit of burying the dead in the churchyard. Land in the city centers was too valuable to be taken up by graveyards; in addition, the graveyard itself produced sanitary problems for a community that derived its drinking water from wells. The infrastructure of a modern city, with its storm drains, streets, and other amenities, arrived in fits and starts, usually after out-breaks of deadly epidemics. Green Mount was one of the first parklike, rural cemeteries in the United States, the first being Cambridge's Mount Auburn Cemetery, dedicated in 1831, and the second, Laurel Hill Cemetery, established 1836.

Robert Cary Long Jr. was employed to design the plan of the cemetery (he also designed the gate), which, in the sentiment of the times, was to be an earthly recreation of paradise, a park in which the tombs of the departed were buried. In practice the funeral was performed at the church of the deceased, and then the procession arrived at the cemetery for the rite of interment. At Green Mount Cemetery, the chapel was conceived as a symbolic interment place, which was also practical and convenient during inclement weather, allowing actual burial at a later time by cemetery personnel. It was seen as an earthly representation of the heavenly mansion.

The chapel is very beautifully located in the cemetery. Set high among the trees, it overlooks the Jones' Falls Valley about fifty-feet above Greenmount Avenue and is visible for blocks around. It is highly picturesque, a quality evident in many other works of Niernsee & Neilson, such as Clifton, where the house and its tower seize the landscape so that the building

NIERNSEE
AND NEILSON

FIG. 53. Green Mount Cemetery Chapel, interior. Green Mount Cemetery

GREEN MOUNT
CEMETERY
CHAPEL

not only dominates the natural surroundings but also augments the scene's romanticism. The sense of the picturesque is never overlooked in a Niernsee & Neilson architectural conception. Many buildings of earlier architects, such as Benjamin Henry Latrobe, are self-contained and are designed irrespective of the urban or landscape context in which they are built. Niernsee & Neilson's buildings are clearly conceived for their site. Niernsee's strength as a designer is distinguished not only by the stylistic qualities (albeit not always original) of his buildings but also by their relationship to their setting.

The chapel is not the only building built by Niernsee & Neilson at Green Mount Cemetery. A year prior to the design of the chapel, Niern-

FIG. 54. Purviance Tomb, Green Mount Cemetery. Frederic C. Chalfant

NIERNSEE
AND NEILSON

see was commissioned by Judge John Purviance to design the entrance of a vaulted tomb to be built at the cemetery. The tiny building has a monumental Gothic arched entrance and a stairway down to the vaulted space, which contains the Purviance coffin, along with those of the rest of his family (fig. 54). The tomb itself consists of an underground arched-brick vault rising above the ground under a grassy mound directly behind the entryway. Niernsee's design is a structure of neolithic simplicity; marble slabs at the side of the entrance and at the roof make the effect quite primitive and powerful. Three slit windows open on each side of the entrance.

Churches and funerary structures like Green Mount became important symbols of faith and stability for society in a period when radical transformations were taking place in Baltimore. The industrial revolution had changed the city from a mercantile center dependent on shipping into a bustling manufacturing economy powered by steam. At the epicenter of this great metamorphosis was the railroad. And Niernsee & Neilson would get the opportunity to pioneer a completely new building type for this new industry.

SIX

Railroad Stations

The biggest business of all in Baltimore was the railroad—the Baltimore and Ohio, the Baltimore and Susquehanna, and the Baltimore and Port Deposit—fanning out from the city in all directions. By the late 1840s, after their initial construction was complete, railroads were beginning to find themselves on a stronger financial footing and on their way to becoming the nation's most formidable economic and political powers for the next hundred years. Now that the basic infrastructure, such as the track, the freight and engine houses, was in place, the railroads focused on improving the efficiency of freight service and expanding passenger service, which meant new stations.

The key impetus for this new focus in Baltimore was the end of using horse-drawn trains on city streets. Train movements in the center city were handled by horsepower, except during the hours between 9 P.M. and 6 A.M., when locomotives could be used, provided a man walking with a lantern preceded the train. Locomotives were prohibited from city streets because of the danger of boiler explosions, frightening horses, and the economic competition with teamsters. The reason for giving up animal power was the growing perfection of the steam locomotive. It no longer made economic sense to haul increasingly heavy loads with animals, especially up steep grades. All three railroads were improvising stations using existing buildings and stables. Baltimore and Susquehanna passengers bought their tickets at a house that stood next door to the tracks at Guilford Avenue and Saratoga Street.[1]

The B&S developed a business strategy that would not only pay the interest on its debts, but also achieve a profit. It consisted of two parts —a new downtown station and the successful completion of a rail line to Harrisburg. The route would connect to the newly formed Pennsylvania Railroad, which offered the promise to Baltimore businessmen of an earlier access to the Ohio River than the B&O was going to be able to achieve. A new centrally located station would not only generate passenger business but would free the railroad from dependence upon private dispatch companies to haul its freight. The B&S plan resulted in a unique and influential building: Calvert Station.[2]

Part of the B&S success was the result of a fortunate land acquisition by their energetic president, Robert Mitchell Magraw, who bought a lot owned by the Baltimore Water Company on Calvert Street between Franklin and Monument Streets immediately adjoining their tracks on North Street (Guilford Avenue). The site had advantages for passenger service as well, being only five blocks from Barnum's Hotel, the premiere hotel in Baltimore and one of the most famous in the United States. Most importantly, though, the railroad obtained an ordinance from Baltimore City allowing them to operate steam locomotives from Biddle Street, the previous terminus of steam operation, to the terminal lot regardless of the time of day. That having been achieved, a new station plan, designed by Niernsee, was announced on June 17, 1848, and construction began later that summer.[3]

As he had with his houses, Niernsee turned to the Italianate for his design and the result was a symmetrical twin towered composition consisting of a two-story building, 112 feet in width, containing the passenger terminal, freight office

FIG. 55. *(top)* Calvert Station, Baltimore, 1936. E. H. Pickering, Historic American Buildings Survey, Library of Congress

FIG. 56. *(bottom)* Calvert Station Train Shed, 1936. E. H. Pickering, Historic American Buildings Survey, Library of Congress

and the headquarters offices of the railroad. (fig. 55). Connected to the rear of the building was a train shed 315 feet long and 112 feet wide. The buildings were placed diagonally on the block site, because, as Niernsee explained, it "permits the easiest and best access, both for passengers and trains, and offers for future buildings the most frontage on the four streets encompassing the square." He also designed the rear of the complex with great care. Though it was not readily visible from the two main streets, the long gable-roofed shed terminated in a wide

Italianate portal with three large stone arches for the entry of passenger and freight trains (fig. 56).

Terminals marked the end and beginning of a railway journey and served as the architectural gateway to a city. This concept was the key to Niernsee's design of Calvert Station and its relation to the city. An arriving traveler's first impression of a city in the nineteenth century was the architectural presence of the train station. His first glimpse of Baltimore was framed by the handsome triple arched portal of the main building on Calvert Street. The towers call out the importance of the building in each direction from which the station is approached. Since the towers rose above the then-prevailing thirty- to forty-foot roof lines of row houses, they could be seen from a distance. The main station building was quite shallow and compact, but its front façade of round arched windows and projecting center pedimented bay gave the B&S an impressive face at the corner of Calvert and Franklin Streets. Niernsee's slender, pyramidal roofed towers effectively framed the main block of the station. The building, sited at an angle, boldly stood out against the orthogonal street grid, giving it great impact and importance.

A floor plan of the lower floor was contained in the cornerstone, opened in 1948 when the building was demolished to make way for the new headquarters of the *Baltimore Sun* (fig. 57). Through the triple arched entry, a twenty-foot wide center hall, led directly from the street to the tracks behind the station. Flanking the center hall to the left was a monumental stair to the offices above, behind the stairs was a ladies' and gentlemen's waiting room, a small ladies' retiring room and a baggage room. Rooms on the right contained a ticket office in the front and the office of the transportation superintendent. The ladies' retiring room had a toilet room equipped with water closets, which was in the bottom of the left hand tower. Men were forced to go up the main stairs to a toilet located over the women's in the same tower. No upper floor plan was found in the cornerstone. It is only a guess that the boardroom was in the center over the main entrance and that President Magraw had one of the front rooms. Behind these front rooms were large areas well suited for accounting and general offices. Though not apparent on the main elevation, there was a complete third floor reached by a separate stair, which was lit by skylights and

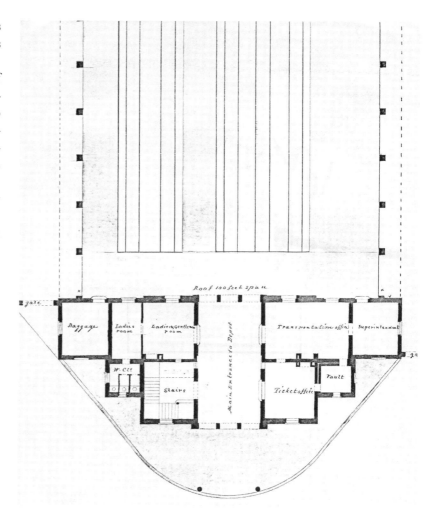

FIG. 57. Calvert Station, plan, 1848. Maryland Historical Society, Baltimore, Maryland

by windows in the rear. Chimneys served fireplaces in the principal rooms.[4]

It was the train shed and the 100-foot span of its trusses that really caught the attention of the press and the public (fig. 58). Baltimore newspapers described it as "without parallel in this section of the country." Actually, there is no record of a larger roof span in the entire nation that year. The trusses, twenty in all, were supported on two colonnades of granite posts about two-feet square and sixteen feet high, complete with bases and capitals. These posts supported continuous timber sills to which the trusses were fastened. The Howe trusses were of composite construction: timber was used for members in compression or bending or for members alternately in compression or tension, and iron was used for connections and members in tension. The working truss, trapezoidal in shape, was what would now be described as a queen-post type with counter braces. On top of each was a kind of annex or "piggyback" truss to complete the triangular outline of the roof; this part resembled a king-post truss. The 100-

foot span was nominal; the shed was 98 feet clear between the granite posts and 99 feet clear between the faces of the wood sills. The whole roof was 112 feet wide. The roof withstood the snow load of the blizzard of 1899, which felled the roof of the President Street Station's train shed. The roof ridge was surmounted by five hip-roofed louvered ventilators equally spaced and each about fifteen feet square. The ventilators do not appear to be adequate to take away locomotive fumes. It is more probable that they served to exhaust the fumes from the gaslights. Nine circular gas jet rings and connecting piping were still in place when the car house roof was dismantled (fig. 59).[5]

Although not entirely complete, the station was opened for public use on June 3, 1850.[6] Tickets were sold from a specially outfitted car. When the Calvert Station was opened, it was the largest railroad terminal building in the United States with the largest clear-span roofed car house in the country. At the beginning of the project the architects had estimated its cost to be $43,000. This estimate was revised in March 1850 to $48,000, including the tracks, walls, fencing and platforms. At the time of the publication of the B&S Railroad annual report in September 1850, the cost had risen to $52,250, partly inflated by the effect of the California Gold Rush.

The city council had raised questions about the cost in March 1850; certain councilmen were suspicious that President Magraw had been lining his purse at the expense of the railroad. (Due to its investment in the line, the city guaranteed the expenses of the railroad at the time.) The railroad made a meticulous reply to the charges, and this is one of the reasons why

FIG. 58. Calvert Station, half elevation (rear). Randolph W. Chalfant, Maryland Historical Society, Baltimore, Maryland

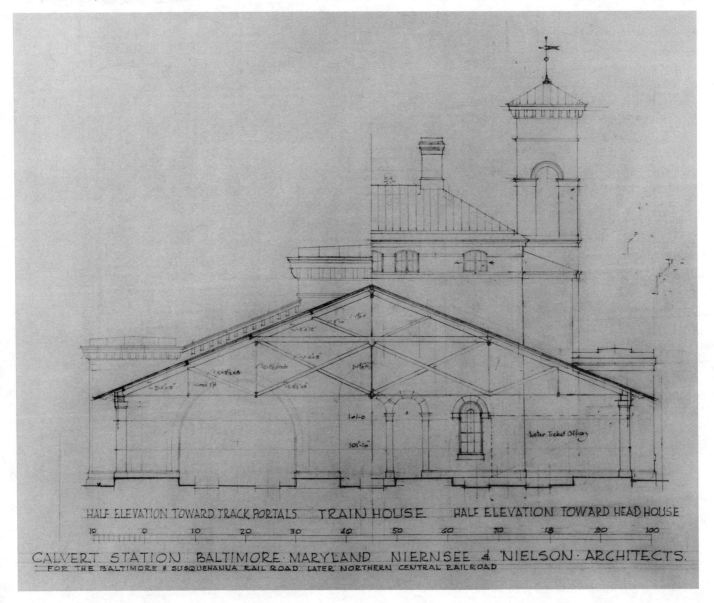

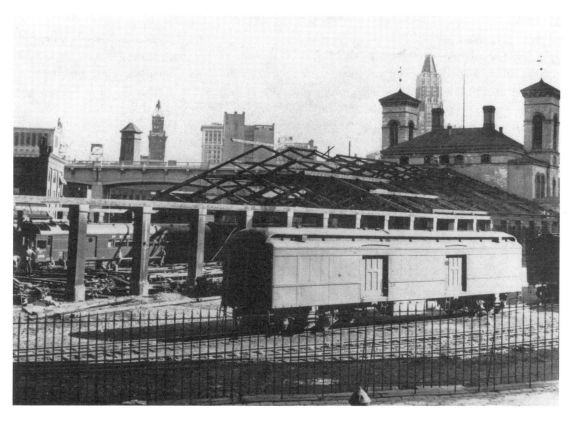

FIG. 59. Calvert Station, 1939. *Baltimore Sun*

so much information is available about the contractors and even about the quantities of work they did for the station building. Niernsee & Neilson appear to have not only prepared the designs for the buildings but also provided a service so that the railroad itself could subcontract the various parts of the work. There is enough information about the actual contract and estimates to show that this was carried out with considerable skill. When the architects were called on by the railroad to defend themselves from accusations of malfeasance in the expenditures on this station, they were able to provide background material that proved the charges to be frivolous.[7]

Niernsee's railroad terminal design would have been completely different if he had designed it in his native Austria. Nothing could indicate more clearly the social differences between the egalitarianism of the United States and stratified European society in this period. In Europe, particularly in the German speaking areas, no terminal station could have been arranged this simply. Four separate classes of passengers and royalty had to be served without making contact with each other. A German station of the same importance as Calvert Station would have had two separate buildings for passengers: one for departure and one for arrival, each with duplicated facilities for each

class of traveler. Initially, there was no alternative for the European architect except to build long rows of buildings on each side of the terminal tracks. Early stations in Berlin, Leipzig, Zurich, Naples, Amsterdam and Prague, for example, featured the end of the train shed as a kind of monumental gateway through which the locomotives of incoming trains steamed into a forecourt containing a turntable where the locomotives pirouetted, so to speak, in front of an audience before going back through the shed to be used for an outgoing train. Although the locomotives were soon banished from view in later terminals, to be replaced by office buildings, hotels and the like in front of the sheds, the actual entrance or exit for passengers would be around on the side despite the monumental appearance of the front.[8]

Calvert Station occupies a significant position in the history of American railroad station architecture. It was undertaken in order to facilitate steam traction from the city center, bringing to an end an era of moving trains by horsepower. It was a prototype of the planned, multipurpose terminal that replaced the previous helter-skelter proliferation of miscellaneous buildings. And it was an early railroad use of the Italianate, which proved so popular for station buildings that it became known as the railroad style. But Calvert Station's tenure as the nation's largest station was brief. Details of the design were reported in the general and technical press before it was completed, and rival buildings were soon constructed that surpassed it in size, but all based their designs on Calvert Station. From the aesthetic point of view, the building served a purpose for which there were no historical precedents. During the railroad age in America, the train station also functioned as ceremonial space for important visitors. Calvert Station ably fulfilled this role as the scene of an elaborate welcome for the Prince of Wales in 1860.

FIG. 60. *(top)* B&O Railroad Station, Washington, D.C., 1872. James D. Dilts Collection

FIG. 61. *(bottom)* B&O Railroad Station, train shed, 1872. James D. Dilts Collection

In 1849, the Baltimore and Ohio Railroad had decided that its present depots were sufficient and that more extensive accommodations could wait until after the line reached the Ohio River. But with the completion of Calvert Station, the B&O realized it could not wait any longer. They felt as if their larger and more important railroad had been outclassed. An enormous amount of capital had to be expended to overcome the weakness in the B&O's terminal areas. They had hired Niernsee & Neilson to design their terminus for the Washington Branch railroad at New Jersey Avenue and C Street NW in 1851 (fig. 60). These facilities eliminated the converted boardinghouse on Pennsylvania Avenue and Second Street and the freight house built in 1842. The New Jersey Avenue station was also an Italianate design and featured a seventy-foot-tall, eighteen-foot-square tower with a clock and bracketed low hipped roof, which raised the profile enough for it to be recognized from several parts of the city. The tower was "the only thing which gives lightness and beauty to the building," reported the *Illustrated London News*.

Niernsee's Washington terminal was much more modest than Calvert Station. It was basically a one-story gable roofed building measuring 106 feet across and 68 feet deep. The projecting cross gable contained a triple arched entry through which passengers entered a 45- by 68-foot hall. The waiting rooms, ticket office and freight office lined both sides of the great space. The stuccoed brick was painted reddish brown with Connecticut brownstone trim. Railroad station spaces for passengers were very similar to parlors of the period. The *Illustrated London News* gave a description of the interior: "The saloons for men and women are small, but commodious. The walls are paneled with wood, painted to imitate oak; and an agreeable mellow light is distributed through the rooms by the use of yellow curtains. The furniture corresponds in colour and character with that of the walls; while the armchairs, benches and etc. are enriched by seats of crimson plush."[9]

This terminal had a large gable-roofed train shed, not quite as large as the train shed at Calvert Station, being only sixty feet wide, which connected to the terminal at an angle (fig. 61). The roof was supported by trusses designed by the B&O's master of the road and developer of the Bollman Truss, Wendel Bollman. It bore on granite piers and had a clerestory along its entire length. At night, the platforms, which the *Baltimore American* noted "render the entrance and exit the trains easy and convenient," were lit by gaslight. Additions were made to the building in 1889 by E. Francis Baldwin, and it was demolished when Union Station was built in 1907–9.[10]

The B&O's Baltimore facilities were located at Charles and Pratt Streets in a series of converted houses and stores. The depot was far too small for the burgeoning freight business the railroad was developing, and the station at Mount Clare was too remote for freight operations, especially since freight and passengers could only be moved there by horses. The company therefore bought a large lot on Camden Street between Howard and Eutaw streets in 1852 for $600,000 for the purpose of developing a new station for both freight and passengers. In 1853, the B&O decided to advertise for plans for the buildings on the new site. The railroad's initial strategy was not to build a passenger station first but rather utilitarian structures to move freight from the harbor and city center to a site closer than Mount Clare where it could be hauled away by locomotive power. The first structures were wooden passenger and freight sheds and engine houses around Howard and Lee Streets designed by Niernsee & Neilson in 1853.[11]

The firm was eventually hired by the railroad to produce preliminary drawings for the main station and came up with a Normanesque design reminiscent of a recently completed building well known to Niernsee, James Renwick's Smithsonian Institution of 1849. A rendering of the new station was first published in Ele Bowen's 1853 prospectus for his *Rambles in the Path of the Steam Horse* (fig. 62). The design was for an extraordinarily ambitious station consisting of a main building with a central tower flanked by two smaller ones and three large barrel-vaulted train sheds to the rear. The purposes for these sheds are not clear, but the eastern shed had a side opening onto Camden Street and it is obvious that the cars emerged onto the right-of-way, which continued up Howard Street almost to Franklin Street.

In June of 1855, Niernsee asked the B&O for a decision on their plan, but the railroad decided "not to accept any plan at this time." Then in March 1856, the railroad appointed a committee to erect a station on the Camden site for $25,000. At this same time, Niernsee

had unexpectedly come upon a choice commission, the South Carolina State House (Chapter 8). In May 1856, he moved from Baltimore to relocate in Columbia, South Carolina to devote his full attention to the project.

This career move would have unexpected consequences for Niernsee, whose station design was placed in another architect's hands. The acceptance of the South Carolina project would reverberate throughout Niernsee's life. It would cost him the opportunity to complete another major building in Baltimore—the Johns Hopkins Hospital (Chapter 10) when he returned again to South Carolina in 1877 to resume work on the State House. When the *Sun* reported on the start of construction of the new Camden Station in May 1856, it credited Joseph F. Kemp, described as "architect of the company."[12] Kemp, a draftsman and carpenter who was employed by the railroad at the time, kept the general massing of the building Niernsee proposed but completely changed the design.

The central pavilion with its 185-foot tower was complete in February of 1857. The *Sun* described it as being in "the Italian bracketed style" and again credited Kemp as architect. John C. Gobright's *City Rambles or, Baltimore As It Is*, of 1857 shows an illustration of the new building signed by "J. F. Kemp, Architect" (fig. 63). In 1864, the two wings designed by Kemp were complete. In general, Kemp's towers are ungainly and out of proportion compared to Niernsee's original design where the three towers rise much more elegantly above the main block (fig. 64). Over the next 128 years, the building underwent numerous renovations including the removal of the original central tower in 1890, which was replaced with a much smaller cupola. In 1992, the station was brought back to its 1865 appearance with a recreation of Kemp's original tower (fig. 65).[13]

The firm designed smaller Italianate passenger stations for other B&O stops. The final rail between Wheeling and Baltimore was laid on Christmas Eve, 1852, and the railroad needed a station as well as other buildings at this important terminus on the levee of the Ohio River. The two-story Wheeling station, which had a three-story tower, was built in 1853 of brick with a waiting room paved in flagstones and offices on the second floor (fig. 66). Though it was the final destination of the 380-mile route from Baltimore that began construction

FIG. 62. *(top)*
Camden Station, 1853
prospectus for Ele
Bowen, *Rambles in the
Path of the Steam
Horse,* 1855

FIG. 63. *(bottom)*
Camden Station. From
John C. Gobright, *City
Rambles, or Baltimore
as It Is,* 1857

CAMDEN STATION.—BALTIMORE AND OHIO RAIL ROAD.

FIG. 64. *(top)* Camden Station, 1872. James D. Dilts Collection

FIG. 65. *(bottom)* Camden Station. James D. Dilts

RAILROAD
STATIONS

in 1828, the station was in no way grandiose. It was a modest design with four arched doorways leading into the passenger waiting room. Niernsee's tower was a toned down version of all his other Italianate designs with a very low hipped roof that had no bracketing. He used cast iron window surrounds in the second story. The station sat at the mouth of Wheeling Creek and its 290-foot train shed extended out on a bridge over the creek. It was replaced in 1908 with a new station.[14] Niernsee & Neilson's 1854 Frederick passenger station at All Saints and Market Streets replaced an 1832 building (fig. 67). This building also had a three-story tower with round arched windows attached to a smaller two-story structure where the passenger waiting area and ticket counter was located. A canopy supported by ornamental iron columns provided cover for arriving and departing passengers.[15] The building still stands in Frederick.

Niernsee seemed to have a corporate identity in mind when he designed the B&O stations.

FIG. 66. *(top)* B&O Railroad Station, Wheeling, West Virginia, 1891. Smithsonian Institution, National Museum of American History

FIG. 67. *(bottom)* B&O Railroad Station, Frederick, Maryland. Frederic C. Chalfant

Niernsee's roundhouse in Martinsburg was apparently completed in 1857, after he departed for South Carolina and probably followed his 1842 plans. It was burned by Confederate troops during the Civil War and was replaced by a somewhat larger building designed by Albert Fink, which remains there today. The complex of railroad shop buildings at Martinsburg is attributed to Niernsee & Neilson by railroad historian John Hankey. He credits several buildings in the complex to the firm. One such building is the casting shop, which is almost exactly the same size as the shed building at Calvert Station. The roof trusses are exactly the same span and appear to be exact copies.

After 1855 there was very little work done by Niernsee & Neilson for the B&O or for any other railroads in the region, which needed to gather more financial backing for their next expansion. But this in no way hurt the firm; in addition to their church and residential work, there came another steady stream of commissions. In the merchant's architectural hierarchy, after family and God, came his place of business, the source of his well-being. He knew the building where he made his money had to reflect well upon him, inspiring confidence in his customers and demonstrating to the public that he was "modern and up-to-date." Niernsee was the man they called upon to create that impression.

Although the buildings were not identical, all shared the same basic massing and one salient design feature, the Italianate tower, which was scaled down for the stations in small towns but still gave the building an imposing architectural presence. Niernsee's 1852 hotel and station in Grafton, Virginia (now West Virginia) was a much larger composition, with the bracketed tower still the main design feature. Instead of placing it to the side of the main block, Niernsee centered the tower on the building.[16]

SEVEN

Places of Business

Commissions for business establishments soon followed John Niernsee's success in Mount Vernon. The young architect began his practice in the best of economic times for Baltimore. The city had prospered in the 1830s from its domestic economy, especially its trade with east coast American markets. But after 1843, its foreign trade accelerated enormously, becoming the driving force behind Baltimore's commercial success. South America became the city's most important trading partner with exports of flour, grain, beef, and textiles. Great Britain revised its trade laws in the 1840s, opening up its markets to foreign grain, which gave Baltimore another key market. The industrial revolution had its full effect on the city in the 1840s and 1850s. Most of the manufacturing and transportation companies incorporated in Maryland used steam power. Baltimore became more than a port city; it now manufactured goods. The number of merchants increased greatly. The 1850 census listed 1,544 merchants and in addition counted seventeen other kinds of merchant specialty, such as "liquor merchant." Though the merchants no longer controlled the wealth of the city, they were by no means poor.[1]

Niernsee's commercial work began in earnest in 1848 with a number of business establishments on Baltimore Street. When Niernsee arrived in Baltimore, Baltimore Street was just beginning to evolve as a commercial thoroughfare. Until then, businesses had been located in row houses; a clothing merchant's store, for example, might occupy the first story rooms. In the late 1840s and especially the 1850s, Baltimore businesses moved out of row houses into buildings tailor-made for conducting trade.

A new business building on Baltimore Street usually had a first-story storefront with plate-glass windows and three to four stories of rental space above. Niernsee's first known project was Martin & Lewis & Company, a menswear store on Baltimore Street completed in 1848. The *Baltimore Sun* described the building as 32 feet in width and 100 feet in depth with a 12-foot diameter dome in the rear of the building. Below the dome was a circular stair that led to the basement level, which dealt with the wholesale trade. "The store fixtures are all of

FIG. 68. Hamilton Easter and Company, Baltimore. William Hollifield Collection

71

oak, giving a rich and finished appearance to the whole interior."[2]

Another Baltimore Street client was Hamilton Easter & Company, a dry goods merchant (fig. 68). The twenty-foot front had two large French plate glass windows. The style of the façade of the store was described as Elizabethan, which, the *Sun* reported, "is once more receiving the attention of the architect and the builder, and certainly will grow more steadily

FIG. 69. *(right)* Patapsco Fire Company Building, Baltimore, 1849. Maryland Historical Society, Baltimore, Maryland

FIG. 70. *(below)* Baltimore Exchange and Custom House. Maryland Historical Society, Baltimore, Maryland

into favor in this city, since the fine display of its beauty has been opened to public view."[3] The James Williams Stores on Gay Street were two four-story buildings with a common thirty-one foot front. The first floor was used for a dry goods business and the upper floors were residences.[4]

The Patapsco Fire Company Building, located on St. Paul Street between East Hamilton and Centre Streets, was another one of Niernsee & Neilson's early projects (fig. 69). In 1849, it housed a volunteer fire company, which at that time was the only way that fire companies were organized in Baltimore, since there was no municipal fire department until the 1850s. The only known representation of the building in its entirety is contained on an engraved certificate of membership in the fire company published in 1849. It shows a churchlike Gothic façade with a tabernacle for fire bells. When the city took over the volunteer fire companies in 1849, the Patapsco firehouse was kept in service until 1866, when it was sold to Michael Roche, a carpenter-builder who flourished between 1845 and 1870. When Roche obtained ownership of the structure, he demolished the Gothic front and converted it into a dwelling and store. The structural walls of the building are still in place although it has been radically altered, with a small retail shop and an upstairs apartment.

In 1852, Niernsee & Neilson received the first of several prestigious commissions to complete the Baltimore Exchange and Custom House, which had originally been designed by Maximilian Godefroy and Benjamin Henry Latrobe. In an age before income tax, the federal government derived most of its tax revenue from tariffs on products. In every major city in America, the custom house was an imposing piece of architecture, signifying its fiscal importance to the government; it was a true mark of respect to get such a project. Benjamin Henry Latrobe's final design primarily comprised the central rotunda and the five-bay-wide façade on Gay Street. The four original wings of the H-shaped plan created by Latrobe had been built in a piecemeal fashion. Niernsee & Neilson's contributions were a one-story addition for the United States government Post Office Department, completed in 1852, and a two-story addition for the Custom House (fig. 70).

Niernsee was not intimidated by Latrobe's design and strove to make his own statement

PLACES OF BUSINESS

with a new entryway. "Perhaps the most striking feature of the structure is the noble portico entrance on Exchange Place; it is of Connecticut brown stone, bold and massive in its details and elaborately wrought in a fine ornamental style," reported the *Sun* in 1853 as the renovation was nearing completion.[5] At the same time, the firm also remodeled the rotunda interior for the purposes of the Custom House Call Room. Niernsee & Neilson also contributed a northwest wing. A new customhouse was built in its place in 1907.

The firm took on a completely new building type when it planned an annex for the Howard House Hotel in 1852 on the west side of the city at Baltimore and Howard Streets (fig. 71). Very little is known about the structure outside of a brief mention in the newspaper.[6]

In 1853, Niernsee received another hotel commission, one that today would be called an adaptive reuse project, to convert the downtown mansion of Thomas Gilmor on Monument Square into a hotel called the Gilmor House (fig. 72). The Thomas Gilmor mansion was actually a luxurious five-bay-wide, three-story town house set slightly above street level and facing Monument Square at the intersection of Calvert Street. Niernsee's program was to convert this handsome house into a six-story hotel—an ambitious endeavor. Three addition-

FIG. 72. (*above*)
Gilmor House, Balti-
more (left). Maryland
Historical Society,
Baltimore, Maryland

FIG. 73. (*right*) Gail's
Tobacco Warehouse,
Baltimore, vignette.
From Robert Taylor,
*Map of the City and
County of Baltimore,
Maryland,* 1857

al stories were built above the original house, and the entire structure extended 165-feet to the rear, to provide 140 rooms and the necessary corridors and stairways. The hotel façade, facing east, was covered with stuccoed brick painted to imitate brownstone and decorated with two stories of highly detailed cast-iron balconies cast by Hayward, Bartlett & Company. The east facing windows also had very elaborate cast iron lintels.

The firm designed an underpinning for the original house, which allowed them to raise the building to install an additional story housing a large public bar, a hair dressing salon, a reading room, and a billiard parlor accessible from the street via three entrances. The main story contained the reception area, separate ladies' and gentlemen's parlors and a dining room, ninety-feet long by twenty-eight-feet wide, which seated

250. A new stairwell and circulation space were added in the rear of the house and a very large wing extended west to the alley. Frescoed ceilings, gold and velvet wallpaper, and richly carved rosewood and mahogany furniture created an elegant and quite memorable setting for this early hotel. Guest rooms did not have their own private bathrooms, so each floor had to share one. "It is difficult to give a complete description of the Gilmor House, so beautifully has it been decorated and furnished—without regard to cost, the various bills of furniture amounting to about $70,000 and which is fully equal to any establishment of the kind in the United States," boasted the *Sun*.[7] The Gilmor House (later renamed Guy's Monumental Hotel and, still later, the St. Clair Hotel) was finished just after Barnum's Hotel opened on the square. It was demolished for the construction of the present courthouse at the end of the nineteenth century.

Industries, especially the tobacco business, needed warehouses to store goods and supplies, and in 1853, the firm designed a small tobacco warehouse in South Baltimore for G. W. Gail, a tobacco importer from Hamburg, Germany. Robert Taylor's 1857 *Map of Baltimore City and Baltimore County* shows a five-story utilitarian building of brick with arched windows and doorway on the front façade (fig. 73). In the 1890s, their building was incorporated into the Gail & Axe warehouse complex by architect Henry Brauns.

Architects who performed well on commercial projects were often asked by their clients to design their personal residences. Gail remembered Niernsee, and in 1875, he commissioned the architect to provide him with an elaborate suburban house on Eutaw Place just south of Druid Hill Park Lake (see Chapter 11).

Niernsee & Neilson designed a large tobacco warehouse for Charles Deford & Company in

FIG. 74. Grocer's Exchange, Baltimore. Maryland Historical Society, Baltimore, Maryland

FIG. 75. *(right)* Spring Grove, Catonsville, Maryland, 1877. Maryland Historical Society, Baltimore, Maryland

FIG. 76. *(below)* Spring Garden Valve House, Baltimore. James D. Dilts

1854, across the street from the Custom House. The 33-foot wide, six-story building of Cheat River stone was 170 feet deep. Ten granite columns carried a girder that supported sixteen-inch deep yellow pine joists. These framed the 16-foot-high main story, which was for the storage of three thousand hogsheads of leaf tobacco. The stories above, supported by cast-iron columns, stored chewing and smoking tobacco and Havana cigars.[8]

New markets in Great Britain and South America increased business greatly for produce merchants. To reflect this prosperity, a building called the Grocer's Exchange was designed by the firm for an old client, Johns Hopkins (fig. 74). Four stories in height with a first-story white cast-iron façade with segmental arches framing a double door and plate-glass windows, it fronted sixty feet on Commerce Street and thirty-five feet on Exchange Place. The upper stories were brick with windows topped with cast-iron surrounds. Hayward, Bartlett & Company supplied the ironwork. Hopkins leased the entire building to White & Elder, coffee merchants. The *Sun* remarked on the building's unique design in March 1856, "The building is entirely different from any of the kind and is certainly most imposing in appearance."[9]

Many of Baltimore's wealthy businessmen served on the boards of various institutions in the city, such as colleges and hospitals, but, interestingly, the firm's ties to the business community brought in little institutional work in the 1850s. But they did receive a major commission to design a hospital building at the new insane asylum in Catonsville, now called Spring Grove. The design of insane asylums took a more humane direction before the Civil War. No longer were they warehouses for the mentally ill, but handsome buildings of great architectural merit. The preliminary designs for this building were completed in 1852. The huge complex was a symmetrical composition of Italianate forms with bracketed roofs, double- and triple-arched windows, and Niernsee's favorite towers. But the plan was not actually Niernsee's; rather, it was based on the work of Dr. Thomas Kirkbride, superintendent of the Pennsylvania Hospital from 1842 to 1883. His "Kirkbride plan" dictated all asylum design in America during the second half of the nineteenth century. An administrative building was at the center of the plan, flanked by wings that were stepped back to allow for natural ventilation and better privacy[10] (fig. 75). The construction of the building began in 1853 but was postponed owing to the onset of the Civil War (when it was used as an army hospital). When construction resumed, it was supervised by Neilson, who revised the design in 1868. This building lasted until 1913, when it was cleared away for a new central building.

At about the same time, Niernsee & Neilson did some work at Mount Hope Retreat on Reisterstown Road in Baltimore County, though very little is actually known about the extent of their contribution to that hospital, which was better known as the Seton Institute. Much of the work was done by the Baltimore firm of Long & Powell in the 1850s. The *Sun* credits Neilson in 1860 with the supervision of the six-story, seventy-six-foot-wide main building, which housed 500 patients. Work was then turned over to Niernsee for a time soon after, but the

remainder of work was accomplished by E. Francis Baldwin, beginning in the mid-to-late 1880s.

A completely different commission came in 1855 with a project to build the new Spring Garden Gas Works on a twelve-acre site at the end of Leadenhall Street.

The firm had never before designed a building whose program was solely dictated by the manufacturing process. The main building, which was called a retort, or manufacturing room, was 200 feet in length and 52 feet in depth. In twenty-four hours it produced 600,000 cubic feet of gas, which was then conveyed by piping to the purifying building, which measured 57 by 75 feet. Both buildings were constructed of brick with iron roofs and cost $300,000. The only building from this group that remains standing is the charming Valve House in the center of the Spring Garden complex (fig. 76). An octagonal brick structure, it contains the distribution valves controlling the flow of gas from the manufacturing mill to the storage units and from there to the system's mains. In

FIG. 77. *(left)* John R. Niernsee, ca. 1855. Mark Cummings Collection

FIG. 78. *(right)* J. Crawford Neilson and child. Maryland Historical Society, Baltimore, Maryland

1979, the Baltimore Gas & Electric Company restored the building.

Niernsee had come a long way from the penniless immigrant visiting the Washington Monument. With Neilson's help, he had created Baltimore's most successful architectural firm. No firm came close to them in the number and quality of their commissions. It seemed they would dominate Baltimore architecture forever. Niernsee & Neilson also had developed the paradigm of the full-service professional practice that prevails to this day. In most of the *Sun* articles describing their buildings, it was noted that they superintended the execution of their designs, acting as agents of the client and insuring that the work was built to their specifications. The age of the gentleman architect and carpenter-builder that Benjamin Henry Latrobe sought to abolish was coming to an end.

With success came a comfortable life, one that Niernsee had only dreamed of in his youthful years as a surveyor in the South. An imposing six-footer with a thick head of dark hair, a walrus mustache, and a graying beard in 1855,

the Austrian immigrant was a successful professional man enjoying the fruits of his labor (fig. 77). His expense book for 1854 listed a total of $3,097 in expenditures, over $64,000 in today's money. Groceries every quarter came to $100, horse livery cost $180 per year and three servants, $216 annually. Niernsee, who now had three children, did spend some on himself; $75 for cigars and $5 per month for his membership in the Germania Club, one of many German-American organizations that had been founded since the great German migration of the late 1840s. J. Crawford Neilson was also enjoying the success of the practice. The lean, bespectacled man had married well and had begun a family (fig. 78).

But in the spring of 1854, some cracks in the foundation of the new South Carolina State House, being built some 400 miles from Baltimore, would change Niernsee's and Neilson's careers forever. John Rudolph Niernsee would make a decision that would bring an end to the successful partnership and affect his personal and professional life for the next thirty years.

PLATE 1. Grace and St. Peter's Episcopal Church, Baltimore, interior, ca. 1910. Grace and St. Peter's Church

PLATE 2. Grace and St. Peter's Episcopal Church. J. Crawford Neilson's pew. Mark Watts

PLATE 3. Evangelical
Lutheran Church,
Frederick, Maryland.
James D. Dilts

PLATE 4. Central Presbyterian Church, Baltimore, original Niernsee and Neilson watercolor rendering, ca. 1853. Central Presbyterian Church, Baltimore, Maryland

PLATE 5. St. Mary's
Church, Emmorton,
Harford County,
Maryland. James T.
Wollon Jr.

PLATE 6. St. Mary's
Church, interior

PLATE 7. St. Mary's
Church, detail

PLATE 8. St. Mary's
Church, original
Niernsee and Neilson
watercolor rendering,
ca. 1851. Maryland
Historical Society,
Baltimore, Maryland

PLATE 9. Church of the Most Holy Trinity, Augusta, Georgia. Church of the Most Holy Trinity

PLATE 10. Church of the Most Holy Trinity, interior. Andrew Chambers

ELEVATION OF GREENMOUNT CHAPEL

PLATE 11. Green
Mount Cemetery,
Baltimore. "Elevation
of Green Mount
Chapel," original
Niernsee and Neilson
watercolor rendering,
ca. 1850s. Green
Mount Cemetery

PLATE 12. Clifton, Baltimore, gatehouse, ca. 1912. James T. Wollon Jr. Collection

PLATE 13. St. Paul's Church, Petersburg, Virginia, ca. 1912. James T. Wollon Jr. Collection

PLATE 14. Academy of Music, Baltimore, ca. 1909. James T. Wollon Jr. Collection

EIGHT

The South Carolina State House and the Dissolution

Construction had been progressing smoothly on the new South Carolina State House. The new building, designed by the Swedish-born architect, Peter Hammarskold, had been eagerly anticipated by the South Carolina legislature, which for years had been working in the decaying old wooden statehouse of 1787. Then in May 1854, cracks appeared in the vaulted brick ceiling of the northwest corner of the new building; these were immediately followed by more cracks in the north and west walls. Hammarskold reported the problem to the commissioners overseeing the construction, and to his surprise, one week later they summarily dismissed him from the project. The commissioners then asked Governor John L. Manning, "to communicate with Mr. Niernsee, the (architect) of Baltimore, and ascertain whether he can be engaged by the Commissioners to examine the Capitol."[1]

Niernsee's formal engineering training and his B&O experience made him a sought-after forensic structural investigator. His first major opportunity came in 1848 with the collapse of the Fayette Street Bridge. In his *Chronicles of Baltimore*, John Thomas Scharf describes the scene as follows: "On Thursday morning, May 25, the new massive cast-iron bridge, which crossed Jones Falls at Fayette street, broke in the centre and fell with a tremendous crash into the water beneath."[2] One newspaper article at the time blamed the collapse on the bridge's materials because cast iron is relatively weak in tension. Soon after, the Baltimore City Council persuaded Niernsee to examine the cause of the collapse and to review new plans with another forensic consultant and architect.

Niernsee's work on the Fayette Street Bridge led to more work as a consultant, such as reviewing cost estimates for marine hospitals for the United States Treasury but most notably in investigating the collapsed vault of the Smithsonian Institution Museum in Washington, D.C., in 1850. Niernsee conducted the investigation along with Edward B. White, an architect from Charleston, South Carolina, and Col. William Trumbull of the U.S. Topographical Engineers.[3] Governor Manning had consulted with White on the statehouse problem. White then suggested that the state hire Niernsee to investigate the situation at the new statehouse.[4]

On June 15, 1854, Niernsee arrived in Columbia, the state capital and reviewed Hammarskold's drawings, which he found to be professionally executed, "describing the best kind of work in every branch," but there were no construction documents for any part of the building above the foundation. It was the actual construction work that did not comply with the drawings and specifications. Instead of hard burned brick for the arches in the north wing, soft brick, which was easier to cut, had been used. The exposed foundation work, which did not match the specifications, was of inferior quality. While working on the State Capitol, Hammarskold had commenced several other projects including the construction of a faculty residence at South Carolina College. Hammarskold probably neglected the statehouse construction, therefore allowing the contractors to ignore the specifications (Bryan, 19).

After submitting his report and his offer to be a consulting architect for $3,000 per year,

Niernsee returned to Baltimore. The commissioners needed a new resident architect and promptly advertised for one. The contractor was ordered to remove most of the new foundation work, but he refused and walked off the job (Bryan, 19).

Of the twenty-nine architects who offered their services, the commissioners chose George Edward Walker, who would take over the design of the building at a salary of $4,000 per year. Walker had served as an assistant on the U.S. Custom House in Charleston and had designed the Charleston Free School. At the time of his appointment as architect of the capitol, he was designing a library for the College of Charleston (Bryan, 19-20).

In architectural practice of the period, it was becoming quite common for an out-of-town architect to be the sole designer of a building. The New York firm of Town & Davis did work all over the country. A local firm, if employed at all, was used only in support (as is the practice today). Unfortunately, in South Carolina, the local firm expected to be the lead architect. The statehouse was the commission of a lifetime for Walker, but Niernsee, an outsider, had been retained as consultant, and the two architects were on a collision course.

Walker was convinced that it was best to completely demolish all of Hammarskold's work, that it would be "unsafe and imprudent to attempt to raise the remainder of the building upon such a miserable base." But the commissioners took Niernsee's advice to demolish only part of the foundation. Thus, the project began badly for Walker, who felt he was being undermined by the governor and the commissioners, who backed Niernsee (Bryan, 21). An architect naturally feels that he should have the final say on design and construction matters. But in this case there were two architects.

Walker's problem with Niernsee was not simply that he was a rival architect, but also, and probably more so, because he was a foreigner with a slight German accent and a Northerner. Things would only get worse for the resident architect, who did not establish a cordial working relationship with either Niernsee or the commissioners. Walker felt that decisions were being made behind his back. The suspicion was justified when he discovered, to his dismay, that Niernsee's salary had been doubled, to $6,000. Walker's structural analysis was vindicated when, in September, Niernsee also admitted that nothing could be saved and that it was best for all the existing work to be removed (Bryan, 22-24).

But Walker's problems continued; in a December 1854 meeting, the governor ordered that Niernsee "be requested to make all plans for the future construction of the New State Capitol." Walker was outraged, and when he argued vehemently in the midst of the meeting that he was being treated unfairly, he was asked to leave the room. Niernsee followed him out and tried to reach a compromise, suggesting that Walker furnish the plans in collaboration with him, but the commissioners rejected the agreement outright. Instead, they ordered that both architects submit plans and specifications in basically what became a competition. Walker vigorously protested and asked the commissioners to reconsider. They did, and they allowed Walker to design the building—but with the troublesome proviso that Niernsee would do drawings on parts of the design with which he disagreed (Bryan, 26).

Walker spent a month designing the statehouse on top of Hammarskold's footprint, which he was directed to use by the commissioners. The review of the drawings got off to a bad start when, to Walker's horror, Governor Manning opened the meeting by having Niernsee display his design, which ignored the building's original footprint. Barely controlling his temper, Walker calmly protested to the governor that he was not in competition with Niernsee. The governor politely responded, "We understand you, Mr. Walker" (Bryan, 27).

The dispute dragged on with another resolution in February 1855 describing some program revisions and giving Walker design control. But Niernsee presented another set of plans for a larger building in March, which overshadowed Walker's smaller scheme. To make matters worse, the commissioners favored Niernsee's tower over Walker's dome, but not for aesthetic reasons. A dome, which would be 100 feet in diameter, would "imply great waste of room and great additional expense." A tower, "by its great height, variety and beauty, and the small outlay required for its erection, presents some advantages over the dome," the commissioners reported to the legislature (Bryan, 29).

The commissioners by now had had enough of Walker. They censured him for not consulting with Niernsee and expected him to resign, but he did not. Finally, on April 11, 1855, Walker was dismissed. Niernsee was now the sole architect of the South Carolina State House, at a salary of $8,000, something John Manning and most of the commissioners had wanted from the very beginning. Niernsee now had his commission of a lifetime and it could not have come at a better time (Bryan, 30).

Niernsee was more than eager to accept this commission. He had never bowed to Walker's request that the South Carolinian be the sole designer. Instead, he had continued to submit plans, probably knowing that with his political connections, he would prevail as architect. It was not just the opportunity to design the most important building of his career, but there was a very practical reason as well. Business in Baltimore had slowed down in the past year. It was around this time that the B&O Railroad was completed to Wheeling. The railroad had been a strong generator of business in Baltimore during the B&O construction years. But by the end of construction, there was no longer such a demand for railroad-related products. As a result, Baltimore had a business downturn in 1855, and Niernsee & Neilson had almost no commissions that year. The South Carolina State House commission was a godsend for Niernsee; he had little work or prospects for the immediate future.

Niernsee used the time before moving permanently to Columbia to dissolve his partnership with Neilson and arrange for him to oversee the remaining construction. He also had to have financial help to relocate and turned to a former client. Niernsee and Thomas Winans had become great friends since the design of Alexandroffsky and Crimea, and it was Winans who lent him the money he needed. He took security in the form of Niernsee's houses on Courtland Street.

The delay in moving did not have an adverse effect on the South Carolina project. In the interim, John A. Kay, Hammarskold's assistant, was deputized as assistant architect, to manage the project. There was a great deal of work to be done in Columbia in the way of removing defective work done under Hammarskold's plans before Niernsee's design could be executed. The South Carolina legislature was eager to wipe away the past failure and have a fresh start (Bryan, 32).

When Niernsee finally arrived with his family on June 1, 1856, he first had to face Columbia's unsophisticated building industry, which

had little experience in building with stone. He immediately reorganized the quarry to operate more efficiently. To prevent its regular flooding by the Congaree River, he built a dam and installed steam-powered pumps to remove excess water in place of the old hand-driven pumps. His railroad experience came into use when he constructed a railroad to transport stone to the building site. The stones were of such a weight and dimension (one architrave weighed fifty-two tons) that they could not be hauled by mules (Bryan, 35-36, 45-47).

Though he had never designed a building of such size and complexity, Niernsee's innate talent and intelligence allowed him to handle such a project easily. It was not just his design ability but also his organizational skills that proved decisive. The labor involved in the stonemasonry was critical; he imported skilled foreign stone carvers in addition to having a slave labor force of stonecutters in the quarries. He also used a reliable source for carving the marble and granite; his friend, Hugh Sisson of Baltimore, signed a contract for $335,000. Niernsee organized the labor force into teams to expedite the masonry work. The skilled carvers were employed solely for shaping stones while common laborers sharpened tools and removed the stone from the quarry. Using mechanical stonecutting tools, Niernsee stockpiled stone and built the new foundation, then began laying bricks for the upper stories. Work progressed impressively under his direction; by 1857, the walls had risen twenty-six feet above the footings (Bryan, 45).

In preparing the final design, Niernsee consulted closely with the commissioners, unlike his rival George E. Walker. Walker considered that he knew best how the statehouse should be planned and did not intend to be hampered by a committee telling him what to do. Niernsee, on the other hand, wisely engaged the commissioners in the design process. He was adroit at what is today called networking and as a result gained the attention and respect of the commissioners by asking their opinion and utilizing their skills in planning the building.

Niernsee's original design, seen only in nineteenth-century prints, principally from *Harper's Weekly* of December 1860, *Frank Leslie's Illustrated Newspaper* of 1861, and an 1861 Confederate bank note (the original drawings were destroyed during the Civil War), was set on a raised base surrounded by a balustrade (fig. 79).

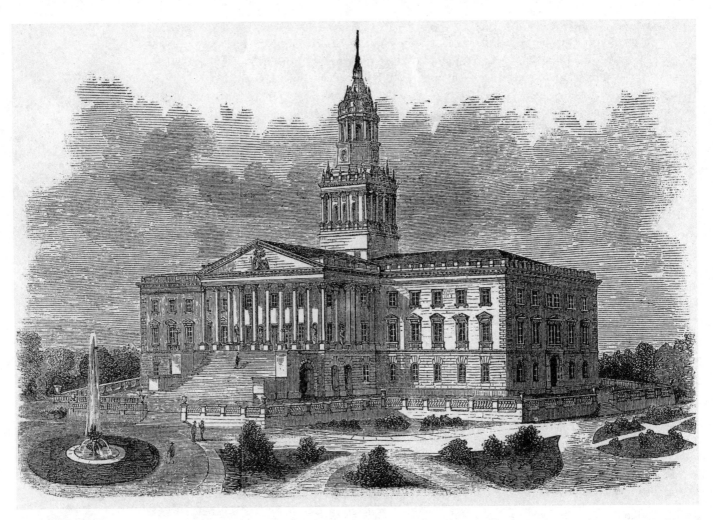

FIG. 79. State House, Columbia, South Carolina. From *Harper's Weekly*, 1860

The building measured 262-feet in length and 172 feet in depth with a height of 63 feet to the cornice. A monumental stair led to a decastyle Corinthian portico. Actual access to the building was from the ground floor and access to the grand lobby, from two staircases.

The floor plan of the South Carolina State House embodied the commissioners' ideas of democracy in action. The library, the repository of information and tradition, was on the left, the house and senate were on the right, and in the center, accessed by a monumental staircase and the grand portico, was the vast vestibule lobby, where the lobbyist, constituent, delegate, and senator could meet when the legislature was in session. The statehouse does not represent a new departure in the design of a legislative building, but Niernsee's great intermediate space distinguishes the State House of South Carolina from all other statehouses built at that time with the exception of the United States Capitol, then being reconstructed by Thomas U. Walter.

The exterior of the main block had a rusticated base with arched windows and tall pedi-

mented windows above. The low hipped roof was surrounded by a balustrade. But the most prominent design feature was the 180-foot tower, which rose above the central lobby. At first glance, it looked like William Strickland's tower for the Tennessee State House, built between 1849 and 1859 at Nashville. Niernsee's design was even more monumental than Strickland's. Niernsee's spire seems to be a copy of Cuthbert Broderick's original design for the Leeds Town Hall of 1853–58.

In addition to Niernsee's design for the building proper and its interior, the commissioners wanted monumental sculpture for the pediments. New York sculptor Henry Kirke Brown, one of the most famous mid-nineteenth-century sculptors, was recruited to model the pediment figures and to supervise the carving of the stone at the site. The design had a central female figure with a star of empire on her crown holding a laurel branch of victory, flanked by figures representing Liberty and Justice. At the ends of the pediment were figures representing South Carolina agriculture—slaves harvesting rice and handling cotton bales. Niernsee had a very good relationship with Mr. Brown; the sculptor recalled that Niernsee still retained a sense of German in his language and demeanor. Unfortunately, the model and half-finished carving were ruthlessly destroyed by Union troops in February 1865 (Bryan, 47-51).

Despite the complexity of the project, Niernsee found the time in 1857 for an important professional commitment—becoming a charter member of the newly created American Institute of Architects. In the spring of 1857, Richard Upjohn and twelve New York architects founded the AIA, a national organization representing architects, to promote the exchange of scientific and practical information and "elevate the standing of the profession."

Thomas U. Walter, the current architect of the U.S. Capitol, insisted (ingenuously) that architects were an artistic elite because their works were totally imaginative. He said that the public would recognize institute membership as an honor and a mark of great distinction. In New York University's Gothic Revival Chapel, designed by Alexander Jackson Davis, the new organization adopted a constitution and membership rules. The original entry requirements were quite elitist. To join the AIA, a candidate could only be recommended by a founder. On April 15, 1857, Niernsee was proposed for membership and on May 5, he was formally elected, a gesture of great respect and recognition for an architect who practiced outside New York. The development of the AIA would be thwarted by the Civil War. Thirteen years after its founding, only 140 of approximately two thousand architects in America were members.[5]

When the Civil War began on April 12, 1861, with the bombardment of Fort Sumter in Charleston harbor, the outside walls of the statehouse had arrived at the cornice line. The carvings for the balustrade had largely been accomplished and stockpiled on the ground. The first floor had been installed, supported by iron columns and masonry walls. The floor was constructed of wrought-iron beams with brick jack arches so as to be fireproof. Neither the roof nor the porticos were in place, but all the engaged columns had been set (Bryan, 56-57).

Construction did not immediately stop with the onset of war. For the next two years, the quarrymen and Sisson worked in exchange for stock issued by the state that paid 6 percent interest. Henry Kirke Brown left, never to return

to South Carolina. Niernsee stayed on as architect at a reduced salary of $2,000. He knew it was just a matter of time before all work on the project ceased, and he worked hard to complete all the stonecutting before the quarries were allowed to flood and the skilled stone carvers left to escape the war. The state had reduced its workforce to two carpenters and 128 black quarry men supervised by two whites. As Niernsee stockpiled materials, the Confederate Army began to requisition material such as bricks for a powder works in Charleston (Bryan, 56-57).

Finally, in April 1862, Niernsee left the building site to become a military engineer. Prior to receiving the statehouse commission, the Austrian immigrant had never displayed any proslavery sentiments. In his diaries of the 1830s, Niernsee never wrote with any malice about the slaves he encountered in the South, some of whom had accompanied his survey trips as cooks and helpers. His decision to join the Confederate Army seems not to have been out of any great moral consideration, but because of who his client was: the government of South Carolina. The statehouse was his greatest commission, the dream of every architect, and he continued with its construction as long as he could. He would do anything (as would most architects) to see it built. When the war made this impossible, Niernsee simply went to work for his client in another capacity, not because of his support of slavery but out of loyalty to South Carolina, whose government had made every effort to build his design. In addition, he was not in the position to move his family back to Baltimore in the midst of a war. This would have caused a rift within his own family; both his sons had immediately enlisted in the Confederate Army when war was declared. Even during his wartime service, his overwhelming desire probably was that the fighting would come to an end so he could continue his beloved building.

Niernsee's principal mission as an engineer in the Confederate Army was to explore potential invasion routes and prepare reconnaissance maps of the western parts of the Carolinas. He essentially became a surveyor in the South again, as he had been twenty-four years before. Upon his return a month later, he was ordered to build obstructions in the Santee River. In the following months, Niernsee conducted more reconnaissance missions and wrote recommendations for defensive plans, none of which was ever acted upon. Even with a drastically reduced workforce, quarrying and stonecutting continued at the statehouse site while Niernsee was away in 1862 and 1863. Sisson had completed the granite Corinthian capitals for the porticos (Bryan, 57-59).

By 1864, the building site was turned over to military production of bandages and bedding. By then, the war had become a disaster for the Confederacy. Atlanta fell to General William T. Sherman in September 1864; Sherman then began his march toward South Carolina, bypassing the western routes Niernsee had mapped. Governor Andrew Gordon McGrath ordered Niernsee to create fortifications to protect Columbia. With the governor's approval, he commenced construction of eight miles of trenches and batteries on the western side of the Congaree River (Bryan, 63-66).

But time ran out and in February 1865, Columbia fell to Sherman's army. Emma Josephine, Niernsee's seven-year-old daughter, who lived in town with mother, sister, and brother, remembered the shelling: "I remembered my Mother, Miss Clark & the maids all falling down on their knees and crying. I don't remember being afraid, when they (shells) whistled overhead, I wanted to go out & look for them." Shells smashed into Niernsee's house and the family fled into a field and watched part of Columbia burn to the ground. But his house was left standing (Bryan, 66-67).

The statehouse itself was barely damaged during the attack, but much of the stockpiled stone was ruined, including sixty Italian marble capitals and all the Tennessee marble columns. The quarry was flooded and its buildings burned. Losses, Niernsee reported to the legislature, amounted to $700,000. He made recommendations to protect the work in place until construction resumed, but with the calamity of defeat, the statehouse was not a priority (Bryan, 73). In the years after the Civil War, to Niernsee's dismay, his building would stand unfinished and unroofed until 1870.

Luckily, Niernsee only suffered professionally, not personally from the attack. His two sons, Frank and Rudolph, who fought for the Confederacy, survived. But his entire office in his home was destroyed by the Union Army, including all the statehouse drawings and his personal architectural library. The *Phoenix*, one of the first papers in Columbia published after Sherman's attack, reported on April 14, 1865, on Major John R. Niernsee's misfortune: "This gentleman, the highly able State Architect, is one of those sufferers at the hands of the Yankees, in a professional as well as pecuniary way, whose losses are, in large measure, public as well as private: since the scientific library, the models, designs, and implements of an architect, are sources of common information and intelligence, to which all students have need to repair at seasons. And it is not easy to replace such collections as accumulate during a term of years in the hands of the professor—difficult in any period—impossible at present."

Niernsee was now out of work. In 1866, he applied for the job to finish the customhouse in Charleston, but it was given to A. B. Mullett, a U.S. Treasury architect. Since it was apparent that the state was not ready to continue construction on the statehouse, Niernsee had no choice but to return to Baltimore in order to earn a living. When Niernsee wrote his letter of resignation to Governor McGrath, he did not hesitate to criticize the Confederate military, saying that he had had little assistance from them in planning for the defenses of Columbia (Bryan, 72).

Niernsee wrote to his former partner, Neilson, in Baltimore and also to Thomas Winans, who held the mortgage on his house on Courtland Street, to make sure he would have a secure home if he did indeed return to Baltimore. Somehow money was found to take his family back to Baltimore, and by the middle of 1866 they were successfully established at their previous residence on Courtland Street.

Neilson's career had not suffered as a result of the firm's breakup in 1856. On the contrary, he had prospered on his own. He had come into the partnership in 1848 as a construction administrator and office manager, but with experience and time, he developed his design skills as an architect. The firm had always been known as Niernsee & Neilson and had established a reputation for excellence and reliability, so it was natural that many still sought out Neilson for work even after Niernsee's departure. Clients would recall Neilson as a genial man with "an engaging sense of humor" who quickly made friends, a personality well suited to the profession of architecture, in which social skills are as important as design talent in securing clients.[6] In addition to completing work that Niernsee had designed, his former partner became an accomplished architect in his own right. The mix of commissions was similar those of the partnership: houses, stores, and especially churches.

Unlike Episcopalians and Presbyterians, Methodists initially resisted the idea of architecturally extravagant churches, but slowly they shifted from their simple early meetinghouse structures. Beginning in the early 1840s, well-to-do Methodist congregations built increasingly ornate churches, eventually accepting the Gothic Revival after the Civil War. In 1864, Neilson designed his first Methodist church, Trinity Independent Methodist Episcopal church, in the Gothic Revival style. Located on the northeast corner of Preston and Madison Streets, the brick and brownstone building had two towers flanking the gable-roofed auditorium, a very tall steeple on the north, and a shorter tower on the south. The church, which accommodated six hundred congregants, was raised above street level to provide a spacious basement for Sunday school and other church functions. Neilson designed a ventilation system that moved hot air from the upper part of the cathedral ceiling out through the rear of the church during the summer months.

The building was drastically remodeled, either by Trinity or another church, with the removal of both towers and the application of classical detailing. It was later converted into a bakery and then into a bottling plant for the Try-Me Beverage and Compound Company in the 1920s before being demolished.[7]

In 1864, Neilson received another Methodist commission, Starr Church, at Poppleton

and Lemmon Streets near the B&O Railroad's Mount Clare shops in west Baltimore. Built of brick with a nave containing four aisles, the building could seat 1,200 worshippers including pews in the galleries, which were supported by cast-iron columns. The columns extended to an arched ceiling thirty-five feet above the main floor.[8]

Zion Episcopal Church on the northwest corner of Gilmor and Baltimore Streets was an 1859 commission done in the Gothic style with a large circular window and an arched entry.[9] Three years later it adopted the name Mount Zion, and in 1873 it was reorganized as All Saints' Church. In 1855, Neilson designed St. James' Protestant Episcopal Church in Trap, four miles north of Churchville in Harford County, Maryland. The wood-frame structure burned in 1869 and was replaced with a stone church of Neilson's design. His wife's family home, Priestford, was near by, and it seems her connections got her husband the commission. Neilson did play an active role in raising the $1,500 needed to construct the 1855 church.

Neilson had enough confidence in his design ability to submit a design to the 1857 competition for Baltimore's most prestigious building of the period, the Peabody Institute (fig. 80). Endowed by a wealthy dry goods merchant and one of America's first investment bankers, George Peabody, the bequest called for the establishment of "an extensive Library," a lecture series, "an Academy of Music," and "a Gallery of Art."[10] The trustees announced they would not consider the Gothic style for the new building, which was to be built on East Mount

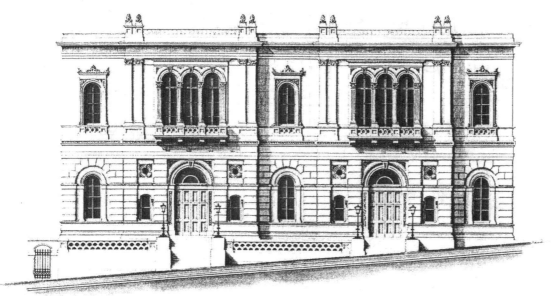

FIG. 80. Peabody Institute, Baltimore, 1857. Archives of the Peabody Institute of the Johns Hopkins University

Vernon Place. Neilson and his fellow architects instead turned to the Renaissance Revival or Italian palazzo, a style popularized by the English architect Charles Barry. The rendering of the elevations of his submission shows a skillful handling of a symmetrical façade with a rusticated base with two identical projecting entrances. The firm of Lind & Murdoch won the competition. Both Niernsee and Neilson would later act as consulting architects for the Peabody Institute. Neilson was a consultant on the original building and Niernsee for the library addition in 1878.[11]

It was his public and commercial commissions, though, that really established Neilson's practice during his separation from Niernsee. The 1856 Bank of Baltimore was a highly prestigious project, as was all bank work (fig. 81). Barry's palazzo style had become very popular for American banks beginning in the late 1840s, and Neilson used it for his project, which was located at St. Paul and Baltimore Streets. Veneered with brownstone, the bank stood 75 feet high, 37 feet wide, and 105 feet deep and housed three separate banking establishments plus rental office space. The first floor contained the banking house of McKim & Company, in a 40-foot by 32-foot palatial banking hall finished in walnut. The Bank of Baltimore occupied the second story, boasting a twenty-foot-tall banking hall and cashier's office. Also in the second story was the Mechanics' Savings Bank. The

third and fourth stories were let as office space to lawyers.[12]

Neilson did other commercial work on Baltimore Street. For the dry good businesses of Howell & Brother and Cushing & Bailey, he designed in 1856 a five-story palazzo building with a cast-iron storefront on the first story and brownstone above. First-story windows, thirteen feet in height and seven feet wide, with three-quarter-inch-thick French plate glass, allowed light into the showrooms, which displayed expensive interior furnishings imported from France. Above, segmentally arched windows framed by engaged columns of slender, intricately carved brownstone gave the façade an impression of being a window wall. Howell & Brother hosted a dinner for their customers and the press to present the new building. This would become a common practice for businessmen beginning before the Civil War and continuing into the late nineteenth century.[13]

The repeal of Britain's corn laws had reinvigorated the Baltimore grain market. Organized in 1851, the Corn Exchange prospered until it needed a building of its own in 1859. Neilson designed the $30,000 Baltimore Corn and Flour Exchange on South Street at Bowley's Wharf. A large building, 52 feet wide by 139 feet deep, it had a cast-iron storefront with foliated columns and a brownstone doorway in the first story, with brick above. The first story was divided into offices and storerooms with the second story containing the exchange, which was accessed from South Street by a broad staircase. Nine round-arched windows and four skylights lit the 100-foot-deep hall. Fifty small tables filled the room, whose interior woodwork was grained as imitation walnut and whose walls were frescoed.

Neilson designed another exchange building on Bowley's Wharf, the Fruit Exchange (fig. 82), at about the same time. Three times a week, fruit from local farmers and southern suppliers was sold in the two-story building. Like the Corn and Flour building, tall windows lit the exchange hall in the second story.[14]

Neither Niernsee nor Neilson did much cast iron work in the 1850s. Their ironwork was usually restricted to first story storefronts. However, Neilson's Hodges Brothers Store of 1856, which sold hosiery, linens, and gloves on South Hanover Street, had a complete cast-iron façade produced by Hayward Bartlett & Company (fig. 83). John C. Gobright in *Baltimore As*

FIG. 81. Bank of Baltimore

It Is gave a description of the façade, including its paint scheme, in 1857:

> It has a front, which is of iron, presenting an imposing aspect, the lower portion being of fluted columns, while handsomely wrought arches adorn the upper portion. At each floor there is a beautifully tesselated cornice. The arches of the front rest over the doors imparting to them a light and elegant appearance. The whole is surmounted by a massive cornice sustained by richly wrought trusses (brackets). The lower portion of the iron work is bronzed on a green surface, which, in contrast with the upper portion, which is of snowy whiteness, gives to the entire front a pleasing appearance. The sashes and doors are painted in imitation of oak.[15]

The building, which also housed the J. S. Inloe Store, a clothing merchant, had a complete cast-iron window wall of pairs of double-arched sashes within an arched opening giving the façade a dynamic rhythm. In the upper stories, salesrooms displayed dry goods and provided for storage of merchandise. Neilson designed a hoist in the rear of the building to move goods from floor to floor. Businessmen like the Hodges Brothers were quite proud of their new buildings and often featured them in their advertisements.

The five-story Tracy & Son Building that Neilson designed in 1861 had a forty-foot-wide cast-iron front fabricated by Hayward, Bartlett & Company. The *Baltimore Sun* described it as "a mixture of Romanesque and Renaissance, with Moorish columns." The heavily bracketed cornice was seventy-five feet above the street.[16]

Cast iron had been hailed in Baltimore as the building system of the future by the *Sun*, which was building its own cast-iron headquarters in 1850. "The subject of building warehouses, dwellings, public edifices & etc., of cast iron is beginning to attract considerable attention throughout the country," the newspaper noted on August 5, 1850.

A. S. Abell, the founder of the *Baltimore Sun*, employed a New York architect, Robert G. Hatfield, who was designing buildings with inventor James Bogardus. Bogardus, an iron founder, had patented a system of iron construction consisting of an iron curtain wall on the street, iron columns and beams, and masonry floors. The newspaper championed the ease of erection, the

detailing that could be attained, and above all, security—iron presented "no food for fire."[17] Bogardus and Hatfield's Sun Iron Building, completed in 1851, is considered by many local historians to be the first iron-framed building in Baltimore. However, it also employed timber beams and joists for the floor structure. The Sun building was destroyed in the 1904 fire, as were almost all of Niernsee & Neilson's downtown buildings.

It would be Neilson who would get the opportunity to design a hospital before Niernsee's Johns Hopkins commission. The Union Protestant Infirmary on Division and Mosher Streets in West Baltimore was a three-and-a-half-story brick structure with segmentally arched windows (fig. 84). A ten-foot-wide vestibule led to an apothecary shop, a twenty- by thirty-foot reception area for patients, doctors' offices, and a dining room. The upper two stories housed seven wards and nine rooms for individual patients. Four of the seven wards accommodated five patients and the remainder, three patients. A cupola exhausted "impure air" out of the wards. The basement contained the kitchen, laundry, and furnace room. The infirmary, which cost $24,000 to build, later became Union Memorial Hospital.[18]

The Maryland Club, an elite men's club, purchased the former Hoffman House, designed by Robert Mills, on the northeast corner of Franklin and Cathedral Streets in 1859 and hired Neilson to handle the $12,000 conversion. "The

FIG. 82. Merchant's Fruit Exchange, Baltimore. From George W. Englehardt, *Baltimore City, Maryland*, 1895. Enoch Pratt Free Library /State Library Resource Center, Baltimore, Maryland

FIG. 83. Hodges Brothers, Baltimore. From George W. Howard, *The Monumental City: Its Past History and Present Resources*, 1873

NIERNSEE
AND NEILSON

main building is being entirely remodeled into brilliant supper and other rooms after plans by J. C. Neilson, Esq.," reported the *Sun*.[19] An addition was built at the rear of the house for billiard and smoking rooms. The east, west, and south façades were kept intact, including the elegant arched entrance portico. The Maryland Club occupied the building until 1891, when its new building at Charles and Eager Streets was built. The old clubhouse was given to the Maryland Academy of Sciences, which was formerly housed in Thomas Swann's old house on Franklin Street.

Niernsee & Neilson did not receive many school projects either on their own or in partnership. The earliest one came in 1865, when Neilson designed the Maryland Institute for the Instruction of the Blind at North Avenue and Calvert Street (fig. 85). Originally located on West Saratoga Street, the school needed a larger building and also desired to be in the country, which was where North Avenue (then Boundary Avenue) was in the 1860s. Neilson was evidently aware of the Second Empire style, which took hold in America at the end of the Civil War. Its most salient feature, the mansard roof, topped Neilson's four-story school, a symmetrical design with a projecting central block and half-round windows in every story. The first story contained administration offices, sitting rooms and a dining room, a concert hall in the second story, dormitories in the

third, and storerooms in the fourth story under the mansard. In addition to the main building, there was a superintendent's house, a classroom building, a shop for making brooms, and a one-story gym. In all likelihood, Neilson designed the entire complex, which was constructed from 1865 to 1868. The school was replaced by the Baltimore Polytechnic Institute, which is now the main headquarters of the Baltimore City Board of Education.[20]

Probably Neilson's most important public commission was the Harford County Courthouse in Bel Air in 1858, which replaced a sixty-year-old structure that burned down (fig. 86). The courthouse, which was the second architect-designed building in Bel Air, was a rather subdued, two-story combination of Italianate and classical details with a pedimented central bay. The roof had a small domed cupola housing a fire bell. The building was only fifty-feet wide by seventy-five feet deep with a nine-foot-wide corridor running from front to rear. The second story held a law library and a courtroom. Given what happened to the first courthouse, fireproofing was an important feature of the new building. Iron beams and brick floor arches were used. The courthouse still stands, but in 1904 J. A. Dempwolf, of York, Pennsylvania, designed additions covering the front and rear façades. Only Neilson's round-arched windows can still be seen on the sides between the Dempwolf additions, which encapsulate both end bays.[21]

One of the few commissions Neilson had outside the Baltimore region during this period was the 1860 American Colonization Society Hall on Pennsylvania Avenue and Fourth Street in Washington, D.C. Organized in 1817, the society's mission was to raise funds to start a colony in Africa for freed blacks. Many abolitionists believed this would be a path for gradual emancipation of slaves. With the help of such well-known men as Charles Carroll of Carrollton, James Madison, Henry Clay, and John H. B. Latrobe, the society began transporting blacks to Africa in 1820. In 1822, the colony of Liberia was created, shortly followed by an adjacent colony called "Maryland." The two combined to form the independent nation of Liberia in 1857. More than six thousand blacks had settled in the country by 1862.

After forty years of meeting in rented spaces, the society hired Neilson to design its permanent quarters (fig. 87). The four-story palazzo

FIG. 85. *(top)* Maryland School for the Blind, Baltimore, 1926. Maryland Historical Society, Baltimore, Maryland

FIG. 86. *(bottom)* Harford County Courthouse, Bel Air, Maryland, ca. 1900. Historical Society of Harford County, Inc.

FIG. 87. American
Colonization Society,
Washington, D.C.
The Historical Soci-
ety of Washington,
D.C.

NIERNSEE
AND NEILSON

style building of brownstone had bold projecting window surrounds supported by slender
columns. The society occupied only a small portion of the building; the rest was used for rental
income. It was torn down in 1930.[22]

Neilson was quite magnanimous when he
agreed to restart the partnership. He had been
successful on his own and could have rebuffed
his old partner. Neilson, who had originally been
the administrative partner, had been designing
on his own for nine years. He was not about to
give up that task and must have reached an understanding with Niernsee that the situation
was not the same as it had been from 1848 to
1856, when Niernsee was the principal designer.
From then on, the partnership would be equal
in terms of design responsibility. Even though
Neilson knew better than anyone else the value
of Niernsee's skills, he would also be a designer.
Instead of designing a building together, each
would design his own projects. With this new
arrangement, Neilson still believed the two
could be as successful as they were before the
war. His decision to rejoin forces with his former partner would be a wise one. The partnership began its second life in Neilson's office at
207 North Charles Street.

NINE

The Second Partnership, 1865 to 1874

Niernsee came back to a city that was set to explode with prosperity. Unlike Columbia and most of the cities of the South, Baltimore was unscathed by the Civil War. But being in the precarious position as the biggest city in a border state, its economy had been put on hold during the war, whereas cities farther to the north were out of harm's way and boomed with wartime industry. With a population of 350,000, Baltimore was ready to serve the markets of a ravaged South, which needed everything from clothing to building materials to canned oysters to architectural services.

The city was still a major transportation hub. The B&O Railroad, damaged but intact after the war, conducted an enormous amount of business, transporting goods to and from markets in the west. First-class steamers made daily runs loaded with goods to Havana and Liverpool as well as trips to Boston, New York, and New Orleans. The mills along the Jones Falls Valley dominated the nation's cotton duck industry. In such a highly charged business environment, the firm had no trouble attracting commissions.[1]

Niernsee & Neilson did relatively little residential work in its reincarnation, but the firm still designed a few town houses for the wealthy in the Mount Vernon section of Baltimore. These houses reflected a stylistic shift to the Second Empire style, whose mansard roofs were the key design feature in Baron Haussman's rebuilding of Paris in the 1850s. The firm's designs typically featured marble veneered fronts and were three stories high; a "French attic," which had ten feet of clear headroom, contained servants' rooms and storage space. The Louis

McLane Jr. House, on the northeast corner of Charles and Chase Streets, was a huge marble and brick mansion with a colossal three-story bay window on Chase Street, stretching back almost 130 feet to Lovegrove Alley (fig. 88). The commission is interesting because the correspondence of Louis McLane Jr. to his wife, Sophie, contains his frustrations about the project and also his opinions about Niernsee:

Sept. 1, 1868
I telegraphed him yesterday asking what progress Niernsee has made with my house to stir him up ... I do not expect much work to be done until I am on the ground, if then. I could meet the demands of workmen, but do not care to entrust the power to old Niernsee who though honest as the world ... is slow as the city he lives in and is disposed to ride my purse as long as I'll permit him in view of the slow progress of the house on Charles Street.

Oct. 1, 1868
Niernsee is slow, awfully slow. His explanations are excuses, mere excuses though of course they have to be excepted [sic]. Had I been on the ground, I would have dispensed with the marble entirely than wait on it ...

December 1, 1869
... Niernsee doesn't understand the meaning of the word 'economy' when other men's money is used.[2]

McLane's sentiments about architects are often echoed today by clients. But the architect

FIG. 88. *(top)* Louis McLane Jr. House, Baltimore, 1922. Maryland Historical Society, Baltimore, Maryland

FIG. 89. *(bottom)* Row Houses, St. Paul Street, Baltimore. Charles Belfoure

only designs the house, he does not actually build it; he must rely on the workmen. When they do not show up or work slower than expected, the wrath of the client usually falls upon the architect. The McLane House may have been built by a general contractor, but from McLane's letters it seems that the work was done by subcontractors who would have been under Niernsee's direct supervision. Fifty-four years after completion, the house was torn down to build the Monumental Life Building.

After the Civil War, west Baltimore rapidly developed into an upper middle class neighborhood of three-story row houses, but the firm is known to have designed only one house in this burgeoning section of the city, the now demolished William F. Burns House of 1870, at 1125 West Madison Street. In the second partnership, Niernsee & Neilson did not do any work for the rowhouse developers who were building large amounts of working- or middleclass housing in Baltimore. When they did do speculative housing, it was usually for well-to-do buyers like the three speculative row houses built for Hugh Sisson in the Gothic Revival style on St. Paul Street north of Chase Street in the early 1870s (fig. 89). As one might expect from a marble merchant, "an unusually large amount of plain and variegated marble [was] used in these houses in place of wood, and found not to exceed the cost of the latter," reported the *Baltimore Sun*.[3] Not only were the front façades faced with marble ashlar, but so were the stoops and railings, the walls, the ceiling and floor of the vestibules, and the wainscoting of the dining rooms. Averaging twenty-two feet in width and seventy-eight feet in depth with back buildings, the houses were of the usual design, with a six-foot main hall off of which opened the parlor, connected by sliding doors to a sitting room, and a dining room, which had a bay window looking out over the rear yard. The bedrooms were in the second and third stories, and the servant's quarters in the "French attic."

Opportunities for country house commissions were also scant, with the exception of a large house in Towson called Aigburth Manor, built for John E. Owens, the first well-known American vaudeville comedian to earn more than one million dollars (fig. 90). His best-known role was that of Solon Shingle in the play *The People's Lawyer*, which he performed over two thousand times in theaters across

America. In an era before movies or television, the theater played an extremely important part in American life. Owens became one of the best-known actors of the day.

He commissioned the firm to build this large, roomy Second Empire country house in 1868 for his use as a permanent residence upon retirement. Built of timber with flush-boarding finish, it has two stories and a mansard third story with dormers and a faux tower. Aigburth Manor is extremely picturesque and worth noticing. The mansard on this house is quite elegant; the dormers are fitted with heavy, recessed jambs, which allow the face of the windows to be set halfway into the mansard, giving a special character to the roof, which has attracted artists and photographers over the years.

Owens entertained many famous theatrical, literary, and political figures at Aigburth Manor during the summer, when he rested after extensive touring. He owned the Baltimore Museum and Gallery of Fine Arts, a theater at Calvert and Baltimore Streets where he put on light comedies. Beset by financial problems, he took the risk of staging the first performance of *Uncle Tom's Cabin* south of the Mason-Dixon Line in 1855; it was a great success and saved him financially.[4] After Owen's death in 1886, the 197-acre property was sold to a company that tried to convert it into a summer resort with the house as a hotel. Aigburth Manor then became a private mental hospital, but its best-known use came in 1949, when it was the headquarters of the Baltimore County Board of Education. In 2000, the building was converted into housing for the elderly.

The revived firm only did a tiny fraction of the church work they once had done. Built in 1870, the Church of Our Saviour, a Protestant Episcopal church on Broadway and McElderry Street, was their major religious work of the second partnership (fig. 91). The brick exterior of the fifty- by eighty-five-foot building had deeply recessed windows with marble sills, which gave "a massive appearance to the building." The ground story was raised above street level and could accommodate 600 to 700 Sunday school students. The thirty-five foot tall nave, which could seat 500, was accessed by a six-foot wide stairway and presented "a pleasing and attractive effect, without conforming to any one order of architecture exclusively."[5] The building was demolished for a replacement

church, which was in turn was demolished for the expansion of the Johns Hopkins Hospital.

It was commercial work that the firm thrived on in the post–Civil War period. But the responsibilities of the architect had shifted; important changes in architectural practice and building construction had taken place. Before the war, Niernsee & Neilson had functioned as designers of projects and also as general contractors. Now more projects were handled by general contractors who would oversee the entire construction of a building and the architect would receive a percentage of the construction cost or a flat fee. But Niernsee & Neilson still insisted that construction supervision be part of their services, and they kept close watch over the contractor's costs to the client. The firm kept accurate records of the construction costs of their buildings, even comparing them to buildings in other cities. Cubic foot costs were the standard measurement of the day in contrast

FIG. 90. (*top*) Aigburth Vale, Towson, Maryland. James D. Dilts

FIG. 91. (*bottom*) Church of Our Saviour, Baltimore, ca. 1907 or later. John McGrain Collection

to square foot costs used today. The firm listed the following cubic foot costs of some of their Baltimore buildings in cents:

Grace Church	$.17
Calvert Station	.16
Savings Bank of Baltimore	.17
Bash and Hodges Warehouses	.06 ½
Dr. Buckler's House	.11
3 very plain houses on Courtland St.	.10
Messrs. Eaton & Schumacher	.19
G. H. Williams	.11
Mr. Neilson's Dwelling	.16
Bank of Baltimore with vaults	.16
Dr. Thomas Dwelling	.22

Despite Louis McLane Jr.'s charge that Niernsee did not know the meaning of the word economy, the firm apparently knew the cost of what they were designing from the outset of the project.

The construction of commercial buildings in Baltimore began to accelerate rapidly, along with the city's economy in the late 1860s. The firm received a commission in 1869 to design

the Adams Building on property owned by Union Bank, the site of the present Blaustein Building, on Charles and Fayette Streets. Developed and built by the Adams Brothers, local construction contractors, the building was a large block of five stores facing Charles Street. The bank, which actually owned its space, had its own white marble entrance on Fayette Street. The sixteen-foot banking hall and directors' room took up the entire first story, topped by two stories of rental space. Each store had a twenty-one foot wide marble front that ran 100 feet deep, with skylights illuminating the rear of the stores. The building was a handsome block-long composition with a mansard roof with round-top dormers framed by projecting bays on both ends of the block.

After the Civil War, the nature of real estate development also changed. Instead of individual men of wealth developing and building properties, general contractors now controlled more of the development process by constructing multiple projects on their own account. This was the case of the Adams brothers, who used Niernsee & Neilson as designers of their buildings, almost in what would today be called a design-build arrangement. The Adams' knew the firm was reliable and could deliver a building on budget. In turn, the partners would recommend them as contractors on their projects. They did this for the College of Notre Dame, a commission they received in 1873. The firm and the Adams brothers also worked together on the Morse Building in 1871, a thirty-four-foot wide, two-story structure on Fayette Street with a cast-iron façade.[6]

Another major bank commission in 1869 was the Citizens' National Bank at Hanover and Pratt Streets. The two-story marble building had a corner entrance with plate glass windows fourteen feet high and five feet wide. Over the entry was a semicircular parapet bearing the name of the bank. The banking hall was forty-two feet square and paneled in walnut.[7]

The firm's Franklin Bank at South and German (now Redwood) Streets was a handsome four-story building on a lot twenty-six feet wide (fig. 92). The customer entered a vestibule two feet below street level through plate-glass doors that were protected after hours by sliding walnut doors. The twenty-three- by fifty-five-foot banking room was two-stories high and decorated in colored marbles. The cashier's office on a mezzanine allowed a full view of the room below. Banks usually used only the first story for their business and the upper stories for rental income. A cast- and wrought-iron stairway, accessed through a separate entrance off the street, led to the upstairs offices. In order to make them desirable rental properties, these spaces were large and well designed. The second story had a front room measuring twenty by twenty-eight feet with a sixteen-foot ceiling, and the third story was one large twenty-three-foot by fifty-five-foot open space with a seventeen-foot ceiling. The palazzo-style façade was done in white marble with tall arched windows.[8]

In 1869, an old client, Johns Hopkins, called on the firm to design a building for him on the corner of Holliday and Water Streets. The Rialto Building, as it was later known, had two stories of offices and a meeting hall on the third story, for a total building height of eighty feet. A new building by the city's most prominent benefactor was a cause for notice: "The building is being erected as an ornament to that part of the city, through the liberal enterprise of Mr. Hopkins, who has already done so much

towards the commercial quarter of Baltimore," reported the *Baltimore American*.[9]

The Maryland Life Insurance Company hired Niernsee & Neilson to design its new headquarters on South Street, which had become the location of many leading Baltimore financial and insurance institutions. The marble-fronted building was twenty-four feet in width and 100 feet in depth.[10]

Cast iron was still popular for building façades after the war. The firm used the material for John B. Morris's three-story building on South Street in 1867. Many new buildings in Baltimore's business district were now essentially speculative real estate ventures rented out to service industries, in particular, the life insurance business. Morris rented most of the space in the South Street building to the Atlantic Fire and Marine Insurance Company and the Connecticut Mutual Life Insurance Company. All needed separate entrances to their spaces, including the office in the third story, so each had its own stairway.[11]

Dr. Ferdinand Edme Chatard, a well-known physician in town, promoted a speculative build-

FIG. 93. Chatard Building, Baltimore. Jacques Kelly Collection

ing on the southwest corner of Charles and Lexington Streets. It was taken over in 1882 by O'Neill's Department Store, which became known as one of the finest department stores in the city (fig. 93). Niernsee & Neilson's building for Chatard had a prominent first story of cast iron with the upper stories faced with Cockeysville marble. The design was one of the few commercial buildings the firm did for a corner site. Both façades had simple segmentally arched windows with heavy marble sills. The frieze board of the cornice between the brackets was curved to match the arch of the windows below.[12] The store was demolished for the One Charles Center office building in 1954.

In such an active business climate, warehouses were in even greater demand by the city's merchants. Sharp Street, south of Baltimore Street, became a warehouse district after the war. Niernsee & Neilson did one four-story cast-iron front building there for Francis T. King and two for Galloway Cheston in 1869. The iron façades came from the foundry of Bartlett, Robbins & Company. A shoe factory, a silk merchant, and a paper merchant rented the space.[13]

The firm also did the Shockoe Warehouse and Richmond Tobacco Exchange in Richmond, Virginia, in 1867 (fig. 94). The two-story brick building, which was demolished in 1995, housed storage space in the first story and an exchange hall on the second, where tall half-round arched windows brought in a great deal of natural light. The commission was most likely obtained by Neilson and designed by him before the reunification of the firm.[14]

Perhaps the most notable of the commercial buildings designed and built under the aegis of Niernsee & Neilson was the Carrollton Hotel, on the site of the old Fountain Inn, in 1872 (fig. 95). The owners of the inn were a consortium referred to as the Fountain Associates, who decided to name the new hotel after Charles Carroll of Carrollton, one of Maryland's signers of the Declaration of Independence.[15] A very large mansard roofed five-story hotel, with a partial iron frame and masonry walls, it had a rather sophisticated structural system for its time. The building was one of the earliest to have true curtain wall construction. The hotel's street front had a cast iron curtain wall with an iron frame supporting the interior beams and carrying the marble facing of the building. The Carrollton was considered the first "modern" hotel of the post–Civil War period, the "only Hotel in Baltimore of the New Style, embracing Elevators, Suites of Rooms with Baths, and all conveniences; perfect ventilation and light throughout."[16] The hotel appears to have been the first in Baltimore to feature a safety elevator. The single elevator provided access from the main lobby to each of the hotel floors for customers and must have been considered a very posh addition to the hotel service of the city.

At the time the hotel opened, it was not considered appropriate for any well-bred lady to appear below Baltimore Street without an escort. However, Baltimore Street was alive most weekdays with unescorted ladies doing their shopping and other chores. The hotel, desiring this clientele, provided a women's entrance to the hotel via Baltimore Street with stairs to the women's lounges, lavatories, and related facilities in the second story. In that way, ladies could go to the hotel for luncheon without having ever violated the social taboo of an unaccompanied presence below Baltimore Street.[17] The Carrollton Hotel was destroyed in the 1904 Baltimore fire.

In the early 1870s, the firm designed a number of very important institutional projects, chiefly, the Academy of Music on North Howard Street (plate 14). One of the building's main promoters was another old client, Dr. John Hanson Thomas, for whom Niernsee & Neilson had designed an impressive residence in West Mount Vernon Place in 1851. A large and properly equipped theater was considered to be an important civic improvement and it

FIG. 94. Shockoe Warehouse and Richmond Tobacco Exchange, Richmond, Virginia. Valentine Richmond History Center

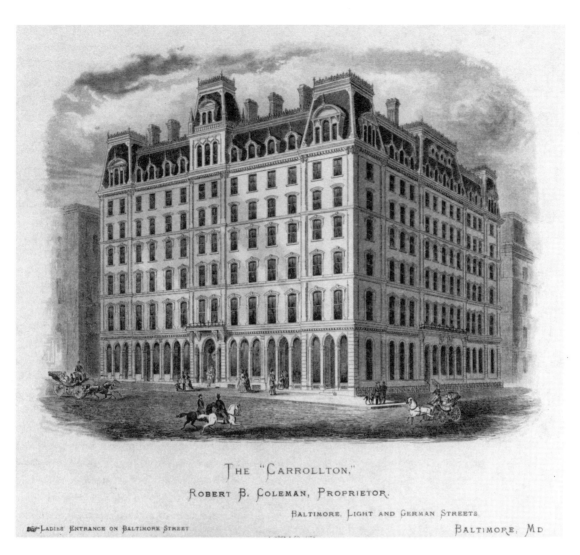

FIG. 95. Carrollton Hotel, Baltimore. James D. Dilts Collection

THE "CARROLLTON,"

ROBERT B. COLEMAN, PROPRIETOR.

BALTIMORE, LIGHT AND GERMAN STREETS.

☞ LADIES' ENTRANCE ON BALTIMORE STREET

BALTIMORE, MD

was financed by subscription, the city's leading businessmen being contributors. The $400,000 theater building, built of red pressed brick and Ohio freestone trim, had a mansard roof with round-arched dormer windows and cresting; it was 120 feet wide and 250 feet deep.

The patrons entered a triple-arched entry-way covered by a canopy that led to a thirty-foot-wide entrance hall with two fourteen-foot-wide grand stairways. There were two main spaces, a 100-foot-long concert and lecture hall with a twelve-hundred-seat capacity in the second story, and the Grand Opera House in the first story, with an eighty- by eighty-foot audi-torium and two sixteen-foot-deep galleries that seated seventeen hundred (fig. 96). The seven-ty- by eighty-foot stage was huge, "affording sufficient room for the representation of any kind of spectacular or other performances."[18] An elaborate chandelier was suspended from a circular skylight, and the ceiling was deco-rated in frescoes depicting "divine art." Behind the large stage, which was 130 feet in height,

were backstage facilities suitable for the high-est quality touring shows at that time.

More than four thousand people, including the governor of Maryland, attended the open-ing of the building. Although it was completed before the second dissolution of Niernsee & Neilson, the litigation over contract payments continued for several years afterward. The com-mission was an example of how design respon-sibilities were allocated in the second partner-ship. Neilson, not Niernsee, was the principal architect of the building. There was a general contractor on a project of this size and com-plexity. The Academy of Music was Baltimore's main social and theatrical center until it was superseded by the Lyric Theatre and the Ly-ceum in the Mount Royal Avenue district. It survived until 1926, when its foundation was used to build an ornate motion picture palace called the Stanley, which was eventually torn down.[19]

The Young Men's Christian Association Building, which still stands (although much al-

NIERNSEE
AND NEILSON

style, expressed by its semi-collegiate character of the uses for which it is intended—an
inviting, home-like retreat for social and recre-
ative purposes, as well as study and instruction
in its ample halls," wrote the *Sun* in 1875.[20] It
was an extremely well planned facility, containing a two-story lecture hall seating 1,700 and
an ample gymnasium, as well as classes and
dormitory facilities for bachelor members of
the organization. The third story contained a
24,000-volume library and a boardroom for the
trustees. To provide revenue for the YMCA,
most of the ground story was given over to
rental stores.

An elaborate octagonal turret at the corner
of the intersection, which extended above the
mansard roof with its own tall spire, was the
focus of the design. Along Saratoga Street, two
Gothic-inspired turrets flanked the main entry
and the gymnasium in the second story. They
were also used as thermo-siphon ventilators for
both the gymnasium and its locker room. The
theater was in the center of the block and was
accessed from the second floor. Such an impressive building was an event in Baltimore. The *Sun*
complemented Niernsee & Neilson: "Altogether
it is a worthy monument of its designers' skill."

When the building was completely remodeled in 1908, all the turrets were removed. The
revisions also included shearing off a projecting bay in the center of the Charles Street façade, which marked the former entrance to the
facility. The building was transformed into an
office building and, in the late 1990s, remodeled
into loft apartments.

The College of Notre Dame was one of the
few educational commissions the firm received
(fig. 98). Located on an elevated site on upper
Charles Street, near the intersection of Homeland Avenue, the college was designed initially
as a tall, narrow, four-story central block extending back from a tall and strikingly handsome ninety-three-foot mansard tower. The
girls' school was one of about a hundred such
schools run by the Sisters of Notre Dame at
the time of its completion in 1873 and was designed with future additions in mind.

As initially built, the school had a refectory
and chapel in the third story with the mansard of the building supplying the added ceiling height for these rooms. There was also a
grand staircase located inside the front tower
entrance (fig. 99). Fire safety was an important
consideration; fireplugs and hoses were in ev-

tered) on a triangular site at the northwest corner of Charles and Saratoga Streets, was a bold
design of red brick and sandstone with corner
towers and a sixteen-foot-high mansard roof
(fig. 97). "This massive and imposing edifice
is designed in the modified, 'French Medieval'

ery story and four stairways provided a safe means of egress from the building. Most of these features vanished with the construction of the wing designed by E. Francis Baldwin some twenty years later. Ironically, the unenclosed grand staircase was eliminated in the 1950s as a fire hazard.

It has been customary to assign this building to Neilson. When the firm broke up for the second time, he was the one who took charge of the remaining details for its completion. But more likely in this case, Niernsee was the designer, especially when one looks closely at the mansard of the tower cupola, which is very droll for a Roman Catholic college, because it is in the shape of a Hindu mandap, the sanctuary of a Hindu temple.

Niernsee relied on architectural references, as most architects did (and still do). Over the course of his career, he built up a personal library; his account books show that he spent money annually for architectural books. He saw historic design elements as having iconic meaning and used them, whether Gothic arches or Hindu temple roofs as inspiration for important features of a building. The $150,000 building, now called Gibbons Hall, was constructed by the Adams brothers, for whom the firm had designed several commercial buildings.[21]

Niernsee & Neilson also did considerable work in connection with Baltimore's new water system, which was developed after the Civil War. No longer able to rely directly on the Jones' Falls as the main supply of water, the city had to build new reservoirs, with Lake Roland serving as the anchor of the system and Druid Hill Park Lake Reservoir acting as the main distribution source. A pump house, built of marble with a gabled slate roof, was located north of the reservoir. Inside, a boiler room powered a pump engine. The building may still be seen at the top of Druid Hill Park near the Reptile House at the present Baltimore Zoo. The firm also designed the Garrett Bridge in 1870 in Druid Hill Park, on the grounds of the zoo (fig. 100).[22]

By the 1870s, the best commissions no longer automatically went to Niernsee & Neilson. Before the war, the firm had unquestionably been the dominant architectural firm in Baltimore, but in the post–Civil War period, they were subjected to considerable competition from younger men, many of whom they had trained themselves. Knowledge of the staff-

ing practices of the office is unknown, since no internal office records of the firm remain. No one knows how many assistants were kept on at any period of time or what their wages were. The firm probably had no more than four to six draftsmen. An architect of national stature like Richard Upjohn had only eleven employees before the Civil War. Not until the 1870s was the modern architectural office, with a large staff, created by New York architects like George B. Post and McKim, Mead, & White.

In the 1850s, architects made the transition from practicing alone to hiring employees. Although many men desired their own practices, they found they could survive financially only by working for another architect. The drafting

FIG. 98. *(top)* College of Notre Dame, Baltimore, 1987. Stephen McDaniel, Archives of College of Notre Dame of Maryland

FIG. 99. *(bottom)* College of Notre Dame, interior. Archives of College of Notre Dame of Maryland

room was the center of activity, taking the designs of the principals and transforming them into construction drawings and specifications. Most of the time, though, the work involved the monotony of copying drawings in ink. Before the invention of blueprinting in the 1880s, draftsmen were basically tracers. But in doing this task, they learned how to draw and also how a building was constructed.

Men in Niernsee & Neilson's office were fortunate to work on some of the most prestigious and complex commissions in the city. Both partners were very skilled in design and construction and thus were excellent models to emulate. The architectural firm of the nineteenth century was a place not only to work but also to learn the profession; the first architectural school, at the Massachusetts Institute of Technology, was not established until 1868. Niernsee, with his high level of education and training, was most likely an excellent mentor and teacher. Judging from the diaries of his youth, Niernsee greatly valued education and may have treated his draftsmen more as apprentices than employees. This is borne out by the architectural genealogy that can be traced from the firm's beginning in 1848 and continuing into the first half of the twentieth century (fig. 101).

The most influential Baltimore practitioner trained by Niernsee & Neilson was E. Francis Baldwin, who worked in Neilson's office from 1856 to 1867. Along with Baldwin was Bruce Price, a Cumberland native, who would become one of America's most famous Shingle Style architects. Both men stayed on when the firm reunited in 1865 and were joined by another

FIG. 100. Garrett Bridge, Druid Hill Park, Baltimore. James D. Dilts

future Baltimore architect, Thomas Buckler Ghequier. Baldwin, who went out on his own in 1867, would become the city's most prominent architect, much as Niernsee & Neilson had been in the 1840s and 1850s. Baldwin, in his own right, would train another generation of Baltimore architects.

The tradition of great architects working for other great architects has a long history in the United States. Robert Mills and William Strickland worked for Benjamin Henry Latrobe; Carrère and Hastings, Cass Gilbert, and John Galen Howard were all alumni of the era's most influential office, McKim Mead & White. Most famously perhaps, Louis Sullivan was Frank Lloyd Wright's employer. Not all the men Niernsee & Neilson employed opened their own practices, but the two partners, who had created the city's first professionally run architectural office, laid the basis for future firms that would take work away from them. When the B&O Railroad needed an architect for its headquarters on Calvert and Baltimore Streets in 1873, it turned to Baldwin, and to Niernsee only as the consulting architect. It was fitting that in 1870, Niernsee and Neilson, together with former employees Baldwin and Price and fourteen other Baltimore architects and engineers, founded the Baltimore Chapter of the American Institute of Architects.

In 1873, Niernsee had the opportunity to return to his native country when President Ulysses S. Grant appointed him as a United States Commissioner to represent America at the Vienna International Exhibition in 1873. It must have been a happy return for the immigrant engineer who had left thirty-seven years before and become extremely successful in his adopted country. Besides visiting his homeland, he was able to study building conditions in Austria, and in 1875 he published his "Report on the Construction and Embellishment of Private Dwellings in Vienna," complete with plans and elevations of apartment houses (fig. 102).

But there was a dark side to the trip. Niernsee left his elder son, Rudolph, with power of attorney to act on his behalf. When Niernsee and his son Frank, who went as his father's personal secretary, returned from their two-month holiday in Vienna, the partnership, which had worked so smoothly and effectively, was in disarray. Both of Niernsee's sons had wanted to become architects. Rudolph, the elder, had attended the University of Virginia (not yet with an archi-

FIG. 101. Niernsee
and Neilson genealogy

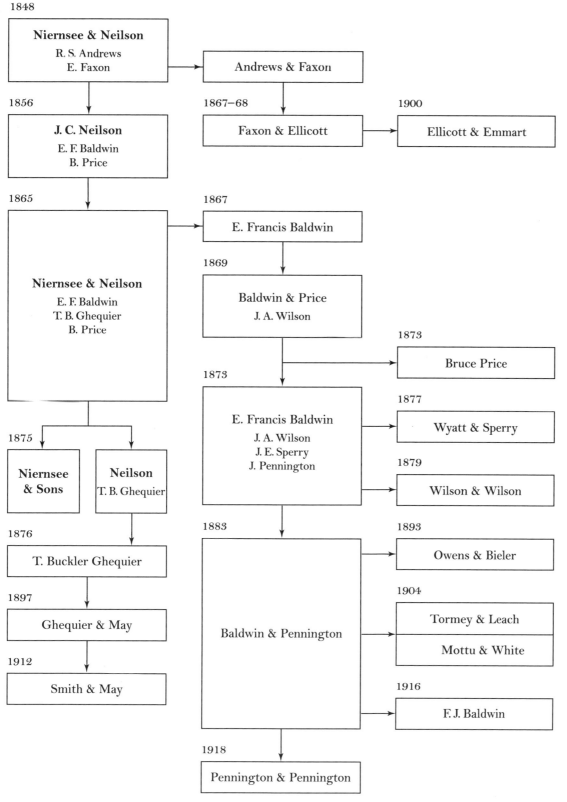

FIG. 101. Niernsee and Neilson genealogy

THE SECOND
PARTNERSHIP
1865 TO 1874

tectural school) and had come back home to the Baltimore office, apparently to study under the aegis of his father and Neilson. There is no record concerning the next series of events pertaining to the quarrel, but it is plain from comments in the narrative of Virginia Niernsee Floyd that her brother, Rudolph, overstepped his boundaries with Neilson in the administration of the office. The results of this dispute upset Niernsee as well as Neilson, and the account that Rudolph wrote to his sister was most likely biased in his favor. Rudolph was an alcoholic, which probably exacerbated his problems with his father's partner.[23]

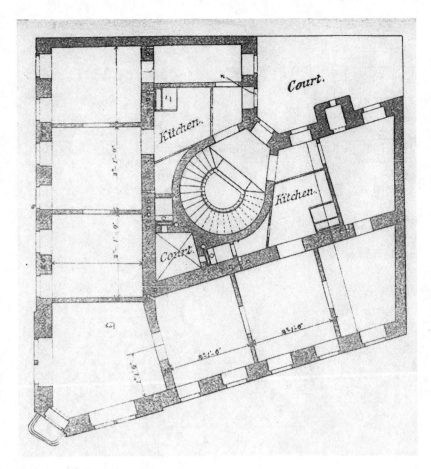

FIG. 102. Apartment
House Plan, Vienna,
1875

Niernsee had gone to Vienna at a particularly bad time, during the Panic of 1873, which plunged businesses across the country into bankruptcy. The effect was not catastrophic in Baltimore, largely due to the efforts of Johns Hopkins, who shored up the city's financial markets with his own funds, but it did initiate a depression and business downturn. Even a dominant firm like Niernsee & Neilson was affected. The panic just compounded the troubles between the partners.

On April 21, 1874, in the worst of economic climates, a legal notice appeared in the *Sun*: "The firm of Niernsee & Neilson has been dissolved by mutual consent on the 15th April. John R. Niernsee will continue the practice of architecture under the name of Niernsee & Son, at the old office, No. 39 North Charles Street. The unfinished works of last year will be completed by the old firm."

In the end, blood was thicker than water, but instead of Rudolph, Niernsee chose his younger son Frank, who had studied engineering at the University of Virginia, to be his partner.[24] Neilson had been successful on his own before and he knew that he could succeed again. The two architects, who had produced some of Baltimore's greatest buildings, would never work together again.

TEN

The Johns Hopkins Hospital

Despite the dissolution of the firm, John R. Niernsee was still considered the dean of Baltimore architects, and his reputation continued to draw important clients. In 1874, he was called on to design one of the most important and prestigious institutions the city had ever seen—the Johns Hopkins Hospital.

When Johns Hopkins, the wealthy Baltimore merchant and financier, died in 1873 and left $7 million to be divided equally to construct a university and a hospital, the trustees of the estate turned to a man for whom Hopkins had had a great deal of respect for over twenty years. It was a highly coveted commission. "It is learned that the claims of several prominent architects in other cities were urged with the Trustees, but after careful consideration of the merits of all the claimants the appointment was awarded to a citizen of Baltimore," reported the *Gazette*.[1] The president of the board of trustees, Francis T. King, was also aware of Niernsee's skill; Niernsee had designed a warehouse for him in 1869.

The hospital, which would become a great symbol of pride for Baltimore, was to be a group of about twenty buildings on a fourteen-acre site along Broadway in the eastern section of the city. For Niernsee, who was hired in 1874, the design process would be similar to his experience at Spring Grove Hospital, where he had been required to follow the medical thinking of the day and design the complex based on the "Kirkbride plan." Hopkins had instructed the trustees "to obtain the advice and assistance of those at home and abroad who have achieved the greatest success in the construction and management of hospitals."[2] Now, Niernsee would design the complex in consultation with John Shaw Billings, the

trustees' medical advisor and an army surgeon assigned to the United States Surgeon General's office.

Prior to 1854, there was no theory linking the design of a hospital to the health of patients. Hospitals had been designed to look like other public buildings, such as courthouses. Then Florence Nightingale, the English nurse who cared for the wounded in field hospitals during the Crimean War, introduced the "miasma" theory of disease. It posited that patients could not be exposed to "bad" air full of germs. During the Civil War, Billings had also used mobile army field hospitals to effectively combat infection for wounded soldiers. The flaps of the tents allowed for a constant airflow that seemed to have a therapeutic effect on his patients. As a result, he became a firm believer in a "village" concept of hospital design. Combating and preventing airborne "disease germs" was of the utmost importance to Billings. This was the basis of Billings' forty-six page proposal in 1875 for constructing the hospital: "The results of the experience of military surgeons with wood barracks and tent hospitals, especially in the late war in this country, and in more recent contacts in Europe, led to the recommendation that similar structures should be adopted for all hospitals."[3]

Billings provided very basic floor plans with his proposal for the administrative building and the two-story pavilions serving as wards, noting that "the plans of this building are simply rough sketches, intended to indicate in a general way only, the number and relative size of the rooms required"[4] (fig. 103). He in no way intended to act as architect on the project, but his drawings served as the basis of Niernsee's design.

FIG. 103. Sketch Plan
of Arrangement for
Johns Hopkins Hospi-
tal, 1875. Alan Mason
Chesney Medical
Archives, The Johns
Hopkins Medical
Institutions

NIERNSEE
AND NEILSON

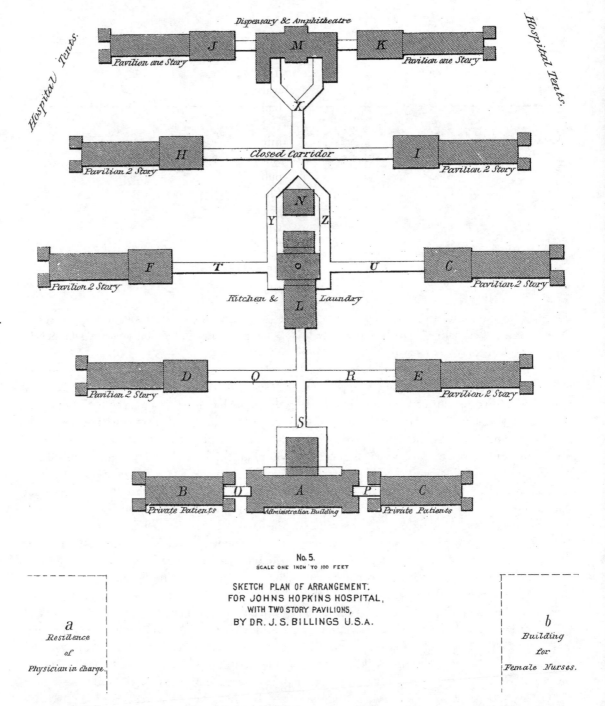

The Johns Hopkins Hospital was to be de-signed as a pavilion hospital, consisting of a village of buildings rather than one very large building containing multiple uses. Billings pro-posed a main administrative building flanked by separate men's and women's private patient wards facing Broadway. To the rear of this com-plex would be a series of separate two-story brick common wards. A glass enclosed connect-ing corridor much like a veranda linked all the wards, which would be fully exposed to light and air. "Light is a powerful tonic and stimulant agent, with peculiar powers and modes of ac-tion, which as yet cannot be said to be well understood," wrote Billings.[5] Most important-ly, the separate wards were to eliminate all in-fectious airborne particles. There would be wards for obstetrics, physical traumas, and in-juries, as well as pathological and physiological laboratories and central facilities providing meals and other support to the hospital. Bill-ings used no elevators for fear of contamina-tion from the shafts. Rounded wall corners were intended to prevent the accumulation of dust and dirt. Initially, the most infectious cases would be housed in tents. Because Hopkins also requested that the site be "laid out and planted with trees and flowers as to afford solace to the sick," Niernsee arranged the wards on either side of a large central garden in the space Billings planned for a kitchen and laundry.

Billings gave a great deal of thought to the ventilation and heating of the complex; each ward would have its own system, so that air from one ward could not contaminate other parts of the hospital. He also incorporated a medical school into the scheme, complying with Hopkins' wish that the hospital be part of the medical school of the university. The two interests, he felt, were inseparable. With Niernsee's help, he submitted the plans to the trustees and was hired on

July 1, 1876. In December of 1876, Niernsee and Billings's hospital design appeared in *American Architect and Building News*, December 16, 1876. The site plan (fig. 104) showed the separate wards and individual floor plans (fig. 105) of the buildings, but there were no elevations shown.

Niernsee, who put much time and thought into the design, was greatly angered by an incident that occurred before the drawings were published. He had helped to found the Baltimore Chapter of the American Institute of Architects in 1870 in the hope of educating the public about what architects actually do. The AIA held its

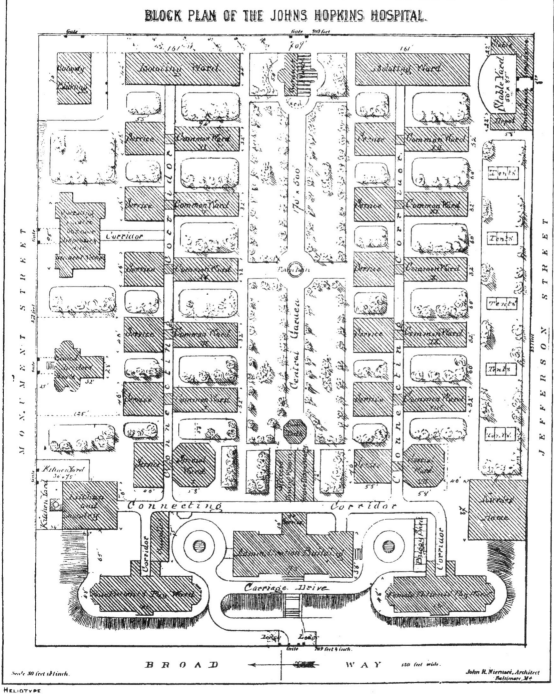

FIG. 104. The Johns Hopkins Hospital, site plan, 1876. From *American Architect and Building News*, 1876

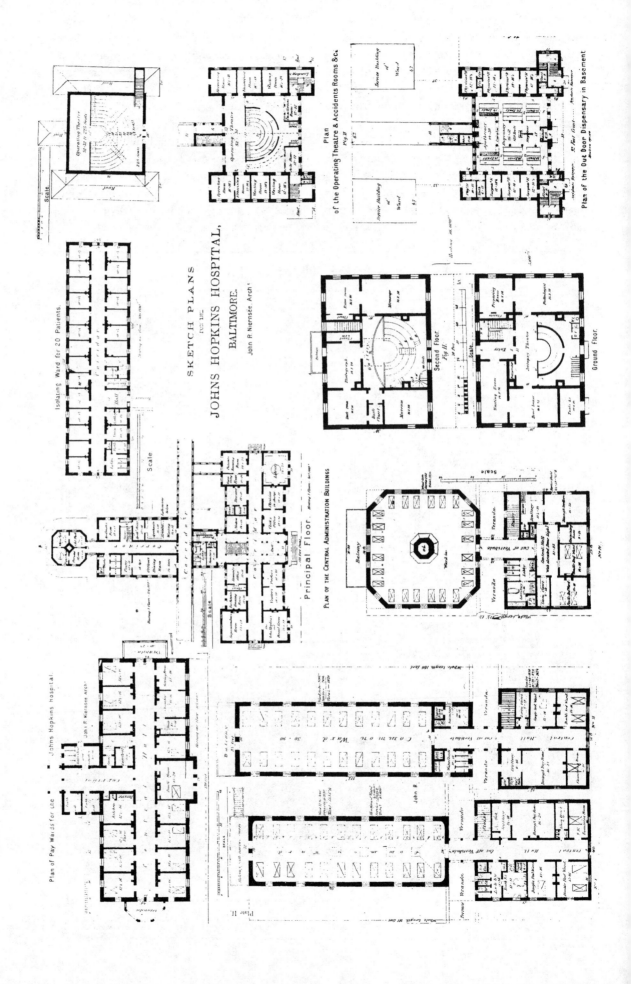

SKETCH PLANS
FOR THE
JOHNS HOPKINS HOSPITAL,
BALTIMORE.

John R Nierneste. Arch'

annual convention in the city in 1875, an event that generated a great deal of press coverage stressing the skill and knowledge required of an architect. But a speech by one of the most honored scholars in the world in September 1876 illustrated how misunderstood the role of the architect still was.

For the dedication of the new Johns Hopkins Institute of Graduate Studies in Baltimore, the famous English science scholar Thomas Huxley was invited to give the dedication address, which was presented at Niernsee & Neilson's Academy of Music. The *Baltimore American* published the speech the following morning. Huxley congratulated the trustees of the university for not building a brand new campus all at once. He thought that they should get "an honest bricklayer" to build only buildings they believed were necessary at the school's beginning. If they had a spare one hundred thousand dollars in the future, they could call in an architect and have him add a façade around what was already constructed.

The idea that "an honest bricklayer" was all that was required to build the first stages of a building was a notion that irked Niernsee. He wrote a letter to the editor, finding it "astonishing" that such a learned man "should fall in the great misconception of recommending a bricklayer as the proper person to devise, arrange, and construct the numerous and important buildings for a great university, and propose calling in an architect afterwards to put a façade on them."[6] It took a great deal of skill and planning to plan a university, including heating and ventilating the buildings, he explained. To Niernsee's relief, Johns Hopkins did not heed Huxley's advice, but hired E. Francis Baldwin to plan and design its first campus at Howard and Centre Streets beginning in the late 1870s. Niernsee would be dismayed to learn that even now, 130 years later, many people still share Huxley's perception of architects.

Niernsee's hospital drawings, now in the Chesney Medical Library at the Johns Hopkins Hospital, were engraved and printed with numbers so that they could be circulated for criticism and discussion amongst professionals concerned with the planning and execution of the Hopkins bequest. After Niernsee had completed his drawings, he was paid off and the project for the hospital lay dormant until the Hopkins estate had accumulated sufficient funds for construction.

Then in 1877, the trustees hired the Boston firm of Cabot & Chandler to design the hospital complex. The reason for the switch in architects may have been that an old project again beckoned to Niernsee. The occupation by Union troops of South Carolina ended in the spring of 1877 and Governor Wade Hampton turned his attention to finishing the statehouse.

Niernsee was the obvious man to be a consultant and he was sent for. His sons had served in Hampton's regiment during the war, and he had great admiration for the former general. The leaking roof needed immediate attention, so on February 20, 1878, Niernsee arrived in the state capitol to advise the legislature on the roof and spent weeks preparing estimates for completing the work, but in the end, nothing was done until 1883.

The Hopkins trustees may have wanted Niernsee's full time attention to their project, and not getting it turned elsewhere. It was not uncommon for architects to lose major commissions because of their involvement with another large project. Heins & Lafarge won the competition for the Cathedral of St. John the Divine in New York in 1891, only to lose it in 1905, when the church decided that the firm's New York subway commission was taking up too much of their time.[7]

It is interesting to note the pull the South Carolina commission had on Niernsee all those years. He essentially would give up authorship of the Johns Hopkins Hospital for the statehouse project as he had done with Camden Station. Niernsee probably felt an honor-bound obligation to South Carolina in addition to the hope of seeing his design finally completed. A statehouse was perhaps the most prestigious commission an architect could have. For whatever reason, Cabot & Chandler, using Niernsee's floor plans and site plan as the basis of their scheme, designed the entire Johns Hopkins Hospital complex, including the famous three-story administrative building and wings and all the wards. Construction began in 1877.

Built of red brick with Cheat River stone trim, the hospital's main administration building is a robust Queen Anne composition with a central dome and roof towers, dormers, pediments, and chimneys. The structure of the 150-foot-high dome is of ribbed cast iron clad in slate. The drawings in the Chesney archive, many of which beautifully detail the dome of

FIG. 105. *(opposite)* The Johns Hopkins Hospital, floor plans, 1876. From *American Architect and Building News*, 1876

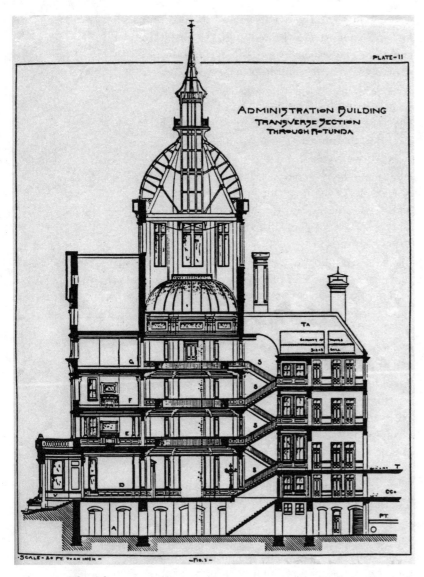

PLATE-11

ADMINISTRATION BUILDING
TRANSVERSE SECTION
THROUGH ROTUNDA

FIG. 106. The Johns Hopkins Hospital, Administration Building. *Description of the Johns Hopkins Hospital by John S. Billings, M.D.*, 1890

the main building, were executed by Cabot & Chandler (fig. 106). On some of the drawings, Niernsee is listed as a consulting architect. The July 27, 1889, issue of *American Architect and Building News* credited Cabot & Chandler as designers. *Harper's Weekly*, September 8, 1888, published front and rear perspectives of the Johns Hopkins Hospital (figs. 107, 108).

Since none of Niernsee's elevations survives, there can be no comparison of the 1889 final design with his original 1876 design. The final site plan, 1890, basically followed Niernsee's scheme of 1876, with the same disposition of the main buildings and the layout of the separate wards, each with a sun parlor overlooking a central garden (fig. 109). The wards were still connected by walkways but were more elongated in proportion. The 1889 administration building did follow the cruciform plan and rear wing extension of Niernsee's 1876 scheme. The first story held the library, reception room, offices, and ex-

amination rooms; the second story housed the living quarters for the superintendent and the resident physicians; bedrooms for the resident students were in the third story. The flanking pay wards for men and women also follow Niernsee's original proportions and layout.[8]

In 1889, when the hospital was about to open, *AABN* noted that it was successful in its "scientific and hygienic theories." The design, however, was not deemed an architectural success. The main buildings on Broadway, which today are widely admired, were given a negative review in the country's main architectural periodical: "The effect produced is not impressive, and recognizing the attempt, the result is almost frivolous. Nevertheless, the public is repeatedly called upon to admire even its smallest detail of design and ornament." The critic wanted to find simplicity, mass, and character in the buildings but found that "these characteristics are not suggested in the architecture of Hopkins Hospital."[9]

The final design followed Billings' independent heating and ventilation system, in which air, drawn from a basement duct, was blown over heating coils and into the ward through a register. There were six miles of underground drainage pipes and fifty miles of supply and gas piping. The pipes for the hot-water system were twenty-six inches in diameter, insulated with an inch of felt, and set on rollers to account for movement due to expansion and contraction. Niernsee's and Billings' plan, of which little remains today, was a pioneering step in American hospital design and was considered the most modern hospital of its time. The design was the result of the first thorough study to identify the necessary elements of a modern hospital, where doctors and nurses could be taught at the same time patients were being treated. Billings' approach to hospital hygiene and infection has been replaced by new innovations including the use of disinfectants. Over the years, the hospital has demolished the older buildings, with the exception of the ones on Broadway, and replaced them with more modern facilities. Only a tiny part of the central garden survives.[10]

The Hopkins bequest also included a provision for an orphanage for black children. In 1875, the trustees hired Niernsee to design a building on a site in Remington, near the future Homewood campus of the university, but it was never built. The drawings for the building are in the Legislative Reference Library in Baltimore City Hall.

With the appointment of Cabot & Chandler, Niernsee became a consultant and oversaw the construction of the Johns Hopkins Hospital complex until his death in 1885. It must have been a bitter pill to take. He had returned from South Carolina around 1878 when it was apparent that the legislature was not going to continue work on the statehouse. The design of the hospital project had officially been given to Cabot & Chandler, and Niernsee could do nothing but act as an advisor. He was no longer the designer of record. The building of the hospital lasted for twelve years, until 1889, because the construction costs could only be paid for by the interest generated from the bequest. Unfortunately, Niernsee's invaluable contribution to the design of the Johns Hopkins Hospital has been overshadowed by Billings' work. The fact that he died four years before the complex was completed may account for his diminished involvement. Even as early as 1877, there was a public misperception about proper design credit

FIG. 107. *(top)*
The Johns Hopkins Hospital, front. From *Harper's Weekly*, 1888

FIG. 108. *(bottom)*
The Johns Hopkins Hospital, rear. From *Harper's Weekly*, 1888

FIG. 109. The Johns
Hopkins Hospital,
site plan. *Description
of the Johns Hopkins
Hospital by John S.
Billings, M.D.,* 1890

NIERNSEE
AND NEILSON

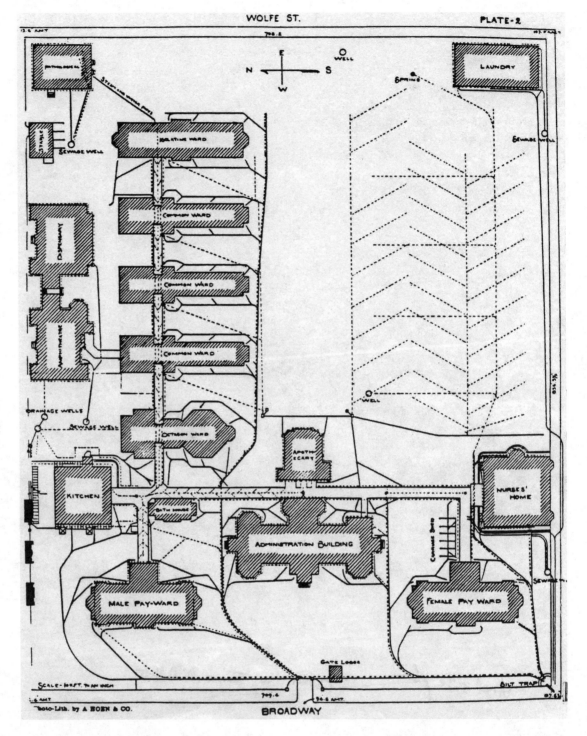

for the hospital. As Niernsee wrote in a letter to the editor of the *Baltimore Sun*:

Personal—Mr. John R. Niernsee, architect of the Johns Hopkins Hospital, takes exception to the words in yesterday's *Sun*. "It is known that the plans of the Johns Hopkins Hospital, prepared by Dr. Billings, with some modifications by the trustees, will be carried out." Mr. Niernsee writes that it would be more correct to say "That the plans of the hospital designed by John R. Niernsee, have been ac-

cepted as being in accordance with the views of the building committee, with some modifications suggested by their medical advisor, Dr. J. S. Bllings."[11]

For an architect, there is nothing more disappointing than having someone else get credit for one's design. But unfortunately for Niernsee, in the end, history would be on Billings's side; the famous domed administrative building is now called the John Shaw Billings Building.

ELEVEN

The Final Years

The final break between John Rudolph Niernsee and James Crawford Neilson was not beneficial to either man. They soon discovered that they had been stronger as a team than they were on their own. After the split, they divided the responsibility for work in progress, with Neilson supervising the Academy of Music and Notre Dame projects, while Niernsee finished the YMCA Building and undertook some other minor jobs.

While Niernsee was working on the Johns Hopkins Hospital, other important commissions came into the office of Niernsee & Son. The Maryland Jockey Club purchased a parcel of land next to its track at Pimlico and hired Niernsee to design a first-class clubhouse (fig. 110). Built exclusively for club members and their families in 1874, Niernsee's $20,000 hip-roofed building measured fifty feet by fifty feet with a twelve-foot-wide veranda on all four sides. Members could climb to the cupola and view the city to the south. The design, which became a beloved landmark in the racing world, especially at Preakness time, resembled the Mansion

FIG. 110. Pimlico Clubhouse, Baltimore, 1965. Library of Congress

House at Druid Hill Park and sported elaborate woodwork on the veranda and cupola. "The new clubhouse," reported the *Baltimore Sun*, "is three stories in height and presents a fine architectural appearance, being an ornament to the grounds." Old Hilltop, as the clubhouse was named, was built in only ninety days. It burned down in 1966.[1]

St. John's Church in Beltsville, Maryland, designed by Niernsee in 1877, has a gable roof with an interesting stick style bell tower, a popular form of wood-frame detailing in this period. The church demonstrates the firm's adept handling of another new post–Civil War style and is the only known building for which the firm used this particular style.

One of Niernsee & Son's most important commissions of the 1870s was made possible by a former employee. In 1878, August Forsberg, the city engineer of Lynchburg, Virginia, who had worked for Niernsee on the South Carolina State House, recommended him to design an opera house for his city. Two wealthy tobacconists, Messrs. Hancock and Moorman, had contributed $550,000 so that Lynchburg could have a first class entertainment venue, "equal to any of the kind in Northern cities," reported the Lynchburg paper, the *Virginian*. When it

was completed, in 1879, theatergoers entered the 60-foot-wide and 132-foot-deep building through a grand foyer and made their way up to the second-floor auditorium, thirty-five feet high with a gallery supported on iron columns. Boxes lined the sides of the auditorium, and the entire interior was finished in stucco and gilt with the ceiling painted to look like a dome surrounded by cherubs carrying garlands of flowers. One newspaper source specifically credited Frank Niernsee with the design, indicating that his father was now giving his son more design responsibility. Like any young architect, Frank Niernsee did not want simply to execute his father's designs or just supervise construction. The elder Niernsee probably critiqued his son's work and made suggestions on the design.

The opera house was an object of great civic pride. The *Virginian* proudly noted that the *Richmond State* admired their new building, cautioning that "if we are not careful some of these more energetic and enterprising Virginia cities will get ahead of us in more ways than building a handsome opera house." Crowds formed a line for tickets two hours before the theater's premier production of *Julius Caesar* presented by John T. Ford, the Baltimore impresario who owned a theater in Baltimore as well as the ill-fated Washington theater where Lincoln was shot. The waiting crowd became so unruly that the police had to be called. In 1902, the building was converted into a warehouse, and then in 1912 it was renovated into a movie theater, which became the Warner Theater in 1951. The building still stands.[2]

Houses for the wealthy had once been a staple of the firm, but probably due in part to the depression spawned by the 1873 panic, residential commissions were now few and far between. The only real house of note Niernsee & Son did in these years was for a former client, G. W. Gail, the tobacco merchant, on Eutaw Place at Ducatel Street, near Druid Park Lake, in 1875 (fig. 111). The $80,000 gray stuccoed twenty-five-room mansion was designed in "a modern Italian Villa style," according to the *Sun*, which added that the architects "have combined the imposing outlines of a castle with all the modern conveniences of the best first class city dwellings." The three-story house had a very bold asymmetrical composition—the south façade, on Ducatel Street, had an imposing veranda at the entry and very tall windows. The façade facing Eutaw Place had a large bay window in the first story and porches in the second and third stories. A grand stair, lit by a stained-glass skylight, a main parlor, a library connected to the veranda, a dining room, and a sitting room, led off a large central corridor. On the north façade, there was a porte cochere, the entire house being surrounded by lawns and gardens.[3] The Gail Mansion had a short life; it was torn down and replaced by an apartment house in the early twentieth century.

The Corn and Flour Exchange turned again to Niernsee in 1882 for their new Chamber of Commerce building at Holiday and Water Streets (fig. 112). The name of the building was misleading, as it was actually a replacement for the exchange's old building designed by Neilson (see Chapter 8). For the exterior, Niernsee & Son used a Renaissance Revival design that recalled the medieval guildhalls of Europe. The large four-story corner building was faced with granite in the first story and pressed brick above. Windowsills and lintels were also done in granite, as was the cornice. A portico supported by four polished granite columns with capitals decorated with corn and wheat motifs framed the main entry, above which was a large arched window.

A main fourteen-foot corridor ran the entire north-south length of the building with a cross corridor, thirteen feet wide, running east to west. A twenty-foot-wide grand central stair and a hydraulic elevator provided access to the

upper stories. The exchange hall, where trading took place, was 76 feet wide by 146 feet long with adjoining offices and a gallery for spectators. The building had its own telegraph office and a pit where corn and wheat could be examined and fifty-eight rooms in the lower stories

for exchange members to conduct business. In the 1880s, more buildings in America were beginning to make use of iron framing systems in place of traditional timber construction. For the Chamber of Commerce building, the floor was constructed of rolled-iron beams infilled with brick and tile arches for fireproofing, because iron yielded badly in fires and had to be protected. The roof was framed in iron, as were all the staircases. The total construction cost was $220,000.[4] This building burned in the Great Baltimore Fire of 1904 and was rebuilt with a different exterior designed by Charles E. Cassell. The Baltimore International College occupies it now.

In 1882, the Merchants Club on German (now Redwood) Street held a design competition and chose Niernsee & Son over J. A and W. T. Wilson, Charles Cassell, and Neilson to design their clubhouse (fig. 113). The purpose of the club was "social and the maintenance of confidential relations between those engaged in similar or parallel pursuits, and also the promotion of those traits of hospitality and culture for

which Baltimore has been so justly famous in the past."[5] The three-story design of red brick featured a full height prominent pediment with many Queen Anne–inspired details, such as pairs of double-hung windows with stained-glass transoms and square multipaned divided lights. The tympanum of the main pediment had a wide arched window. The building shows that Niernsee (or, more likely, his son Frank) had kept up with stylistic changes in American architecture; the Queen Anne had become quite popular by the early 1880s. This building was replaced by the present Merchants Club on Redwood Street, also now occupied by the Baltimore International College.

Although the number of their commissions had declined, the firm of Niernsee & Son was not without a considerable amount of consulting work. John R. Niernsee became a consultant on the B&O's new Central Office Building at Baltimore and Calvert Streets designed by his former apprentice, E. Francis Baldwin, as well as to the Roman Catholic Archdiocese of Baltimore for Baldwin's addition to the basilica. In 1878, he worked with Edmund Lind, the original designer of the Peabody Institute, on the library addition. Niernsee and his son entered into many competitions to secure projects: a chamber of commerce in Atlanta, a city hall in Richmond, a cotton exposition building in New Orleans, and the Georgia statehouse. All of these offered compensation, or "premiums," for designs, ranging from $1,000 to $250 for the Richmond City Hall. In the past, architects had protested against speculative competition work, with only the winner being paid for his design work. The AIA had long discouraged its members from entering competitions without compensation. The creation of the Baltimore Chapter of the American Institute of Architects in 1870 came about because of a protest by the city's architects over an uncompensated competition for the Frederick School for the Deaf and Dumb.

Neilson's career also continued successfully, as it had after the first parting. He had a steady stream of work, especially churches. After his St. James' Protestant Episcopal Church in Trap, four miles north of Churchville in Harford County, burned down in 1869, Neilson designed a stone replacement in 1875 (fig. 114).

An eighteenth-century country house known as Lansdowne, located near Darlington, Harford County, was sold by the Jewett family in 1865 to Joseph King, who would become the first president of the board of directors of the Johns Hopkins Hospital. He died, and his son Thomas, a bachelor merchant of considerable wealth who lived most of the time in Europe, returned in 1876, bought out his brother and co-heir, and moved to Lansdowne permanently. King changed the name of the house to Kenton and employed Neilson to put an annex on the two-and-a-half-story farmhouse and make additions and modifications to the general form of the building (fig. 115). The addition contained a kitchen and pantry with servants' bedrooms and "a large and first-class bathroom" with a copper tub set in walnut and maple.

The house was quite popular in its day, with extensive articles in the Bel Air *Aegis and Intelligencer* describing the work. The mantel in the parlor was especially impressive, "one of the handsomest pieces of ornamental carving … we have ever seen."[6] King, a Quaker and a founding member and principal benefactor of the Darlington Orthodox Friends Meeting House also hired Neilson to design a new meetinghouse in 1877 (fig. 116). As befitting the values of the denomination, the meetinghouse was a simple strong structure built of native stone with a slate hip roof. The porte cochere had a gabled roof supported by bracketed posts. The scale of the design is deceiving; the meetinghouse was not small—the interior had an extremely high ceiling and tall, segmentally arched windows.

In 1884, Thomas King died, leaving Kenton to his brother, who sold it back to the Jewett family in 1886. Hugh Judge Jewett, the retired president of the Wheeling and Lake Erie Railroad, hired Neilson to make another addition

FIG. 114. *(opposite, top)* St. James' Protestant Episcopal Church, Trap, Maryland. James T. Wollon Jr.

FIG. 115. *(opposite, bottom)* Lansdowne (Kenton), Darlington, Maryland, ca. 1880. Photo courtesy Ann H. Gregory

FIG. 116. *(above)* Darlington Orthodox Friends Meeting House, Darlington, Maryland, 1877. Photo courtesy Ann H. Gregory

FIG. 117. *(top)*
Lansdowne (Kenton),
ca. 1950. Private
collection

FIG. 118. *(bottom)*
Osmun C. Latrobe
House, Baltimore.
James D. Dilts

to the house (fig. 117). Using a totally different style, it took the form of a massive, cruciform Queen Anne structure added to the east end of the original house, with a stone first story with shingles above. A massive gable and hipped roof with dormers of all sizes covered the addition. At the same time, the original house received a second remodeling, largely obliterating Neilson's earlier 1879 work. The building became a kind of triumph of Neilson's architectural talent, showing how skillfully he could handle the Queen Anne style's picturesque massing and intricate detailing.

Neilson's other residential work included the Osmun C. Latrobe House at 1205 St. Paul Street in 1881 (fig. 118). The three-story house, designed in a vaguely Queen Anne style and costing $18,000 to build, has a mansard roof and a façade of pressed brick set in black mortar with Cheat River stone trim. The builder was George Blake, well known as a builder of both private and speculative houses in Upper Mount Vernon in the late nineteenth and early twentieth centuries. With a frontage of forty feet, it served as a two-family house, in which Neilson himself lived for a time.[7]

Neilson also worked on the Eastern Shore, renovating the Queen Anne's County Courthouse in Centreville, Maryland, in 1876–77. Emmanuel Episcopal Church in Chestertown was restyled by Neilson in 1880. The two-story colonial church of the 1760s was transformed into a tall one-story Romanesque design by lowering the original roof structure about twelve feet in one intact piece and altering the windows—all for the sake of style. The colonial church is depicted in a map vignette (fig. 119). Neilson's renovations were illustrated in an 1898 book (fig. 120). The photograph shows the current appearance of the church (fig. 121). Neilson had two more important projects in Chestertown: the Kent County Jail in 1884 and the three-story Wickes House in 1885.

Neilson seemed to be constantly adding to or renovating his family home in Priestford, Harford County, from 1875 until his death in 1900. His notebooks are filled with architectural sketches of new buildings and floor plans for his estate (fig. 122). As was his usual practice, Neilson spent summers running his farm and socializing in the neighboring community with his wife.

Neilson's best-known Baltimore building after the firm's final dissolution was the Western Maryland Railway's Hillen Street Station, located between High and Front Streets (fig. 123). After dissolving their partnership, both men were forced to realign themselves with clients. Neilson was fortunate enough to have John Mifflin Hood, the president of the railroad, choose him to design the line's new in-town freight and passenger depot. Built in 1876, the three-story building had a low-pitched, bracketed Swiss chalet–style roof, with a dramatic spire topping its main projecting gable. The Hillen Street Station consisted of a general office and passenger station adjoining a long train shed and adjacent freight station and general warehouse. The main entry sports double segmental arched openings, supported by a short column. The station handled forty-two trains a day. It was demolished in the mid-1950s, when train travel in America was coming to an end.[8]

Perhaps the most important commission of national scope given to Neilson during this final period in his career was the first Ellis Island Immigrant Station of 1891 (fig. 124). It is not known how he got the project. When the federal government took over the responsibility of processing immigrants from New York State's

immigration agency in 1890, it decided to move the immigrant station from Castle Garden, a fort in lower Manhattan, to Ellis Island.

Neilson designed a vast wood-frame structure built directly along an artificial quay on

FIG. 119. *(top)* Emmanuel Episcopal Church, Chestertown, Maryland, vignette. From Simon J. Martenet, *Map of Kent County*, 1860

FIG. 120. *(center)* Emmanuel Episcopal Church. From Fred C. Usilton, *History of Chestertown*, 1898

FIG. 121. *(bottom)* Emmanuel Episcopal Church. James T. Wollon Jr.

117

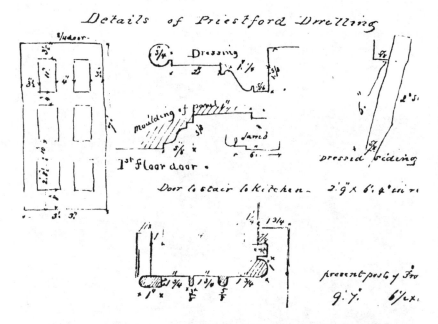

FIG. 122. *(top)* Priestford, Harford County, Maryland, floor plans. Maryland Historical Society, Baltimore, Maryland

FIG. 123. *(bottom)* Western Maryland Railway Station, Hillen Street, Baltimore, ca. 1880s. Baltimore Architecture Foundation

Steerage passengers went to the second story, lit by a continuous clerestory, for medical inspection and interrogation, and then were separated into ten lines for further examination. An 1882 act of Congress prohibited convicts, lunatics, paupers, contract laborers, or anyone with a contagious disease from being admitted to the United States, and many who disembarked were sent home. After passing inspection, the immigrants moved into one of two enclosure pens, depending on whether they were heading for New York City or to other parts of the country. A lunch stand, telegraph office, and railroad ticket offices were conveniently located in the second story. It was reported that four million board feet of lumber went into the construction of the building. There was also a large brick detention building next to the main structure, in addition to other ancillary buildings, such as a dining hall and quarters for immigration officers. Neilson's building lasted fewer than five years but processed about 1,644,000 immigrants. When it burned down in three hours in 1897, all of the immigration records from 1855 to 1897 were destroyed. The present Ellis Island immigration building was constructed in 1898, replacing Neilson's building. It operated as a processing station until 1954 and was converted into a museum in 1990.[9]

Neilson's biggest and most prestigious source of commissions was from Washington and Lee University in Lexington, Virginia. A small private liberal arts college founded in 1749, the school was saved from financial failure when George Washington gave it an endowment of $20,000 in stock in 1796. In gratitude, the school changed its name to Washington College.

After the Civil War, in 1865, Robert E. Lee reluctantly accepted the position of president, although he was afraid he "might draw upon the school a feeling of hostility." Lee died in 1870, but in his brief tenure, he established a law school and introduced a business curriculum. After his death, the board of trustees voted to change the name of the college to Washington and Lee University.

A statue, a recumbent figure of Lee, was commissioned by the university, which was finished in 1875, but a suitable mausoleum was needed to house it. Because of his admiration for the Confederate general, Neilson offered to design the building free of charge in 1877. With great difficulty, funds were raised for the construction of the mausoleum, which was finally fin-

Ellis Island so that steamers could directly unload immigrants for processing and also to take them back to Manhattan or New Jersey. The 440-foot-long, 150-foot-wide shingle style building had a long gable roof of blue slate; the exterior walls were painted a buff color. A central cross gable marked the entry and was flanked by two small towers, with larger towers at all four corners of the station.

The first story, thirteen feet in height, could handle the baggage of 12,000 immigrants a day.

ished in 1883. Neilson's building, an extension to the chapel where Lee was buried, matched the existing building's roof and detailing. He removed the rear wall of the chapel to create a Tudor arch framing the statue, depicting Lee in repose on an army field bed. As a result of this generous act, Neilson began a friendship with G. W. Custis Lee, the son of Robert E. Lee. This friendship led to commissions to design a group of buildings for the college, beginning in 1876 with renovations of the former Robinson Hall into what is now Brooks Museum.[10]

In 1881, Mrs. Warren Newcomb donated money to the university for a new library in memory of her husband. Neilson, apparently hampered by the limited amount of funds, designed a rather plain academic building, which took only a year to build (figs. 125–127). Newcomb Hall had offices and a reading room with a picture gallery in the second story; the wings at the rear of the building housed book stacks and classrooms. "It will not be the handsomest structure of its kind in the country, but will be I think, as convenient and well-adapted to its uses as any," wrote Custis Lee about the new building, whose only adornment was some pilasters and a glazed cupola, very similar to the ones Niernsee favored for his country houses like Crimea.

Neilson's next commission was for a professor's residence in 1887 (fig. 128). The brick house, which cost $4,500, was done in a typical Queen Anne residential style with tall corbelled-brick chimneys and a turned-wood front porch. The house was larger than the president's residence, which annoyed some members of the

board of trustees who hoped that "the growth of trees in front … would hide this fault."

The school had been without a proper gymnasium since 1874, even using the second story of Newcomb Hall as a recreation space, until the board authorized a new gym in 1890. Neilson's design was a very utilitarian two-story hip-roofed structure with exposed timber framing and a projecting two-story pediment at the entrance (figs. 129, 130). But during construction, the entrance was moved to the side end of the building and the overall size of the gymnasium was reduced. All of Neilson's buildings are extant with the exception of the gym, which burned down in 1913.[11]

In 1888, Neilson was called on to provide a design for the remodeling of the Baltimore Exchange and Custom House complex on Exchange Place, Latrobe's original building that Niernsee & Neilson had added to in the 1850s. The building had been used as a post office and courthouse since that time. An illustration of the design was shown in the *Baltimore American* and showed a massive tower atop the building (fig. 131). The alteration was never built.[12]

Fifteen years after John R. Niernsee abandoned the Johns Hopkins Hospital commission for the South Carolina State House, the old project in Columbia beckoned him again. In 1883, Governor Hugh S. Thompson summoned Niernsee to prepare a cost estimate to complete the statehouse. He was paid $600 for the estimate, which stated that the building could be finished for $738,475 without the tower; an additional $163,454 could be deducted if the projection of

THE FINAL YEARS

FIG. 124. Ellis Island Immigrant Station, New York. From *Harper's Weekly*, October 24, 1891

FIG. 125. *(top)* Washington and Lee University, Lexington, Virginia, Newcomb Hall (left), chapel (right), ca. 1884. Special Collections, Leyburn Library, Washington and Lee University Archives, Lexington, Virginia

FIG. 126. *(center)* Washington and Lee University, Newcomb Hall, left, ca. 1880s. Special Collections, Leyburn Library, Washington and Lee University Archives, Lexington, Virginia

FIG. 127. *(bottom)* Washington and Lee University, Newcomb Hall, J. C. Neilson, 1882. Special Collections, Leyburn Library, Washington and Lee University Archives, Lexington, Virginia

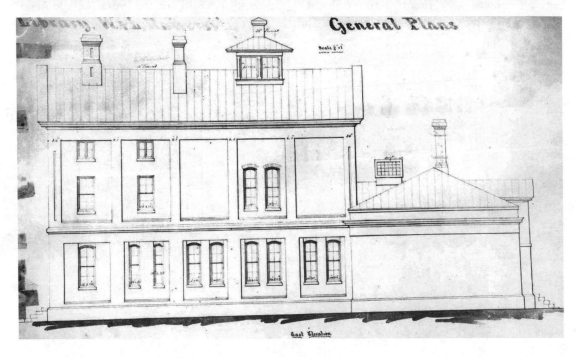

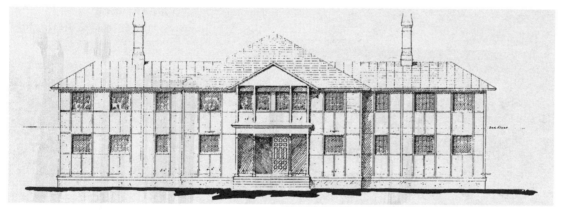

the portico was reduced and the steps leading
up to it were eliminated (the staircases provided access from the ground level). The original
plans had been destroyed during the war, and
Niernsee advised the legislature that since he
could not construct the building from memory,
he needed six months to prepare a set of plans.
He also urged that convict labor not be used on
the project.[13]

Over the years of inactivity, the weather had
battered the building and eroded the subsoil
around the foundation. In 1885, Niernsee was
again officially appointed architect, and he left
Baltimore to open an office in Columbia. With

the help of Gustavus Theodore Berg, a German émigré architect, he prepared new drawings only for the completion of the entablature and cornice, which were advertised for bid in May 1885 (Bryan, 93).

Niernsee, seventy-one years old, had been in ill health for a long time. Old age had finally caught up with him. In addition to his health problems, he had been injured in a train acci-

dent in 1883. While boarding a train at Relay, Md. he had been thrown onto the platform, striking his head on the ground. He spent months at home recuperating. Niernsee was in poor health in the spring of 1885, when he returned to Columbia. In the last week of May, he suffered from an attack of inflammation of the stomach (Bryan, 92).

John Rudolph Niernsee died on June 7, 1885. He left a wife and six children. His funeral took place at St. Peter's Catholic Church in Columbia. State officials, including the governor and comptroller of South Carolina, served as pallbearers.

Obituaries universally hailed Niernsee and his accomplishments. South Carolinians especially appreciated the old Confederate Major's efforts to continue building the statehouse during the upheaval of the Civil War. In the end, though, the finest accolade came from Niernsee's colleagues. *American Architect and Building News* called him "one of the oldest and most respected architects in the United States" and cited his major works on the first page of its July 4, 1885, edition. The article ended with a tribute: "In private life, Mr. Niernsee was one of the most amiable and honorable of men, devoted to his profession and zealous for the interests of its members. He was one of the earliest

FIG. 131. *(top)* Exchange and Custom House, Baltimore, 1888, proposed improvements

FIG. 132. *(bottom)* State House, Columbia, South Carolina, 1960. Jack E. Boucher, Historic American Buildings Survey, Library of Congress

THE BALTIMORE CUSTOM-HOUSE.

The Design of Mr. J. Crawford Neilson for a Vast Improvement.

members of the American Institute of Architects and did much to gain for it the reputation and authority of which his successors now enjoy the benefit"[14]

With no drawings to complete the statehouse, the commissioners turned to Neilson, who was hired in July 1885 at a salary of $2,500 and did not have to live in Columbia. An on-site assistant was hired to oversee the project. But being a nonresident architect would prove to be Neilson's undoing. Neilson was pitched headlong into the same kind of bickering that plagued his old partner's introduction to the job (Bryan, 94).

Since Niernsee's original plan was thirty years old, it had some deficiencies—no interior bathrooms and too few offices. Neilson proposed an alternative plan to increase the number of offices, including using the basement. He also offered an alternative to the exterior design; the tower would be replaced with two more stories, thus creating additional space. The legislature did not act on his recommendations, and Neilson largely became a construction administrator, completing the walls and Niernsee's roof (Bryan, 95).

Neilson faced insurmountable problems in this task. Convict labor, which he opposed on the grounds that it was unskilled, was used for the construction. Because much of the building material—for example, the steel frame of the

NIERNSEE
AND NEILSON

roof—could not be produced locally, Neilson had to seek out-of-state vendors, which prompted charges that he was treating "home enterprise" unfairly. Politicians brought pressure on Neilson and the commissioners to award bids to local firms even though they were not the low bidders. Then an earthquake in 1886 called the building's structural integrity into question. With great difficulty, Neilson convinced the authorities that the building was sound (Bryan, 96-99).

Work progressed on the interior until a disagreement over paint colors arose. The South Carolinians favored a more subdued scheme instead of the Victorian polychromed interior Neilson had already completed. This imbroglio, coupled with the fact that he was not on site to deal with day-to-day problems, precipitated his dismissal. In 1887, the legislature passed a residency requirement, which meant Neilson could no longer serve as statehouse architect (Bryan, 100-101).

Frank Niernsee applied for the position of resident statehouse architect in partnership with Edwin I. White, of Charleston, which he won in October of 1888. Niernsee then dissolved the partnership, and he alone was appointed to the position at a salary of $2,100. Niernsee's main task was to design a fireproof interior, something his father felt was an absolute necessity in a building of such importance. He removed wooden floors and replaced them with hollow terra cotta tile set between iron beams topped with two courses of brick covered by a marble floor (Bryan, 102-4).

Frank Niernsee spent considerable time designing the library, its cast iron stairs, balconies, pressed-metal ceiling, and galleries. He also devised a completely new color scheme for the interior, believing that "one color should dominate and that this dominating color should be a primary or a secondary and the other colors must be subsidiary to it." Other offices were completed, including committee rooms and the secretary of state's office. Plumbing and electrical systems were installed by Niernsee, who also built a sewer that ran down to the Congaree River (there was no public sewage system). In just two years, the interior was complete. Frank Niernsee provided the legislature with an estimate for continuing the work, but they rejected his proposal (Bryan, 101-11). The exterior of the building his father had begun in 1856 would not be completed until 1903.

Frank P. Milburn, a South Carolina architect who had designed many courthouses throughout the south, submitted plans, along with two others, and was selected to finish the project. John R. Niernsee's tower was never built, as Milburn's design called for an elaborate dome (figs. 132, 133, 134). The final construction phase was not without its share of controversy, the state suing Milburn for shoddy construction and calling in an outside expert who declared Milburn's work "a parody upon the science of architecture, an insult to the fame of John R. Niernsee, and a disgrace to the State of South Carolina" (Bryan, 121). Niernsee's piers, meant to support the tower, had not been used for the dome, which instead was supported by cantilevered steel beams. The Office of the Supervising Architect of the U.S. Treasury, however, made an examination and confirmed that the dome was safely supported. The state's suit against Milburn ended in a mistrial; angry at the way he had been treated, he left South Carolina for good in 1907 (Bryan, 120-23).

With Milburn's dome and other interior alterations, Niernsee's original design (see fig. 79) had been compromised, a sad fact given that he had devoted thirty years to the project. And the commission had come with a high price. It precipitated the dissolution of Baltimore's most successful pre–Civil War architectural firm, neither member of which was afterwards as successful as before. The statehouse project probably caused Niernsee to relinquish design control of the Johns Hopkins Hospital, with the unfortunate consequence that Billings and Cabot & Chandler would always be credited with the final design.

Frank Niernsee never returned to Baltimore. He established a practice in South Carolina while working on the statehouse. From 1893 to 1896, he formed a partnership with A. Gamewell LaMotte, designing many residences, schools, the York County Courthouse in South Carolina, and the Laden Presbyterian Church in Columbia. He died at the age of fifty in 1899.

Neilson lived until 1900, dying at the age of eighty-four at his home in Harford County, where he is buried, with his wife, in her family cemetery at Priestford. His last major commission was the ill-fated Ellis Island immigration station of 1891, quite an important project for a seventy-four-year-old architect. He spent the last ten years of his life at Priestford, content-

edly designing new renovations and additions to his family estate.[15]

The two men who created the first modern professional architectural practice in Baltimore were gone. Younger men, some of them trained by Niernsee & Neilson, took their places as the preeminent architects in the post-Civil War decades. Instead of regarding John Rudolph Niernsee and James Crawford Neilson as elderly anachronisms, these men always understood the great debt they owed to the partners who were primarily responsible for establishing the architectural profession in their city. To the end of their careers, Niernsee and Neilson's work, in partnership and individually, was well respected. Both men adapted to the changes in architectural styles that occurred from the 1850s to the 1890s and produced outstanding work. Niernsee and Neilson were transitional architects, instrumental in the evolution of the profession from the early days of Benjamin Henry Latrobe, Robert Mills, and Maximilian Godefroy to the formation of the American Institute of Architects and its attempt to regularize the practice of architecture and establish it as a true profession.

On February 7, 1904, a fire began in the Baltimore warehouse of J. E. Hurst & Company, on the corner of Liberty and German (now Redwood) Streets. The building, which stored highly flammable goods, was in the center of the city's retail district. With the help of a high wind blowing from the southwest, the fire quickly spread in a northeasterly direction engulfing everything in its 140-acre path, including most of Niernsee & Neilson's downtown buildings. Their commercial work vanished (fig. 135) with the single exception of the Chamber of Commerce building, which survived the Baltimore Fire of 1904 and was rebuilt. The fire substantially diminished the architectural heritage of Niernsee & Neilson. Their original designs for Camden Station, Johns Hopkins Hospital, and the South Carolina State House were all vastly altered by others. Nevertheless, their churches and almost all of their imposing residential designs in Mount Vernon survive largely intact. Country houses like Clifton and Crimea also stand in their original state. Green Mount Cemetery Mortuary Chapel, maybe their greatest creation, is unaltered and now undergoing restoration.

The two young B&O Railroad engineers who met on a tour of the line in December 1839 had no idea what they would achieve together. John Rudolph Niernsee and James Crawford Neilson felt fortunate to be making three dollars per day working on what was then America's greatest engineering effort and could not have imagined the effect they would have on Baltimore's architecture or on the development of the architectural profession. The city's architectural legacy is richer as a result of their designs and their training of Baltimore's young architects. Niernsee & Neilson showed pre–Civil War Baltimore that the architect was not the same as a carpenter-builder or a gentleman-architect, but a professional with a unique combination of artistic talent and technical skill.

APPENDIX

Building List

Note: Unless noted, building is extant. Date indicates year completed or opened for use. Current street numbers are used.

Period I: Before 1848

JOHN R. NIERNSEE

Baltimore & Ohio Railroad Engine House, Frederick, MD
  1842. Demolished
Baltimore & Ohio Railroad Freight House, Second and B Sts., NW, Washington, DC
  1842. Demolished
Benjamin H. Latrobe Jr. Houses, 606 and 608 S. Washington Place, Baltimore
  1846. Demolished

Period II: 1848–1856

NIERNSEE & NEILSON

Town Houses

Edmund Didier House, 16 W. Mount Vernon Place, Baltimore
  1848, remodeled by Charles Carson, 1888, and Joseph Evans Sperry, 1896
John H. Duvall / Walters House, 5 W. Mount Vernon Place, Baltimore
  1848
George Tiffany House, 12 W. Mount Vernon Place, Baltimore
  1848
John S. Gittings House, NE corner of St. Paul and Monument Sts., Baltimore
  1849. Demolished

Thomas Swann House Addition and alterations, 200 block of W. Franklin St., Baltimore
  1850. Demolished
Robert Campbell House, 15 W. Mount Vernon Place, Baltimore
  1850
John S. Gittings Speculative Houses, 104–112 E. Madison St., Baltimore
  1851
John H. B. Latrobe House, 901 N. Charles St., Baltimore
  1851. Demolished
Decatur Miller House, 700 Cathedral St., Baltimore
  1851
John Hanson Thomas / Jencks / Hackerman House, 1 W. Mount Vernon Place, Baltimore
  1851
James Carroll Speculative Houses, SW corner of Monument and Howard Sts., Baltimore
  1852
John R. Niernsee Speculative Houses, 404–408 Courtland St., Baltimore
  1853. Demolished
William E. Mayhew House, 12 E. Mount Vernon Place, Baltimore
  1855
A. H. Schumacher / Asbury House, 10 E. Mount Vernon Place, Baltimore
  1855

Country Houses

Elmington—J. Prosser Tabb House, Gloucester County, VA
  1848

Fairy Knowe—John H. B. Latrobe House, Elkridge, MD
  1851. Demolished
Alexandroffsky—Thomas DeKay Winans House, 30 Hollins St., Baltimore
  1852. Demolished 1926
Clifton—Johns Hopkins Country House, Harford Rd. (Clifton Park), Baltimore
  1852
Stoneleigh—Robert P. Brown House, York Rd., Towson, MD
  1852. Demolished 1956
Frederick Harrison House (Anneslie), Dunkirk Rd., Towson, MD
  Between 1848 and 1856
Woodburne, Baltimore County, MD
  1856
Crimea (Orianda)—Thomas DeKay Winans House, Windsor Mill Rd. (Leakin Park), Baltimore
  1857

Churches and Cemetery Structures

St. Charles Borromeo Roman Catholic Church, Church Lane, Pikesville, MD
  1849. Demolished
Har Sinai Verein Synagogue, 148–150 High St., Baltimore
  1849, altered 1856. Demolished
Judge Purviance Burial Vault, Green Mount Cemetery, Baltimore
  1849
St. Mark's Church (Protestant Episcopal), W. Lombard and Parkin Sts., Baltimore
  1850. Demolished
St. Luke's Church (Protestant Episcopal), Carey and Lexington Sts., Baltimore
Nave, aisles, and, tower base
  1851
Spesutia Church. (Protestant Episcopal), St. George's Parish, Perryman, Harford County, MD
  1851
St. Mary's Church (Protestant Episcopal), Emmorton, Harford County, MD
  1851
Grace Church (now Grace and St. Peter's Episcopal Church), Monument St. and Park Ave., Baltimore
  1852
Second Presbyterian Church, Baltimore and Lloyd Sts., Baltimore
  1852. Demolished
St. Michael's Roman Catholic Church, Pratt

and Regester Sts., Baltimore
  1852. Demolished
Mount Calvary Church (Protestant Episcopal) North addition to nave, N. Eutaw St. and Madison Ave., Baltimore
  1853
Emmanuel Church (Protestant Episcopal), Cathedral and Read Sts., Baltimore
  1853, altered 1914 and 1919
First Constitutional Presbyterian Church, Green and German (now Redwood) Sts., Baltimore
  1854. Demolished
Evangelical Lutheran Church, East Church St., Frederick, MD
  1854
Central Presbyterian Church, SW corner of Saratoga and Liberty Sts., Baltimore
  1855. Destroyed in Clay St. fire, 1877
Martin's Brandon Church (Protestant Episcopal), Burrowsville, Prince George County, VA
  1855
St. John the Evangelist Roman Catholic Church, SE corner of Eager and Valley Sts., Baltimore
  1856
Christ Church (Protestant Episcopal) Church and McMarine Sts., Elizabeth City, NC
  1857
Green Mount Mortuary Chapel, Green Mount Cemetery, Baltimore
  1857
St. Paul's Church (Protestant Episcopal), 102 Union St., Petersburg, VA
  1857

Railroad Stations

Calvert Station—Baltimore & Susquehanna Railroad, Calvert and Little Franklin Sts., Baltimore
  1850. Demolished 1948
Frederick Station—Baltimore & Ohio Railroad, All Saints and S. Market Sts., Frederick, MD
  1852
Washington Depot—Baltimore & Ohio Railroad, New Jersey Ave. and C St., NW, Washington, DC
  1852. Demolished 1907
Camden Station—Baltimore & Ohio Railroad, original design, Howard and Camden Sts., Baltimore
  ca.1852
Grafton Hotel and Station—Baltimore & Ohio Railroad, Grafton, WV
  1853. Demolished

Wheeling Station—Baltimore & Ohio Railroad, Wheeling, WV
  1853. Demolished

Public and Commercial Buildings

Hamilton Easter & Company Store, 13 E.
Baltimore St., Baltimore
  1848. Destroyed by fire in 1904
James Williams Stores, Gay St., Baltimore
  1848. Destroyed by fire in 1904
Martin Lewis & Company Store, 5 W. Baltimore St., Baltimore
  1848. Destroyed by fire in 1904
Mexican War Monument Obelisk, Calvert and
Saratoga Sts., Baltimore
  1849. Demolished
Patapsco Fire Company Building, St. Paul St.
near Hamilton St, Baltimore
  1849. Drastically remodeled beyond
  recognition
Baltimore Exchange and Custom House
Additions, Lombard, Commerce, and Gay Sts.,
Baltimore
  1852. Demolished 1907
Howard House Hotel Addition, Howard and
Baltimore Sts., Baltimore
  1852. Demolished
Old Main Building—Spring Grove State
Lunatic Asylum, Catonsville, MD
  1852. Demolished ca.1950
William Gail Tobacco Warehouse, Barre St.,
between Light and Charles Sts., Baltimore
  1853. Demolished
Charles D. Deford & Company Store, Gay St.,
Baltimore
  1854. Demolished
Gilmor House Hotel, Court House Square,
Baltimore
  1855. Demolished 1893
Spring Garden Gasworks Valve House and
buildings—Gaslight Company of Baltimore,
Baltimore
  1855. Only Valve House is standing.
Baltimore Grocers Exchange, Exchange Place,
Baltimore
  1856. Destroyed by fire in 1904

Period III: 1856-1865

JOHN R. NIERNSEE

South Carolina State House, Columbia, SC
  1856–85

The Most Holy Trinity Roman Catholic
Church, Augusta, GA
  1857–63. Spire completed 1894
St. Mary's Roman Catholic Church, Edgefield, SC
  1858

J. CRAWFORD NEILSON

Churches

St. James Church (Protestant Episcopal), Trap,
Harford County, MD
  1855. Destroyed by fire in 1869
Mt. Zion Episcopal Church, Baltimore and
Gilmor Sts., Baltimore
  1859. Demolished
Starr Church (Methodist), Poppleton and
Lemmon Sts., Baltimore
  1864. Demolished
Trinity Independent Methodist Episcopal
Church South, Preston and Madison Sts.,
Baltimore
  1864. Demolished

Houses

Dr. John Marshall Snyder House, 3051 N St.,
NW, Washington, DC
  1858
Washington A. Danskin House Addition,
410 W. Fayette St., Baltimore
  1864

Public and Commercial Buildings

Bank of Baltimore, St. Paul and Baltimore Sts.,
Baltimore
  1856. Destroyed by fire in 1904
Hodges Brothers Store and J.S. Inloe Store,
S. Hanover St., Baltimore
  1856. Destroyed by fire in 1904
Howell Brothers—Cushing & Bailey Store,
32–34 W. Baltimore St., Baltimore
  1856. Destroyed by fire in 1904
Peabody Institute design competition entry,
E. Mount Vernon Place, Baltimore
  1857
Union Protestant Infirmary, Mosher and
Division Sts., Baltimore
  1857. Demolished
Harford County Courthouse, Bel Air, MD
  1858. Drastically altered
Baltimore County Courthouse Repairs,
Washington St., Towson, MD
  1859

Maryland Club Additions, Franklin and Cathedral Sts., Baltimore
   1859. Demolished
Merchants' Fruit Exchange, Bowley's Wharf, Baltimore
   1859. Demolished
American Colonization Society Building, Pennsylvania Ave. and 4th St. NW, Washington DC
   1860. Demolished 1930
Baltimore Corn Exchange Company Building, 209–211 South and Woods Sts., Baltimore
   1860. Destroyed by fire in 1904
New Mount Hope Asylum (Seton Institute), Patterson Ave., Baltimore
   1860
Tracy & Son Building, Baltimore and Calvert Sts., Baltimore
   1861. Demolished
Maryland Institution for the Instruction of the Blind, North Ave. and Calvert St., Baltimore
   1868. Demolished in 1905

Period IV: 1865–1874

JOHN R. NIERNSEE AND
J. CRAWFORD NEILSON

Town Houses

Louis McLane Jr. House, NE corner of Charles and Chase Sts., Baltimore
   1868. Demolished 1925
House, Decker St., Baltimore
   1869
House, Eutaw Place and Mosher St., Baltimore
   1869
Houses on Madison Ave., Baltimore
   1869. Demolished
William F. Burns House, Madison St., Baltimore
   1870. Demolished
Henry James House, SE corner of Charles and Chase Sts., Baltimore
   1870. Demolished 1903
James L. McLane Speculative Houses, Park Ave., Baltimore
   Date uncertain
Hugh Sisson Speculative Houses, 1123–1127 St. Paul St., Baltimore
   1873

Country Houses

John E. Owens House (Aigburth Vale), Towson, MD
   1868

Music Hall at Alexandroffsky, Hollins and Baltimore Sts., Baltimore
   1871. Demolished 1925

Churches

Church of Our Saviour (Protestant Episcopal), SW corner of Broadway and McElderry Sts., Baltimore
   1870. Demolished
Churchville Presbyterian Church, Churchville, MD. Tower, porches, and apse
   1870
St. John's Church (Protestant Episcopal), Beltsville, MD
   Ca. 1870s

Public and Commercial Buildings

High Service Pumping Station, NE corner of Charles and Chase Sts., Baltimore
   1866. Demolished
Atlantic Fire & Marine Insurance Company, South St., Baltimore
   1867. Destroyed by fire in 1904
Dr. Ferdinand Edme Chatard Store, SW corner of Charles and Lexington Sts., Baltimore
   1867. Demolished
Shockhoe Warehouse, Richmond Tobacco Exchange, 13th St. and Shockhoe Wharf, Richmond, VA
   1867. Demolished
National Fire Insurance Company Building, NW corner of Holliday and Second Sts., Baltimore
   1868. Destroyed by fire in 1904
Clark Y. Davidson Store Building, North Liberty St., Baltimore
   1869. Destroyed by fire in 1904
Franklin Bank, South and German Sts., Baltimore
   1869. Destroyed by fire in 1904
Cheston Galloway Shipping Agency, Sharp St., Baltimore
   1869. Destroyed by fire in 1904
Issac Greenbaum & Sons Warehouse, SE of Hanover St. near German St., Baltimore
   1869. Destroyed by fire in 1904
Francis T. King Warehouses, Sharp St., Baltimore
   1869. Destroyed by fire in 1904
John B. Morris Building, South St., Baltimore
   1869. Demolished
Office and Warehouse Building, west side of N. Charles St., between Lexington and Saratoga Sts., Baltimore
   1869. Demolished

Union Bank. Adams Block, Charles and
Fayette Sts., Baltimore
 1869. Destroyed by fire in 1904
Garrett Bridge, Druid Hill Park, Baltimore
 1870
Citizens National Bank, Hanover and Pratt
Sts., Baltimore
 1871. Destroyed by fire in 1904
Eight Warehouses, Light and Pratt Sts.,
Baltimore
 1871. Destroyed by fire in 1904
Maryland Insurance Company Building, South
St., Baltimore
 1871. Destroyed by fire in 1904
Morse Building, Fayette St. opposite City Hall,
Baltimore
 1871. Destroyed by fire in 1904
Office Building, Pratt and Light Sts., Balti-
more
 1871. Destroyed by fire in 1904
Rialto Building, Water and Holiday Sts.,
Baltimore
 1871. Destroyed by fire in 1904
Carrollton Hotel, Baltimore, Light, and Ger-
man Sts., Baltimore
 1872. Destroyed by fire in 1904
Academy of Music, N. Howard St., between
Centre and Franklin Sts., Baltimore
 1873. Demolished
New High Service Reservoir Pump House,
Druid Hill Park, Baltimore
 1873
Notre Dame Academy—Gibbons Hall,
Homeland Ave. and Charles St., Baltimore
 1873
Warner Building, W. Baltimore St., Baltimore
 1873
YMCA Central Building, NW corner of
Charles and Saratoga Sts., Baltimore
 1875. Altered

Period V: 1874–1886

JOHN R. NIERNSEE & SON

Houses

Gail Mansion, Eutaw Place at Ducatel St.,
Baltimore
 1875. Demolished

Churches

Chapel of the Convent of Valle Crucis, Columbia, SC. Original design
 1882

Public and Commercial Buildings

Maryland Jockey Club Clubhouse, Pimlico
Racetrack, Baltimore
 1874. Destroyed by fire in 1966
Baltimore & Ohio Railroad Central Building,
Baltimore and Calvert Sts., Baltimore
 1875. Consultant to E. Francis Baldwin.
Destroyed by fire in 1904
Johns Hopkins Colored Orphan Asylum
Design, Remington Ave., Baltimore
 1875. Never built
Spiller Building, W. Baltimore St., between
Charles and Hanover Sts., Baltimore
 1877. Destroyed by fire in 1904
Johns Hopkins Hospital, Broadway, between E.
Monument and Jefferson Sts., Baltimore
 1877–89. Original design executed by
 Cabot & Chandler
Peabody Institute Library Addition (Consul-
tant), Mount Vernon Place, Baltimore
 1878
Opera House, Lynchburg, VA
 1879. Demolished
Chamber of Commerce Building, Holiday and
Water Sts., Baltimore
 1882. Gutted by fire in 1904 and
 reconstructed
Merchants Club, German St., between Calvert
and South Sts., Baltimore
 1882. Destroyed by fire in 1904

J. CRAWFORD NEILSON

Houses

John H. B. Latrobe Residence, NE corner of
Charles and Read Sts., Baltimore
 1877. Demolished
Kenton, Thomas King Residence (formerly
Lansdowne, ca.1770), Alterations and
additions, Darlington, Harford County, MD
 1879
Neilson/Osman C. Latrobe House, 1205 St.
Paul St., Baltimore
 1881
Lansdowne (formerly Kenton), Alterations and
additions, Darlington, Harford County, MD
 1886
Priestford Additions and Alterations (Neilson
family residence), Priestford, Harford County,
MD
 1875–1900

Churches

St. James Church (Protestant Episcopal), Trap, Harford County, MD
 1875. Replaced Neilson's 1855 church, which was destroyed by fire
Darlington Orthodox Friends Meeting House, Darlington, MD
 1877. Drastically altered
Lexington Baptist Church, Lexington, VA
 1879
Emmanuel Episcopal Church Alterations and Additions, Chestertown, MD
 1880
St. Thomas' Episcopal Church, White Sulphur Springs, WV
 1884. Demolished ca. 1930
Grace Church Parish House, Monument St. and Park Ave. Baltimore
 1889. Demolished

Public and Commercial Buildings

Academy of Music, Baltimore Alterations
 1874. Demolished
Hillen Street Station (Western Maryland Railroad), Hillen St., between High and Front Sts., Baltimore
 1876. Demolished 1948
Male and Female Grammar School No. 12, Ridgely St., Baltimore
 1876
Robinson Hall (now Brooks Museum), Alterations, Washington and Lee University, Lexington, VA
 1877
Queen Anne's County Courthouse, Centreville, MD. Alterations
 1877

Tobacco Exchange, Shockoe Slip, Richmond, VA
 1877, Demolished 1995
Newcomb Hall, Washington and Lee University, Lexington, VA
 1882. Altered 1907
Robert E. Lee Memorial Chapel Mausoleum, Washington and Lee University, Lexington, VA
 1883
Kent County Jail, Chestertown, MD
 1884. Demolished
Professor's Residence, Letcher Ave., Washington and Lee University, Lexington, VA
 1887
South Carolina State House Senate and House Chambers, Columbia, SC
 1887
Albion Hotel Alterations, Cathedral and Read Sts., Baltimore
 1888
Baltimore Exchange and Custom House, Proposed additions Baltimore
 1888
Gymnasium, Washington and Lee University, Lexington, VA
 1890. Destroyed by fire 1913
Western State Hospital for the Insane, SE corner of Rte. 11 and 250, Staunton, VA
 1890
United States Immigration Station, Ellis Island, New York, NY
 1891. Destroyed by fire in 1897

Notes

Introduction

1. Kathryn Elizabeth Holliday, "Leopold Eidlitz and the Architecture of Nineteenth-Century America," Ph.D. diss., University of Texas, 2003.

2. The history of German architectural emigration remains to be written in full. An important building block is Kathleen Curran, *The Romanesque Revival: Religion, Politics, and Transnational Exchange* (University Park: Pennsylvania State University Press, 2003). Also see Michael J. Lewis, "Der Rundbogenstil und die Karlsruhe-Philadelphia Achse," in *Dauer und Wechsel: Festschrift für Harold Hammer-Schenk* (Berlin: Lukas Verlag, 2004), 128–38. For an overview of German architectural events in this period, see Eva Börsch-Supan, *Berliner Baukunst nach Schinkel, 1840–1870* (Munich: Prestel, 1977).

3. Heinrich Hübsch, *In What Style Should We Build?*, trans. Wolfgang Herrmann (Santa Monica, CA: Getty Center for the History of Art and the Humanities, 1992), 99.

4. See Carroll L. V. Meeks, *The Railroad Station: An Architectural History* (New Haven, CT: Yale University Press, 1956). For Tefft, see the exhibition catalogue *Thomas Alexander Tefft: American Architecture in Transition* (Providence, RI: Department of Art, Brown University, 1988). For Collins and Autenrieth, see *Drawing Toward Building: Philadelphia Architectural Graphics*, ed. J. F. O'Gorman (Philadelphia: University of Pennsylvania, 1986), 114–16.

5. See Michael J. Lewis, "Wilhelm Lorenz: Die Hannoversche Schule in Amerika," *Günther Kokkelink Festschrift*, ed. Stefan Amt (Hanover: Institut für Bau- und Kunstgeschichte, 1999), 143–150.

6. Carlos P. Avery, *E. Francis Baldwin: The B&O, Baltimore, and Beyond* (Baltimore: Baltimore Architecture Foundation, 2003).

ONE: Coming to America and the B&O Years

1. Entry for August 31, 1839, Diary of John R. Niernsee, 1836–1841, trans. E. Albrecht, MS 2457. Maryland Historical Society, Baltimore. Hereafter cited in the text, with or without a date.

2. Frances Trollope, *Domestic Manners of the Americans*, 5th ed. (London: G. Routledge, 1839).

3. Mary N. Woods, *From Craft to Profession: The Practice of Architecture in Nineteenth-Century America* (Berkeley: University of California Press, 1999), 9–17.

4. Franz Anton Ritter von Gerstner, *Early American Railroads*, ed. Frederick C. Gamst (Stanford, CA: Stanford University Press, 1999).

5. Diary of John R. Niernsee, July 1, 1838.

6. Ibid.

7. James D. Dilts, *The Great Road: The Building of the Baltimore & Ohio, the Nation's First Railroad, 1828–1853* (Stanford, CA: Stanford University Press, 1993), 63–64.

8. Diary of John R. Niernsee, February 24, March 2, May 8, and June 28, 1839.

9. Ibid., March 2, 1839.

10. Benjamin H. Latrobe Jr. to John R. Niernsee, August 15, 1839. Baltimore & Ohio Railroad Museum, Baltimore.

11. Dilts, *The Great Road*, 160.

12. John Dorsey and James D. Dilts, *A Guide to Baltimore Architecture*, 3rd ed. (Centreville, MD: Tidewater Publishers, 1997), 405.

13. Diary of John R. Niernsee, December 5, 1839.

14. Ibid., October 25, 1841.

15. Gary Lawson Browne, *Baltimore in the Nation, 1789–1861* (Chapel Hill: University of North Carolina Press, 1980), 145.

16. Dorsey and Dilts, *Guide to Baltimore Architecture*, 410.

17. Mary Ellen Hayward and Frank R. Shivers Jr., eds. *The Architecture of Baltimore: An Illustrated History* (Baltimore: Johns Hopkins University Press, 2004), 161–62; Sarah E. Wermiel, *An Unusual Application of Wire Cables from the 1850s: Benjamin Severson's Wire-tied Iron Girders*, OIPEEC (Organisation Internationale pour l'Etude de l'Endurance des Cables) Round Table Conference, August 2001, 219–20.

18. John R. Niernsee, "Cast Iron Truss Roofs in America," *Allgemeine Bauzeitung.* Trans. 1842.

19. Ibid.

20. Ibid.; Woods, *From Craft to Profession*, 158.

21. Edna A. Kanely, "A List of Persons with their Pay in the Service of the Baltimore and Ohio Railroad Company (April 1, 1842)," *Baltimore and Ohio Railroad Employees*, from original manuscript in B&O Railroad Museum.

TWO: The First Partnership and Town Houses in Mount Vernon

1. James D. Dilts, *The Great Road: The Building of the Baltimore & Ohio, The Nation's First Railroad, 1828–1853* (Stanford, CA: Stanford University Press, 1993), 398, 342.

2. *Baltimore Sun*, April 17, 1846

3. Ibid.

4. Mary Ellen Hayward and Frank R. Shivers Jr., eds., *The Architecture of Baltimore: An Illustrated History* (Baltimore: Johns Hopkins University Press, 2004), 124.

5. *Baltimore Sun*, April 17, 1846.

6. Ibid., November 9, 1848.

7. Ibid.

8. Ibid., December 14, 1848, and January 24, 1851.

9. Mills Lane, *The Architecture of the Old South: Maryland* (New York: Abbeville Press, 1991), 223–28.

10. *Baltimore Sun*, December 13, 1849.

11. Ibid., October 18, 1850.

12. Thomas Swann Collection, MS 1826, Maryland Historical Society.

13. Gary Lawson Browne, *Baltimore in the Nation, 1789–1861* (Chapel Hill: University of North Carolina Press, 1980), 143–45.

14. Malcolm Heard, *French Quarter Manual: An Architectural Guide to New Orleans' Vieux Carré* (New Orleans: Tulane School of Architecture, 1997), 10, 43. Much of the cast iron used in New Orleans for its famous balconies came from Baltimore foundries.

15. Decatur Miller Account Book 1849, MS 1627, Maryland Historical Society.

16. Thomas Swann Collection, MS 1826.

17. *Baltimore Sun*, February 10, 1853.

18. John Dorsey and James D. Dilts, *A Guide to Baltimore Architecture*, 3rd ed. (Centreville, MD: Tidewater Publishers, 1997); *Baltimore Sun*, January 24, 1855.

19. Dorsey and Dilts, *Guide to Baltimore Architecture*, 125.

20. *Baltimore News*, April 26, 1850.

21. *Baltimore Sun*, January 22, 1852.

THREE: : Country Houses and Estates

1. The attribution to Niernsee is by the late James Foster, former director of the Maryland Historical Society; Emmie Ferguson Farrar, *Old Virginia Houses* (New York: Hastings House, 1955).

2. Alexandra Lee Levin, "A Russian Railroad made the Winans Family Rich," *Baltimore Sun Magazine*, October 10, 1976; *Woodlawn Franklintown and Hebbville: Three Communities— Two Centuries* (Baltimore: Woodlawn Recreation and Parks Council, 1977).

3. Baltimore Equitable Society Records, book 8, 66–69, MS 3020, Maryland Historical Society. The Sanborn Map of 1880 shows the footprint of the original building incorporated into Niernsee & Neilson's design. An 1813 drawing by Thomas Middleton of St. Mary's Seminary shows the school facing Baltimore Street.

4. The wall was not constructed to hide nude sculpture, as was popularly believed.

5. Ferdinand C. Latrobe, *Iron Men and Their Dogs* (Baltimore, 1941), 12–14.

6. Mary Ellen Hayward and Frank R. Shivers Jr., eds., *The Architecture of Baltimore: An Illustrated History* (Baltimore: Johns Hopkins University Press, 2004), 130–31; John C. Gobright, *The Monumental City, or Baltimore Guide Book* (Baltimore, 1857).

7. Pierre Cabanne, *Whistler* (New York: Crown Publishers, 1985), 92.

8. Winans Papers, MS 916, Maryland Historical Society.

9. *Baltimore Sun*, November 2, 1925.

10. Ibid., February 5, 1852.

11. Ibid.; Hayward and Shivers, *Architecture of Baltimore*, 131–32.

12. *Baltimore Sun*, September 11, 1949, and November 1, 1953.

13. Mills Lane, *The Architecture of the Old South: Maryland* (New York: Abbeville Press, 1991), 226.

14. Ibid., 228; Herman D. Aldrich to William Wyman, June 19, and December 16, 1851; G. H. Cary to Wyman, January 1, 1852, Francis Wilbur to Wyman, May 5, 1852, Wyman Collection, Maryland Historical Society.

FOUR: Churches

1. *Baltimore Sun*, November 3, 1854. The article described the building of Niernsee & Neilson's Central Presbyterian Church at Liberty and Saratoga Streets in Baltimore.

2. Michael S. Franch, "The Congregational Community in the Changing City, 1840–1870," *Maryland Historical Magazine* 71, no.3 (1976): 367–80.

3. Ibid.

4. Phoebe B. Stanton, *The Gothic Revival and American Church Architecture: An Episode in Taste, 1840–1856* (Baltimore: Johns Hopkins Press, 1968).

5. Mills Lane, *The Architecture of the Old South: Maryland* (New York: Abbeville Press, 1991), 166–92.

6. *U.S. Catholic Magazine*, February 3, 1849.

7. *Baltimore Sun*, September 8, 1849.

8. Ibid., August 5, 1850.

9. *Baltimore American*, December 4, 1852.

10. The late Phoebe Stanton, in *The Gothic Revival and American Church Architecture*, 284–86, insisted that Niernsee and Neilson had plagiarized Notman's drawings. *Baltimore Sun*, December 3, 1852; *Republican* (Towson, MD), December 11, 1852.

11. Martin E. Weaver, *Conserving Buildings: A Guide to Techniques and Materials* (New York: John Wiley & Sons, 1993), 62–63.

12. *Baltimore Sun*, January 3, 1852.

13. Michael S. Franch, "Stable and Handsome Public Edifices," Ph.D. diss., University of Maryland, 1984, 194–222; *Baltimore Sun*, January 12, 1852.

14. Stanton, *Gothic Revival*, 298–301.

15. Ibid.

16. Ibid., 300–301.

17. Ibid.; *Baltimore Sun*, August 31, 1853.

18. Christ Church would eventually move into a new building, designed by Baldwin & Price and completed in 1872, which still stands in Mount Vernon at the corner of Chase and St. Paul streets.

19. Franch, "Congregational Community in the Changing City," 367–80.

20. *Baltimore Sun*, October 19, 1854.

21. Ibid., May 3, 1854.

22. John Scharf, *A History of Western Maryland* (Baltimore: Regional Publishing Co., 1968), 156; Abdel Ross Wentz, *The Evangelical Lutheran Church of Frederick, Maryland, 1738–1938* (Frederick, MD: University Publishing Group, 1988), 225.

23. *Baltimore Sun*, April 4, 1855.

24. Ibid., June 11, 1856.

25. *Baltimore American*, December 15, 1855.

26. Christopher Weeks, *An Architectural History of Harford County, Maryland* (Baltimore: Johns Hopkins University Press, 1996), 121.

27. The name *Spesutia* comes from "Utie's Hope," the seventeenth-century land grant to Nathaniel Utie; *spes* is Latin for *hope*.

28. *The Churchman* (Hartford, CT), January 3, 1856.

29. *Citizen News* (Columbia, SC), September 5, 1985.

30. www.themostholytrinity.org/history

FIVE: Green Mount Cemetery Chapel

1. Pat Jolland, *Death in the Victorian Family* (London: Oxford University Press, 1999).

2. *Baltimore Sun*, March 26, 1851.

SIX: Railroad Stations

Early material in this chapter first appeared in Randolph W. Chalfant, "Calvert Station: Its Structure and Significance," *Maryland Historical Magazine* 74, no. 1 (1979).

1. Baltimore City Ordinance 38, May 2, 1845; Chalfant, 11–13.

2. Ibid.; *Baltimore Sun*, April 1, 1851.

3. *Baltimore American*, June 17, 1848; Chalfant, "Calvert Station," 14. Niernsee, now in practice for himself, accepted work from other railroads besides the B&O.

4. Ibid., 19–20.

5. Ibid.

6. The Philadelphia, Wilmington & Baltimore's President Street Station, designed by Isaac Ridgeway Trimble, was completed that same year; *Baltimore Sun*, February 19, 1850; *Baltimore Clipper*, June 4, 1850.

7. Niernsee & Neilson to Robert S. Hollins, on probable cost of Calvert Station, Calvert

Street Station Manuscript, Maryland Historical Society; Chalfant, "Calvert Station," 16–17.

8. Chalfant, "Calvert Station," 17.

9. *Illustrated London News*, April 23, 1853.

10. *American Railroad Journal*, August 28, 1852.

11. B&O Railroad minute books, Baltimore & Ohio Railroad Museum; *Baltimore Sun*, February 4, 1853.

12. *Baltimore Sun*, May 2, 1856.

13. Ibid.

14. James D. Dilts, *The Great Road: The Building of the Baltimore & Ohio, the Nation's First Railroad, 1828–1853* (Stanford, CA: Stanford University Press, 1993), 377.

15. Ibid., 419n18.

16. The B&O Railroad Annual Report of 1851 mentions the construction of a new station at Mount Clare on a fourteen-acre site, costing $85,000, to replace an 1829 facility. The report does not mention the architect. It is assumed by many architectural and railroad historians that the new building at Poppleton and Pratt Streets was designed by Niernsee & Neilson.

SEVEN: Places of Business

1. Gary Lawson Browne, *Baltimore in the Nation, 1789–1861* (Chapel Hill: University of North Carolina Press, 1980), 139–55.

2. *Baltimore Sun*, March 1, 1848.

3. *Baltimore American*, August 25, 1848; *Baltimore Sun*, January 15, 1849.

4. *Baltimore Sun*, February 15, 1849, *Republican and Argus* (Towson, MD), January 11, 1848.

5. *Baltimore Sun*, August 10 and September 7, 1853.

6. Ibid., May 26, 1852.

7. Ibid., October 1, 1855; John C. Gobright, *The Monumental City, or Baltimore As It Is* (Baltimore, 1857), 38-40.

8. *Baltimore Sun*, September 7, 1854

9. Ibid., March 22 and 29, 1856.

10. www.springgrove.com/history.html.

EIGHT: The South Carolina State House and the Dissolution

1. John M. Bryan, *Creating the South Carolina State House* (Columbia: University of South Carolina Press, 1999), 14–17. For more detailed information on the construction of the South Carolina State House, Annual Reports of the Commissioner and Architect of the New State Capitol for the Fiscal Years 1857–1863, (Columbia: R. W. Gibbes, State Printer, 1857–63).

2. John T. Scharf, *Chronicles of Baltimore* (Baltimore: Turnbull Brothers, 1874), 525.

3. Kenneth Hafertepe, *America's Castle: The Evolution of the Smithsonian Building and Its Institution* (Washington, DC: Smithsonian Institution Press, 1984), 106–8.

4. Bryan, *Creating the South Carolina State House*, 18; hereafter cited in the text.

5. Mary N. Woods, *From Craft to Profession: The Practice of Architecture in Nineteenth-Century America* (Berkeley: University of California Press, 1999), 159.

6. *Baltimore Sun*, October 12, 1854.

7. Ibid., January 30, 1865.

8. Ibid., June 11, 1864.

9. Ibid., June 23, 1859.

10. John Dorsey and James D. Dilts, *A Guide to Baltimore Architecture*, 3rd ed. (Centreville, MD: Tidewater Publishers, 1997), 119.

11. Mary Ellen Hayward and Frank R. Shivers Jr., eds., *The Architecture of Baltimore: An Illustrated History* (Baltimore: Johns Hopkins University Press, 2004), 144; Mills Lane, *The Architecture of the Old South: Maryland* (New York: Abbeville Press, 1991), 216–21.

12. *Baltimore Sun*, June 10, 1856, and July 9, 1857.

13. Ibid.

14. Ibid., May 1, 1860; Carleton Jones, *Lost Baltimore* (Baltimore: Johns Hopkins University Press, 1993), 182–83.

15. John C. Gobright, *The Monumental City, or Baltimore As It Is* (Baltimore, 1857), 30

16. *Baltimore Sun*, January 25, 1861.

17. Ibid., August 5, 1850.

18. Ibid., February 3, 1859.

19. Ibid., August 26, 1858.

20. "Then and Now ... The Blind School on North Avenue," in ibid., July 17, 1949.

21. Marilyn M. Larew, *Bel Air: An Architectural and Cultural History, 1782–1945* (Bel Air, MD: Town of Bel Air, 1995); *Baltimore Sun*, April 14, 1858; Christopher Weeks, *An Architectural History of Harford Country*, Maryland (Baltimore: Johns Hopkins University Press, 1996), 132-33.

22. James M. Goode, *Capital Losses* (Washington, DC: Smithsonian Institution Press, 1979), 224.

NINE: The Second Partnership, 1865 to 1874

1. Sherry Olson, *Baltimore: The Building of an American City* (Baltimore: Johns Hopkins University Press, 1980).

2. Fisher-McLane Papers, MS 2403, Maryland Historical Society.

3. *Baltimore Sun*, December 24, 1873.

4. Thomas A. Bogar, "John E. Owens: The People's Comedian from Towsontown," *Maryland Historical Magazine* 7, no. 4 (1984).

5. *Baltimore Gazette*, June 6, 1870.

6. *Baltimore Sun*, November 6, 1869, and September 1, 1871.

7. Ibid., September 16, 1869.

8. Ibid., October 14, 1869.

9. Ibid., October 9, 1869; *Baltimore American*, March 9, 1871.

10. *Baltimore Sun*, December 19, 1868.

11. Ibid., July 31, 1867.

12. *Baltimore Gazette*, December 14, 1867.

13. *Baltimore Sun*, August 4, 1869.

14. Thomas F. Hale, *Richmond: A Pictorial History from the Valentine Museum and Dementi Collections* (Richmond, VA: Hale, 1974).

15. There is a good deal of information concerning the development of this hotel in the Maryland Historical Society; *Prospectus of the Fountain Hotel Company of Baltimore: With a List of Officers* (Baltimore: Innes & Co., 1869).

16. George W. Howard, *Monumental City: Its Past History and Present Resources* (Baltimore, 1873), 64.

17. Mary Ellen Hayward and Frank R. Shivers Jr., eds. *The Architecture of Baltimore: An Illustrated History* (Baltimore: Johns Hopkins University Press, 2004), 189; *Baltimore American*, July 7, 1870; *Baltimore Sun*, November 24, 1871, and November 6, 1869; *Baltimore American*, December 3, 1869.

18. *Baltimore Sun*, October 10, 1873.

19. Hayward and Shivers, *Architecture of Baltimore*, 201; *Baltimore Sun*, October 10, 1873, and December 20, 1874.

20. Hayward and Shivers, *Architecture of Baltimore*, 200; *Baltimore Sun*, June 19, 1875.

21. *Baltimore Sun*, May 31, 1873.

22. Ibid., December 9, 1873.

23. Virginia Niernsee Floyd's own handwritten account of the dissolution, in Chalfant's collection, says that the Panic of 1873, while Niernsee was away, frightened Neilson: "Well the panic got so bad Neilson must have gotten scared or panicked himself, anyway, it appears he got Uncle Rue drunk and had him sign papers, which amounted to him turning all assets of the firm to Neilson. Uncle Rue didn't even remember signing any papers at all." This is obviously a biased account by Niernsee's daughter. In all likelihood, Rudolph, with the power of attorney and a drinking problem, clashed with Neilson over the management of the firm.

24. Neilson's two sons chose careers outside of architecture and engineering.

TEN: The Johns Hopkins Hospital

1. *Baltimore Gazette*, July 1, 1875.

2. Johns Hopkins to the trustees of the Johns Hopkins Hospital, March 10, 1873, Alan Mason Chesney Medical Archives of the Johns Hopkins Medical Institutions.

3. John S. Billings, *Hospital Construction and Organization, Johns Hopkins Hospital* (New York: William Wood & Co., 1875).

4. Ibid.

5. Ibid.

6. *Baltimore American*, September 20, 1876.

7. John M. Bryan, *Creating the South Carolina State House* (Columbia: University of South Carolina Press, 1999), 90–92.

8. Francis T. King address at hospital opening, May 7, 1889; John S. Billings, M.D., *Description of the Johns Hopkins Hospital*, pamphlet (Baltimore, 1890); Alan M. Chesney, M.D., *The Johns Hopkins Hospital and the Johns Hopkins University School of Medicine*, vol. 1, *Early Years, 1867–1893* (Baltimore: Johns Hopkins Press, 1943).

9. *American Architect and Building News*, July 27, 1889.

10. The Chesney Medical Archives at the Johns Hopkins Hospital has nine volumes of construction diaries, beginning in 1879, and also the hospital trustee minutes that cover the construction of the hospital.

11. *Baltimore Sun*, February 7, 1877.

ELEVEN: The Final Years

1. *Baltimore Sun*, March 4 and October 19, 1874.

2. S. Allen Chambers Jr., *Lynchburg: An Architectural History* (Charlottesville: Sarah Winston Henry Branch of the Association for the Preservation of Virginia Antiquities by the University Press of Virginia, 1981), 223–25; *Lynchburg Virginian*, January 24, 1879.

3. *Baltimore Sun*, August 18, 1875.

4. Ibid., February 3, 1882; John T. Scharf, *Scharf's History of Baltimore City and County* (Philadelphia: L. H. Everts, 1881), 443–45.

5. *American Architect and Building News*, September 17, 1881.

6. Christopher Weeks, *An Architectural History of Harford County, Maryland* (Baltimore: Johns

Hopkins University Press, 1996), 136–37; W. Stump Forwood, "Homes on Deer Creek," *Aegis and Intelligencer* (Havre de Grace, MD), May 21, 28, 1880.

7. *Baltimore Sun*, May 2, 1881.

8. Carleton Jones, *Lost Baltimore: A Portfolio of Vanished Buildings* (Baltimore: Johns Hopkins University Press, 1993), 208–9; *Aegis and Intelligencer*, February 4, 1876.

9. *Harper's Weekly*, October 24, 1891; *King's Handbook of New York, 1892* (Boston, 1892; New York: Barnes & Noble, 2001), 53, 412, 79.

10. Royster Lyle Jr. and Pamela Hemenway Simpson, *The Architecture of Historic Lexington* (Charlottesville: Historic Lexington Foundation by the University Press of Virginia, 1977), 22, 167–69.

11. Ibid., 21–22, 169, 191.

12. *Baltimore American*, April 10, 1888.

13. *American Architect and Building News*, July 4, 1885.

14. All information and quotations regarding the completion of the South Carolina State House are from John M. Bryan, *Creating the South Carolina State House* (Columbia: University of South Carolina Press, 1999).

15. *Baltimore Sun*, December 20, 1900.

Bibliography

Archival Materials

Baltimore & Ohio Railroad Museum, Baltimore, MD
Letters
B&O Railroad minute books

Maryland Historical Society, Baltimore, MD
Baltimore Equitable Society Collection, MS 3020
Calvert Street Station Manuscript
Carroll Papers
Fisher-McLane Papers, MS 2403
Diary of John R. Niernsee, 1836–1841, MS 2457
Thomas Swann Collection, MS 1826
Winans Papers, MS 916
Wyman Collection

The Johns Hopkins Medical Institutions
Alan Mason Chesney Medical Archives

Secondary Works

Billings, John S. *Hospital Construction and Organization, Johns Hopkins Hospital.* New York: William Wood & Co., 1875.

Bowen, Ele. *Rambles in the Path of the Steam Horse.* Philadelphia, 1855.

Browne, Gary Lawson. *Baltimore in the Nation, 1789–1861.* Chapel Hill: University of North Carolina Press, 1980.

Bryan, John M. *Creating the South Carolina State House.* Columbia: University of South Carolina Press, 1999.

Cabanne, Pierre. *Whistler.* New York: Crown Publishers, 1985.

Chambers, Jr., S. Allen. *Lynchburg: An Architectural History.* Charlottesville: Sarah Winston Henry Branch of the Association for the Preservation of Virginia Antiquities by the University Press of Virginia, 1981.

Chesney, Alan M. *The Johns Hopkins Hospital and the Johns Hopkins University School of Medicine,* vol. 1, *Early Years, 1867–1893.* Baltimore: Johns Hopkins Press, 1943.

Dilts, James D. *The Great Road: The Building of the Baltimore & Ohio, the Nation's First Railroad, 1828–1853.* Stanford, CA: Stanford University Press, 1993.

Dorsey, John, and Dilts, James D. *A Guide to Baltimore Architecture.* 3rd ed. Centreville, MD: Tidewater Publishers, 1997.

Farrar, Emmie Ferguson. *Old Virginia Houses.* New York: Hastings House, 1955.

Gerstner, Franz Anton Ritter von. *Early American Railroads.* Edited by Frederick C. Gamst. Stanford, CA: Stanford University Press, 1999.

Gobright, John C. *The Monumental City, or Baltimore Guide Book.* Baltimore, 1857.

Goode, James M. *Capital Losses.* Washington, DC: Smithsonian Institution Press, 1979.

Hafertepe, Kenneth. *America's Castle: The Evolution of the Smithsonian Building and Its Institution.* Washington, DC: Smithsonian Institution Press, 1984.

Hayward, Mary Ellen, and Shivers, Frank R., Jr., eds. *The Architecture of Baltimore: An Illustrated History.* Baltimore: Johns Hopkins University Press, 2004.

Heard, Malcolm. *French Quarter Manual: An Architectural Guide to New Orleans' Vieux Carré.* New Orleans: Tulane School of Architecture, 1997.

Howard, George W. *The Monumental City: Its Past History and Present Resources.* Baltimore, 1873.

Jolland, Pat. *Death in the Victorian Family*. London: Oxford University Press, 1999.

Jones, Carleton. *Lost Baltimore*. Baltimore: Johns Hopkins University Press, 1993.

Lane, Mills. *The Architecture of the Old South: Maryland*. New York: Abbeville Press, 1991.

Larew, Marilynn M. *Bel Air: An Architectural and Cultural History, 1782–1945*. Bel Air, MD: Town of Bel Air, 1995.

Latrobe, Ferdinand C. *Iron Men and Their Dogs*. Baltimore, 1941.

Lyle, Jr., Royster, and Simpson, Pamela Hemenway. *The Architecture of Historic Lexington*. Charlottesville: Historic Lexington Foundation by the University Press of Virginia, 1977.

Olson, Sherry. *Baltimore: The Building of an American City*. Baltimore: Johns Hopkins University Press, 1980.

Scharf, John T. *A History of Western Maryland*. Baltimore: Regional Publishing Co., 1968.

———. *Chronicles of Baltimore*. Baltimore: Turnbull Brothers, 1874.

———. *Scharf's History of Baltimore City and County*. Philadelphia, 1881; Baltimore: Regional Publishing Co., 1971.

Stanton, Phoebe B. *The Gothic Revival and American Church architecture An Episode in Taste, 1840–1856*. Baltimore: Johns Hopkins Press, 1968.

Trollope, Frances. *Domestic Manners of the Americans*. 5th ed. London: G. Routledge, 1839.

Weaver, Martin E. *Conserving Buildings: A Guide to Techniques and Materials*. New York: John Wiley & Sons, 1993.

Weeks, Christopher. *An Architectural History of Harford County, Maryland*. Baltimore: Johns Hopkins University Press, 1996.

Wentz, Abdel Ross. *The Evangelical Lutheran Church of Frederick, Maryland, 1738–1938*. Frederick, MD: University Publishing Group, 1988.

Woods, Mary N. *From Craft to Profession: The Practice of Architecture in Nineteenth-Century America*. Berkeley: University of California Press, 1999.

BIBLIOGRAPHY

Index

Randolph W. Chalfant (1919–2004), architect and architectural historian, served in the U.S. Army during WW II and the Korean conflict (in India and Germany respectively), both times in the construction services. In between, he received a degree in architecture from Pittsburgh's Carnegie Institute of Technology (1947). Settling in Baltimore, he worked for the architectural firms of Fisher, Nes, Campbell; Taylor and Fisher; and Tyler, Chalfant, and McShane. The son of an architect, Chalfant had a lifelong passion for architecture as a building art and as the fabric of American culture and history.

Charles Belfoure, architect and writer, graduated from the Pratt Institute and Columbia University. His articles on Baltimore development have appeared in the *Baltimore Sun* and the *New York Times*. He is co-author, with Mary Ellen Hayward, of *The Baltimore Rowhouse* (New York: Princeton Architectural Press, 1999). Mr. Bel-

foure's novel, *Dying by Design*, was published by iUniverse in 2002. He is most recently the author of *Monuments to Money: The Architecture of American Banks* (Jefferson, NC: McFarland & Co., 2005)

Michael J. Lewis has taught American art and architecture at Williams College since 1993. A graduate of Haverford College, he studied at the University of Hanover, Germany, and received his Ph.D. degree from the University of Pennsylvania. Professor Lewis's articles on art and culture have appeared in the *New York Times*, the *Wall Street Journal*, *Commentary*, and the *New Criterion*. His books include *Frank Furness: Architecture and the Violent Mind* (New York: W. W. Norton, 2001) and *The Gothic Revival* (London: Thames & Hudson, 2002). His newest work, a textbook, is *American Art and Architecture* (London: Thames & Hudson, 2006).